HARDY

A COLLECTION OF CRITICAL ESSAYS

Edited by

Albert J. Guerard

Englewood Cliffs, New Jersey London Mexico New Delhi
Rio de Janeiro Singapore Sydney Tokyo Toronto Wellington

Prentice-Hall Inc., *Englewood Cliffs, New Jersey*
Prentice-Hall International (UK) Ltd, *London*
Prentice-Hall of Australia Pty Ltd, *Sydney*
Prentice-Hall Canada Inc., *Toronto*
Prentice-Hall Hispanoamericana S.A., *Mexico*
Prentice-Hall of India Private Ltd, *New Delhi*
Prentice-Hall of Japan Inc., *Tokyo*
Prentice-Hall of Southeast Asia Pte Ltd, *Singapore*
Editora Prentice-Hall do Brasil Ltda, *Rio de Janeiro*
Whitehall Books Ltd, *Wellington, New Zealand*

Printed and bound in Great Britain for
Prentice-Hall International (UK) Ltd,
66 Wood Lane End, Hemel Hempstead,
Hertfordshire, HP2 4RG
at the University Press, Cambridge

2 3 4 5 90 89 88 87

0-13-384065-4

Table of Contents

HARDY

Introduction

by Albert J. Guerard

It may be said of Thomas Hardy (who at times seemed the kind of man to whom nothing happens) that he blundered and stumbled onto greatness. For some years he seemed destined to become, at most, a mildly successful architect. One of his humble ambitions, until fairly late in his novelistic career, was to be considered a "good hand at a serial"; he gave little thought to fiction as an art. And though he always cherished poetry as a fine uncompromising art, he waited many years before publishing a volume of verse. He even seemed, at times, a passive spectator of his own career and life. And yet this apparently shy, reticent, unassuming, even unambitious man achieved almost equal eminence as novelist and poet, and died the Grand Old Man of English letters. A subversive writer without intending to be one, he was honored at the end by the Establishment, with burial in Westminster Abbey and the Prime Minister as a pallbearer. June 2, 1840—January 11, 1928. He had begun his career as a novelist in the days of Dickens and Trollope, yet published a large volume of verse three years after *The Waste Land* and a year before *The Sun Also Rises.* There was an even later, posthumous volume.

The conjunction is a startling one: of popular, even primitive, novelist and austere, experimenting poet. The pattern of the career is still more unusual. Hardy wrote poetry from 1863 to 1868, then turned to fiction and for over twenty-five years wrote comparatively little poetry. There are only six dated poems for 1872-1882. But in 1896—at the height of his powers, and financially secure at last—he abandoned the novel for good. It was long believed he gave up novel-writing because of the harsh moralistic attacks on *Tess of the D'Urbervilles* and *Jude the Obscure.* But one may also argue that in *Jude* Hardy had at last made a full and definitive statement on evil and mischance and self-destructiveness, on the social and the cosmic absurd. He had written openly, moreover, on sexual conflicts and tensions, after years of writing evasively. So where was he to go from *Jude*? [1] John Holloway interestingly remarks that Hardy,

[1] *The Well-Beloved,* though revised and published (1897) after *Jude,* was in conception and to a large degree in writing an earlier book. See the conclusion to A. Alvarez's essay on *Jude the Obscure.*

having lost his faith in the traditional rural order, had "no position to which to retreat." But also it may be affirmed that Hardy had completed his novelist's trajectory with *Jude*. He had realized and exhausted—with such great and different books as *Tess, The Mayor of Casterbridge* and *Jude*—his major fictional impulses, both in subject and form.

The novelist and poet are unmistakably the same man. The melancholy and brooding temperament, the ironic vision and fine eye for absurd discrepancies, the grotesque and macabre imagination, the tenderness and compassion, the wry saddened wisdom—these appear in both. (There is also the odd literary fact, in both novelist and poet, of extreme unevenness, the great chapter succeeded by a wooden one, and the fine stanza by a stanza almost unreadable.) Nevertheless, prose and verse seemed to bring out different facets of that single self. Hardy's novels, though deeply felt, are in one sense impersonal. They are not autobiographical; Jude Fawley is the only intense masculine creation with a large autobiographical component. Michael Henchard, Hardy's greatest hero, seems very different from his creator in impulse, aspiration, and dream. Hardy projects himself more often in the succession of pallid, featureless, unaggressive heroes of the earlier books, those dogged, faithful, and uninteresting men who seem quite unworthy of the unmoral heroines fluttering about them.

This impersonality is not found as often in the verse. There are a number of great traditional poems and ballads of rural tragedy and betrayal, notably in the volume *Time's Laughingstocks* of 1909. But this same volume contains some of Hardy's most personal love lyrics and most nostalgic evocations of the past. The central oddity is that some of Hardy's intimate feelings not only failed to get into the fiction but seem to have been long suppressed, or have gone long unexpressed, in his life. There was a reticence in later years which only the poems could overcome. Hardy's great romance with Emma Lavinia Gifford on the wild Cornish coast had occurred in 1870; they were married in 1872. But they drifted apart, spiritually, and at last quarreled harshly before her death in 1912. Shortly after her death, however, Hardy wrote a series of his most personal and most beautiful poems, astonishing evocations of that romance over forty-two years gone by:

> O the opal and the sapphire of that wandering western sea,
> And the woman riding high above with bright hair flapping free—
> The woman whom I loved so, and who loyally loved me.

Significantly, Hardy referred to these poems as "an expiation." They show, as do so many other lyrics both early and late, an exceptional directness of utterance, an accent of unremittent sincerity, an unmistakable "voice." Even Hardy's most involuted lyrics, or those with the most crabbed and outlandish rhetoric, have this personal accent.

Historically speaking, Hardy the novelist is a major transitional figure between the popular moralists and popular entertainers of Victorian fiction and the serious, visionary, often symbolizing novelists of today. He stands massively between the talented but often compromising Victorian "giants" and the meditative and austere Conrad. The great movement from Victorian to modern is reflected, in fact, within Hardy's own novel-writing career. His first published novel, *Desperate Remedies* (1871), has much in common with the so-called sensation-novel of the Victorians. But with *Jude the Obscure* (1895) we have entered both the more austere aesthetic of the modern novel, and the dark world in which we live. The dismal unfaith and rudderless society of *Jude,* the anxieties of sexual maladjustment and social misemployment, the chronic self-destructiveness of both Jude and Sue, the total vision of weakened vitality and gray despair—all these may give, to the twentieth century reader, a comforting sense of familiarity and home.

The fact is that Hardy was at his best both traditional and modern, rudely archaic yet minutely observant, capable of both scriptural simplicity of narrative and complex psychological insight. This rewarding duality is discussed in several of the essays to follow. Donald Davidson firmly establishes Hardy as a traditional and almost timeless teller of tales, and remarks that the most "literary" of the novels (*The Hand of Ethelberta* and *A Laodicean*) are the weakest. "He wrote as a ballad-maker would write if a ballad-maker were to have to write novels; or as a bardic or epic poet would write if faced with the necessity of performing in the quasi-lyrical but nonsingable strains of the nineteenth century and later." Many of the peculiarities of the novels, perhaps even the fatalistic or pessimistic "meanings" so overstressed by academic critics, are also peculiarities of the old popular ballads. Davidson's argument is highly persuasive. Yet Morton Dauwen Zabel is fully as persuasive in describing Hardy's modern tensions and ambiguities, and his role in freeing the novel from an unenergized realism. "He now appears to us as a realist developing toward allegory—as an imaginative artist who brought the nineteenth century novel out of its slavery to fact and its dangerous reaction against popularity, and so prepared the way for some of the most original talents of a new time. He stands in a succession of novelists that includes Melville, Emily Brontë, and Hawthorne, that takes in James and Flaubert in the wider reach of their faculties, and that has arrived at the achievements of Joyce, Proust, Gide, and Kafka."

Even a single novel may be described as both traditional and modern, most notably *The Mayor of Casterbridge*. John Paterson's masterful essay presents this novel as a traditional tragedy evocative of *Lear, Hamlet,*

Oedipus, and one that assumes in the ancient way "the existence of a moral order, an ethical substance, a standard of justice and rectitude, in terms of which man's experience can be rendered as the drama of his salvation as well as the drama of his damnation." It is the moral order that "will not be satisfied with less than the total humiliation of the offender." Yet this in no way contradicts my own emphasis on a very modern dramatization of an impulse to self-destruction, of what Hardy called Henchard's "self-alienation." In the dynamics of novel-writing the dreaming mind can simultaneously conceive of an ancient ethic that sees punishment as coming from without *and* intuitively observe punishment coming from within . . . which is where it does, after all, so often come from. A chronic and even a preconscious impulse to self-destruction is no invention of modern psychology; it has existed since the dawn of mind and origins of guilt.

Not only the "modern" novelist is prey to tensions and ambivalences, and to radical divergences of feeling and belief, sympathy and judgment. The most important tension for Hardy—the very heart of his aesthetic in fact—was the simple desire to juxtapose plausible human beings and strange uncommon event, the real and the fantastic. He found his immediate master not in another novelist but in the verse tales of George Crabbe, who similarly blended "rural realism" with ironic or tragic mischance. It would have seemed to Hardy impertinent to offer to the reader nothing that escaped the banal and everyday; even macabre coincidence may entertain; a good fiction must be strange. Hardy was a conscious antirealist, opposed to the documentary and the drab, in spite of his minute fidelity to the physical world. He knew that all great art is a "disproportioning," and remarked that the "seer should watch that pattern among general things which his idiosyncrasy moves him to observe, and describe that alone." Hardy's grotesque distortions and ironies are more frequent and more extreme in the short stories than in the novels. But in the novels they are more meaningful; that is, more symbolic of general truths.

One of the commonest conflicts in the modern novelist is between sympathy and judgment, between unconscious allegiance and conscious commitment, between unmoral identification and rational preference. We may dislike those we admire, and feel drawn toward those we condemn. The man in whom feeling and belief wholly coincided might be free from anxiety, but he would probably not write novels. D. H. Lawrence, in his reckless yet brilliant way, notes Hardy's "*prédilection d'artiste* for the aristocrat" and his "moral antagonism" to him. Hardy's "private sympathy" is for the individual against the community, yet he must show that individual destroyed. Expressed more academically—he envied rebellion and nonconformity, and *thought he approved of them.* But (here exactly reversing the order of the nominally conservative Conrad) Hardy in fact identified rather with the docile and the unaggressive. It must at once be added, however, that it is hard to conceive of a great novel without some secret identifying sympathy for the outlaw. Perhaps such sympathy accounts in part for *The Mayor of Casterbridge*'s greatness.

There are other polarities in Hardy's world: between the simple and complex temperament, for instance, or between the rural and the urban. These require no critical comment here—unless to remark that Hardy's attitude toward rural and peasant society was, like that of Wordsworth, to a considerable degree aesthetic. He had remade the real Dorset into a fictional Wessex, with at times as much distortion (and as much truth) as one finds in Faulkner's Yoknapatawpha. It is also worth noting that Hardy maintained a double standard of sexual morality—one code for Wessex and one for the rest of the world. In Wessex seduction and infidelity are "natural," as natural as the seasons. But in the corrupt outside world, or when perpetrated by outsiders and aristocrats, seduction and infidelity seem more reflective, nastier, evil.

To what degree was Hardy's notorious "pessimism"—that pessimism wearily and systematically insisted on by professors in the 1920's and 1930's, with frequent allusions to Schopenhauer—also an aesthetic matter? In 1920 the second Mrs. Hardy wrote that Hardy "is now, this afternoon writing a poem with great spirit: always a sign of well-being with him. Needless to say, it is an intensely dismal poem." One of the wisest statements on the pessimism, and on the common discrepancy between life and art, is Hardy's own:

> Differing natures find their tongue in the presence of differing spectacles. Some natures become vocal at tragedy, some are made vocal by comedy, and it seems to me that to whichever of these aspects of life a writer's instinct for expression the more readily responds, to that he should allow it to respond. That before a contrasting side of things he remains undemonstrative need not be assumed to mean that he remains unperceiving.

And again, a caveat to those who see Hardy's "fatalism" as pure philosophical commitment, there is the following most interesting passage, Hardy's New Year's thought for 1879: "A perception of the FAILURE OF THINGS to be what they are meant to be, lends them, in place of the intended interest, a new and greater interest of an unintended kind."

Much has been written of Hardy's "philosophy," and even such a vivid personage as Arabella in *Jude* has been reduced by some critics to deterministic abstraction. Hardy spoke of "Crass Casualty" and "purblind Doomsters" in one of his earliest poems, and he would never cease to dramatize the discrepancies between man's physical nature and his spirit, or between man's longing for order and justice and the disorderly, seemingly malevolent drift of things. The pessimism and fatalism (and even that "meliorism" with which *The Dynasts* would conclude) are natural nineteenth century responses, and the responses of a sensitive man to the reading of Darwin, Huxley, Spencer, Schopenhauer. The systematic connections between Von Hartmann's *Philosophy of the Unconscious* and *The Dynasts* can be explicated in detail. But the unacademic approach of most of the essayists in this volume seems a more useful one—to regard the philosophy either as intrusive and inert, or at best as a body of speculation aesthetically useful to Hardy in the writing of his novels and poems, but of no great intrinsic interest to the reader of today. At most the "system" made its contribution to the over-all dark vision of things.

It is always tempting to correct the excesses of a previous generation, or to ridicule the somber academic critics with their distaste for Hardy's grotesque qualities, their affection for his obvious formalisms, and their obsessive concern with the "philosophy." Nevertheless, one is compelled to recognize that some wound to the spirit had occurred, and a deeper wound than the reading of Darwin would inflict. The philosophically inclined may follow Hardy to *The Dynasts* for the ultimate workings of The Will.[2] But the general darkening of Hardy's attitude, during his years of novel-writing, cannot be brushed aside; it is interestingly discussed in John Holloway's important essay. An incidental result was that Hardy's view of the agricultural laborer's lot grew more and more pessimistic as he moved through his own career, and as he dramatized later periods of the nineteenth century. (*Under the Greenwood Tree,* 1872, is laid in about 1835; *Tess,* 1891, is laid in 1884-9.) The historical fact, as Hardy himself elsewhere recognized, was that the laborer's lot had improved. The citizen was compelled to note this amelioration. But the writer regretted changes inimical to "the preservation of legend, folklore, close inter-social relations, and eccentric individualities." Why (looking at the matter in more personal terms) Hardy grew more and more pessimistic—as his own fortunes waxed, as he moved toward success both literary and financial—appears to be beyond the biographer's reach.

Hardy the novelist remains a challenge to critics: perhaps as great a challenge as Conrad, Faulkner, and other novelists so much more complex and more ambitious. For he was a great, humane, simple, even primitive novelist, and one who left little to be explicated in the way of elusive symbolic content or technical subtlety. He had the courage and

[2] William R. Rutland's *Thomas Hardy: A Study of his Writings and their Background* (Oxford, 1938) is highly recommended in this connection.

the tact to be both obvious and direct, where the human material was of sufficient importance. Consider the great memorable scenes from *The Mayor of Casterbridge,* beginning with the sale of the wife, a story "as simple as Scripture history," as Henchard himself remarks.

> Unforgettable, surely, is the furmity-seller's appearance before Henchard as Justice of the Peace—charged "with the offence of disorderly female and nuisance"—and her story of the large crime she had witnessed twenty years before. This is, I suppose, the big moment of the book, and the average novelist would give it twenty pages or more: would perhaps go into Henchard's mind, and into the woman's, and would doubtless describe at length the hubbub in the courtroom. Hardy gets over the scene in four pages. Or—what would be a woman's first tumult of feeling as she is turned over to the man who has purchased her? Hardy limits himself to a short sentence: "She paused for an instant, with a close glance at him." And I can still remember, from my schoolboy reading of this novel, a grand vision of Hadrian's soldiers mysteriously reappearing in broad daylight. Now, over a quarter of a century later, I find on inspection that the vision is evoked in one rather pedestrian sentence. The point I want to make is simple enough. Not subtlety or elaboration of art *but the imagined material itself* gives the best scenes of the novel their strength. And Hardy had the instinct or the art to let the material speak for itself. He becomes diffuse and flabbily abstract only when the material is inadequate, or when he is not himself convinced of its truth.[3]

Faced with Hardy's essential unadorned humanity, criticism has often been puzzled, or has found itself disarmed. The journeyman reviewer is helpless in any age when confronted by unfamiliar tones or unpopular attitudes. His Victorian exemplar was consoled to find resemblances between Hardy and George Eliot, for instance, but was repelled by Hardy's stark differences. Hardy was not worse served in his time than most original novelists are, in spite of the collective rejection of *The Return of the Native* and the outcry against *Tess* and *Jude.* It is saddening rather to see the obtuseness of Henry James[4] when confronted by *Far From the Madding Crowd.* In the same year, however, Havelock Ellis wrote the first general article (in *The Westminster Review,* June 1, 1883) on Hardy's novels, and it remains an impressive one. With his particular blend of talents, as psychologist and man-of-letters, Ellis was able to discuss Hardy's women with more subtlety and insight than any of the critics of the 1920's and 1930's.

The very striking impulse of these latter was to try to make Hardy

[3] From my introduction to the Washington Square Press edition of *The Mayor of Casterbridge.*

[4] See A. Mordell, *Literary Reviews and Essays* (New York: Twayne Publishers, 1957), pp. 291-7.

academically respectable: to insist on the formalities and symmetries of his fictional structures, on the faithful realism of his picture of Dorset, on the seriousness of his "philosophy." These critics tended to apologize for the vagaries and eccentricities and audacities of imagining that attract readers today. It may in fact be argued that Hardy had to wait until 1940 (with the special and brilliantly edited centennial number of *The Southern Review*) for anything like an adequate, unpedantic summing-up. It is easy enough to demonstrate the importance of this moment in the history of Hardy criticism. For these many years afterward I find myself drawing upon it for no less than four of the essays for the present collection, and there were several others I was tempted to use.

The poetry, while often praised, has by no means received the attention it deserves. Since 1940, criticism of Hardy the novelist has not been particularly active, partly because *The Southern Review* had covered so much ground, partly because Hardy does not lend himself to the methods of the new critics, the formalists, or the delvers into archetype and the psychic underground. Norman Holland and Robert W. Stallman offered characteristically ingenious essays, the former discovering minute and detailed parallels between Jude and the Christ story, the latter finding intricate patterns of time in *The Return of the Native*.[5] But this is about all. The provocative essay on the individual novel is in fact fairly rare. The brilliant analyses of Dorothy Van Ghent, John Paterson and A. Alvarez to follow, though very different, are isolated exceptions to this rule. What Hardy has particularly encouraged, instead, is the large essay in synthesis represented by various contributors to this volume.

Hardy was praised or blamed by some of his contemporaries for austerity and subtlety, and for a seeming evasion of popular modes. But the Conrads and Joyces and Prousts and Kafkas have intervened to change our view of both the novel and the world. Today Hardy would appear to survive rather as a popular and even primitive novelist, reaching us through pure narrative gifts and antique simplicities of understanding and art. His sluggish schematizing intellect may repel us. But his dark wisdom and brooding temperament prevail. In the 1930's Hardy's gloomy visions seemed perverse; this is hardly true today. The love of the macabre coincidence and grotesque mischance, the cruel imaginings and manipulations, all the bad luck and all the mismatched destinies, the darkness of the physical and moral landscapes, the awareness of dwindling energies, and the sense of man's appalling limitations—all these are peculiarly modern. Yet quite as fundamental are a timeless traditionalism and an

[5] Norman Holland, "*Jude the Obscure:* Hardy's Symbolic Indictment of Christianity," *Nineteenth Century Fiction* IX (June, 1954), 50-60; R. W. Stallman, *The Houses That James Built* (Michigan State Press, 1961), pp. 53-63.

unmodern purity of temperament and a most uninhibited compassion. For behind Hardy's sadistic imaginings and pessimistic declarations lie, of course, a deep concern for the fortunes of his characters, an incorrigible sympathy for all who are lonely and all who long for happiness. Man usually deserved, Hardy believed, more than he received.

All this is but to say that Hardy was both a serious man and a popular traditional story-teller; and that he was, moreover, simultaneously ancient and modern.

The Traditional Basis of Thomas Hardy's Fiction

by Donald Davidson

In the eighty-eight years of his life Thomas Hardy got used to a great many of the oddities of terrestrial experience, and was resigned to most of them, even to the seeming unapproachableness or indifference of the Deity. One thing, however, he never got used to, and was apparently not resigned to. I find a peculiar pertinence in the fact that Mrs. Hardy, in *The Later Years,* has inserted a rather lengthy reminiscence of Hardy's visit to Oxford in 1920, written by Charles Morgan, who was then an undergraduate at the University and one of the leaders in arranging for the performance of *The Dynasts* at Oxford on this particular occasion. After an account of Hardy's visit, Morgan goes on to record a later conversation with Hardy at Max Gate, on the subject of literary criticism. Hardy spoke out against the critics with an animus that startled the younger man. Dramatic criticism, Hardy thought, had some merit because the dramatic critics had less time "to rehearse their prejudices." But Hardy was bitter about literary criticism.

> The origin of this bitterness [writes Morgan] was in the past where, I believe, there was good reason for it, but it was directed now against contemporary critics of his own work, and I could not understand what general reason he had to complain of them. He used no names; he spoke with studied reserve, sadly rather than querulously; but he was persuaded—and there is evidence of his persuasion in the preface to the posthumous volume of his verse—that critics approached his work with an ignorant prejudice against his "pessimism" which they allowed to stand in the way of fair reading and fair judgment.
>
> This was a distortion of the facts as I knew them. It was hard to believe that Hardy honestly thought that his genius was not recognized; harder to

"The Traditional Basis of Thomas Hardy's Fiction." From *Still Rebels, Still Yankees, and Other Essays* by Donald Davidson (Baton Rouge: The Louisiana State Press, 1957). Originally published in the Hardy Centennial number (VI, 1940) of *The Southern Review.*

believe that he thought his work was not read. Such a belief indicated the only failure of balance, the only refusal to seek the truth, which I perceived in Hardy. . . .

But Morgan was wrong, and Hardy was right, and the "bitterness" of the aged poet toward literary criticism, as thus recorded, is something to give pause to the presumptuous critical interpreter. Hardy could not explain himself clearly to the younger man, and perhaps the reference to pessimism comes in only for want of a better verbal statement of the strange misunderstanding Hardy felt he had encountered. There was a real intellectual distance between Hardy and the critics—indeed, between Hardy and almost three generations of critics. The critics had not so much underrated—or overrated—Hardy as missed him, in somewhat the same way as, in our opinion, Dr. Johnson missed John Donne. When we look over the impressive list of those who have made literary pronouncements in Hardy's time and ours, they do not seem to be the kind of people who would have affinity with Hardy. From George Meredith, his first literary adviser, up to T. S. Eliot, one can hardly think of a critic whose view of Hardy's work, however, well-intentioned, would not be so external as to set up a gross incongruity like what we find in Marxian criticisms of Shakespeare.

Possibly the critics have been most in error in not realizing the comparative isolation of Hardy in modern literary history. Misled by the superficial resemblance between his work and the product current in their day, they have invariably attempted to treat him as a current author —or at least as a queer blend of tendencies receding and tendencies coming on. They have been further misled by Hardy's own attempt (not always happy) to shape his work into a marketable form or to bring it up to what he conceived to be a good current literary standard. For Hardy seems to have had little idea of being an innovator or an iconoclast. He sought to please and entertain, and perhaps to instruct, and he must have been amazed to find himself now acclaimed, now condemned, as heretic.

The appearance of Thomas Hardy among the temporal phenomena of the England of 1870 to 1928—that is the amazing, the confusing thing. I believe we ought to begin consideration by admitting that though Hardy was *in* that time, and was affected by its thought and art, he was not really *of* that time whenever he was his essential self. It is not enough to say that Hardy is "old-fashioned" or "quaint." Certainly he did not try consciously to be old-fashioned. Although there are archaisms of language in his poetry and prose, and much general display of the antique in subject matter, there is nowhere in Hardy the affectation of archaism (found in such ironic romanticists as Cabell) or the deliberate exploitation of archaism (found in a great many of the literary specialties offered in America). The old-fashioned quality in Hardy is not in the obvious places, but lies deeper. It is in the habit of Hardy's mind rather than in "folk-lore" or the phenomena of language and style.

Hardy wrote, or tried to write, more or less as a modern—modern, for him, being late nineteenth century. But he thought, or artistically conceived, like a man of another century—indeed, of a century that we should be hard put to name. It might be better to say that he wrote like a creator of tales and poems who is a little embarrassed at having to adapt the creation of tales and poems to the conditions of a written, or printed, literature, and yet tries to do his faithful best under the regrettable circumstances. He is not in any sense a "folk author," and yet he does approach his tale-telling and poem-making as if three centuries of Renaissance effort had worked only upon the outward form of tale and poem without changing its essential character. He wrote as a ballad-maker would write if a ballad-maker were to have to write novels; or as a bardic or epic poet would write if faced with the necessity of performing in the quasi-lyrical but nonsingable strains of the nineteenth century and later.

Hardy is the only specimen of his genus in modern English literature, and I do not know how to account for him. He has no immediate predecessors; and though he has some imitators, no real followers as yet. For his habit of mind has seemingly disappeared in England, and threatens to disappear in America; and without the habit of mind to begin with no real following can be done. I am almost ready to characterize Hardy (if he must be "placed") as an American whose ancestors failed to migrate at the proper time and who accordingly found himself stranded, a couple of centuries later, in the wrong literary climate. In this connection it is amusing to remember that Hardy has been charged with borrowing a description from Augustus Baldwin Longstreet's *Georgia Scenes* for use in *The Trumpet-Major*. The truth is that his general affiliation with the frontier humorists of the Old Southwest is a good deal more discernible than his affiliation with Victorian romantic-realists or with French naturalists. It is an organic affiliation, not a literary attachment, because the southwestern humorists drew their art, such as it was, from the same kind of source that Hardy used, and wrote (when they had to write) under the same embarrassment. If Hardy's distant seventeenth century progenitor had migrated to America at the time of the Monmouth Rebellion—as some of his progenitor's relatives and many of his neighbors did, in all haste, migrate, then Thomas Hardy might easily have been a frontier humorist of the Longstreet school. And then he would never have been accused of pessimism, though he might, to be sure, have caused eyebrows to lift in Boston.

In the two volumes which are the second Mrs. Hardy's Memoir of her husband (*The Early Life of Thomas Hardy* and *The Later Years of Thomas Hardy*) there is a good deal of scattered and fragmentary evidence to indicate the bent of Hardy's mind. It is enough to aid a speculation, though not enough, probably, to prove the case for a professional researchist. I refer to the recorded experiences of Hardy's childhood and youth which seem to suggest his inward preoccupation better than the interests generally emphasized by critics, such as his study of Greek, his knowledge of architecture, or tussle with Darwinian theory and modern social problems. Another age than ours would have made something out of the fact that when Hardy was born he was at first cast aside for a stillbirth and was saved only by the shrewd perception of a nurse; or that when the infant Hardy was reposing in his cradle a snake crawled upon his breast and went to sleep there. These are omens that I profess no ability to read. But the many little items that seem to make Hardy a "crusted character," like so many of the personages of his fiction, are not of minor or dubious importance.

Hardy was born early enough—and far enough away from looming Arnoldian or Marxian influences—to receive a conception of art as something homely, natural, functional, and in short traditional. He grew up in a Dorset where fiction was a tale told or sung; and where the art of music, always important to him, was primarily for worship or merriment. The Hardys, up through the time of Thomas Hardy's father, were "church-players" of the type of the Mellstock Choir—performers on the violin, cello, and bass who adhered to a traditional psalmody and instrumental performance (of which echoes are preserved here today in the music of the "shape note" singers of the South). Thomas Hardy, as a child, was "extraordinarily sensitive to music." He danced to "the endless jigs, hornpipes, reels, waltzes, and country-dances" that his own father played and, without knowing why, was contradictorily moved to tears by some of the tunes. Later he himself could "twiddle from notation some hundreds of jigs and country-dances that he found in his father's and grandfather's old books"—he was an "oldtime fiddler." Young Thomas played the fiddle at weddings and in farmer's parlors. On one occasion he bowed away for a solid three-quarters of an hour while twelve tireless couples danced to a single favorite tune. At one notable harvest-home he heard the maids sing ballads. Among these Hardy remembered particularly "The Outlandish Knight"—a Dorset version of the ballad recorded by Child as "Lady Isabel and the Elf Knight."

And of course he must have heard, in time, many another ballad, if we may make a justifiable inference from the snatches of balladry in the novels and tales, and if Dorset was the kind of countryside we are led to think it to be. Mrs. Hardy would have us believe that upon the extension of the railway to Dorset in the middle nineteenth century "the orally transmitted ballads were slain at a stroke by the London comic songs," but she underestimates the vitality of folk art. As late as 1922, one R. Thurston Hopkins published a book entitled *Thomas Hardy's Dorset,* in which he tells how he found a singing blacksmith at Lyme Regis, in Devon. Hopkins gives the blacksmith's song, but evidently does not know enough of balladry to recognize it. It is a perfectly good version of the ballad known as "Mollie Vaughn" or "Mollie Bond."

For what it may be worth I note that Hardy first conceived *The Dynasts* as a ballad, or group of ballads. In May, 1875, he wrote in his journal:

> Mem: A Ballad of the Hundred Days. Then another of Moscow. Others of earlier campaigns—forming altogether an Iliad of Europe from 1789 to 1815.

This, Mrs. Hardy says, is the first mention in Hardy's memoranda of the conception later to take shape in the epic drama. Again, on March 27, 1881, Hardy referred to his scheme: "A Homeric Ballad, in which Napoleon is a sort of Achilles, to be written."

To evidence of this kind I should naturally add the following facts: that Hardy wrote a number of ballads, like "The Bride-Night Fire," and ballad-like poems; that his poems like his novels are full of references to old singers, tunes, and dances, and that many of the poems proceed from the same sources as his novels; that he is fond of inserting in his journals, among philosophizings and other memoranda, summaries of anecdotes or stories he has heard. Of the latter sort is the following entry:

> Conjurer Mynterne when consulted by Patt P. (a strapping handsome young woman), told her that her husband would die on a certain day, and showed her the funeral in a glass of water. . . . She used to impress all this on her inoffensive husband, and assure him that he would go to hell if he made the conjurer a liar. He didn't, but died on the day foretold.

Such notations should not be unduly emphasized. Yet they appear in his journal with such frequency that we are justified in assuming Hardy's special interest in such material. On the other hand, in the record of Hardy's life thus far available to us, there is little evidence to indicate that, in devising the greater stories, he had some specific literary model before him, or was trying out some theory of fiction, or had, at the beginning of his conception, a particular philosophical or social thesis. Critics may show that such and such a literary influence reached him, or that a theory or philosophy ultimately engaged his mind; but I cannot believe that such elements controlled the original conception or determined the essential character of the greater novels and stories. The poetry offers a somewhat different field of critical speculation, which I do not propose to enter, but it seems worth while to argue that his characteristic habit of mind, early established and naturally developed, has much to do with certain peculiarities of his fiction.

My thesis is that the characteristic Hardy novel is conceived as a *told* (or *sung*) story, or at least not as a literary story; that it is an extension, in the form of a modern prose fiction, of a traditional ballad or an oral tale—a tale of the kind which Hardy reproduces with great skill in *A Few Crusted Characters* and less successfully in *A Group of Noble Dames;* but, furthermore, that this habit of mind is a rather unconscious element in Hardy's art. The conscious side of his art manifests itself in two ways: first, he "works up" his core of traditional, or nonliterary, narrative into a literary form; but, second, at the same time he labors to establish, in his "Wessex," the kind of artistic climate and environment which will enable him to handle his traditional story with conviction—a world in which typical ballad heroes and heroines can flourish with a thoroughly rationalized "mythology" to sustain them. The novels that support this thesis are the great Hardy novels: *Under the Greenwood Tree, Far from the Madding Crowd, The Mayor of Casterbridge, The Return of the Native, The Woodlanders,* and *Tess of the D'Urbervilles*—in other words, the Wessex novels proper. *Jude the Obscure* and *The Trumpet-Major* can be included, with some reservations, in the same list. The novels that do not support this thesis are commonly held to be, by comparison with those named above, of inferior quality: *The Hand of Ethelberta* and *A Laodicean,* for example. These are Hardy's attempt to be a fully modern —and literary—novelist.

The fictions that result from Hardy's habit of mind resemble traditional, or nonliterary, types of narrative in many ways. They are always conceived of as stories primarily, with the narrative always of foremost interest. They have the rounded, often intricate plot and the balance and antithesis of characters associated with traditional fiction from ancient times. It is natural, of course, that they should in such respects resemble classic drama. But that does not mean that Hardy thought in terms of dramatic composition. His studies in Greek (like his experience in architecture) simply reinforced an original tendency. The interspersed descriptive elements—always important, but not overwhelmingly important, in a Hardy novel—do not encumber the narrative, as they invariably do in the work of novelists who conceive their task in wholly literary terms; but they blend rather quickly into the narrative. Action, not description, is always foremost; the event dominates, rather than motive, or psychology, or comment. There is no loose episodic structure. Hardy does not write the chronicle novel or the biographical novel. Nor does he build up circumstantial detail like a Zola or a Flaubert.

Hardy has an evident fondness for what we might call the "country story"—the kind of story *told* by the passengers in the van in *A Few Crusted Characters;* or *sung* in ballads of the type attributed by scholars to the seventeenth and eighteenth centuries and sometimes called "vulgar" ballads to distinguish them from the supposedly more genuine "popular" ballads of an earlier day. In *Under the Greenwood Tree,* the coquettish behavior of Fancy Day is a delicate feminine parallel to the difficulties of Tony Kytes, the Arch-deceiver, related in *A Few Crusted Characters.* The coy maiden, after involvement with the solid farmer Shiner and the excellent Vicar, rejects them both at last for the brisk young country lad, Dick Dewy. Gabriel Oak, in *Far from the Madding Crowd,* is the "faithful lover" of many a ballad, who has many of the elements of a masculine "patient Griselda"; he endures a kind of "testing" not irretrievably remote from the testings that ladies put upon their lovers in romances and ballads; and he is also obviously the excellent lover of "low degree" who aims his affections high and is finally rewarded. Fanny Robin, of the same novel, is a typical deserted maiden, lacking nothing but a turtledove on her tombstone; or perhaps she is the more luridly forsaken girl found in "Mary of the Wild Moor." Her lover, Sergeant Troy, is the soldier (or sailor) of any number of later ballads. And it is worth remarking, in this connection, that Hardy's fondness for soldiers has everywhere in it the echo of many ballads about the military composed in the half-century or more preceding his birth and even in his own time. It flavors strongly, that is, of such pieces as "Polly Oliver," "Bold Dighton," "High Germany," and "Bloody Waterloo."

The Return of the Native gives us far more complexity, but many of its focal incidents are of the stuff in which tale-tellers and balladmakers delight. Mrs. Yeobright is bitten by a snake; Eustacia and Wildeve are drowned in one pool, to make a simultaneous romantic death, and we almost expect to learn that they were buried in the old churchyard and presently sprouted—a rose from her breast, a briar from his. We should not forget that Eustacia disguises herself in man's clothing (as heroines of traditional stories have long done) for the mummer's play.

Henchard, in *The Mayor of Casterbridge,* undergoes the rise and fall traditional in English story from Chaucer to *The Mirror for Magistrates.* More clearly, as the man who sold his own wife, he is of ballad or folk tale quality. And the man to whom he sold her is none other than a sailor, of all persons, who returns from the salt, salt sea to claim his woman, as sailors will do.

The Woodlanders, of the Wessex novels, seems furthest from the type; but again, the love of Marty South for Giles Winterborne is ballad love; and the women of *The Woodlanders,* like most of Hardy's women, have the frantic impulsion toward love, or the cruel and unreasoning capacity to reject faithful love, which we find in balladry. Then, too, Grace Melbury is caught, after the setting of the sun, in a murderous mantrap inadvertently placed in the path by her own lover. Happily she is released, and so escapes the fate of Mollie Vaughn of the ballad; Mollie was *shot* by her own lover, who went hunting after the setting of the sun.

Tess of the D'Urbervilles, whatever else she may be, is once more the deserted maiden who finally murders her seducer with a knife in the effective ballad way. And she, with the love-stricken trio—Marian, Retty, and Izz—is a milkmaid; and milkmaids, in balladry, folk song, and folk tale, are somehow peculiarly subject to seduction.

The high degree of coincidence in the typical Hardy narrative has been noted by all observers, often unfavorably. Mr. Samuel Chew explains it as partly a result of the influence of the "sensation novelists," and partly as a deliberate emphasis on "the persistence of the unforeseen"—hence a grim, if exaggerated, evidence of the sardonic humor of the purblind Doomsters. Let us pay this view all respect, and still remember that such conscious and artful emphasis may be only a rationalization of unconscious habit. The logic of the traditional story is not the logic of modern literary fiction. The traditional story admits, and even cherishes, the improbable and unpredictable. The miraculous, or nearly miraculous, is what makes a story a story, in the old way. Unless a story has some strange and unusual features it will hardly be told and will not be remembered. Most of the anecdotes that Hardy records in his journal savor of the odd and unusual. And occasionally he speaks directly to the point, as in the following passages:

> The writer's problem is, how to strike the balance between the uncommon and the ordinary, so as on the one hand to give interest, on the other to give reality.
>
> In working out this problem, human nature must never be abnormal, which is introducing incredibility. The uncommonness must be in the events, not in the characters . . . (July, 1881).
>
> A story must be exceptional enough to justify its telling. We taletellers are all Ancient Mariners, and none of us is warranted in stopping Wedding Guests (in other words, the hurrying public) unless he has something more unusual to relate than the ordinary experience of every average man and woman.

Thus coincidence in Hardy's narratives represents a conviction about the nature of story as such. Hardy's world is of course not the world of the most antique ballads and folk tales—where devils, demons, fairies, and mermaids intervene in human affairs, and ghosts, witches, and revenants are commonplace. It is a world like that of later balladry and folk tale, from which old beliefs have receded, leaving a residue of the merely strange. Improbability and accident have replaced the miraculous. The process is illustrated in the ballad "Mollie Vaughn" (sometimes Van, Bond, or Baun), in which the speaker, warning young men not to go shooting after sundown, tells how Mollie was shot by her lover. I quote from an American version recorded by Louise Pound:

> Jim Random was out hunting, a-hunting in the dark;
> He shot at his true love and missed not his mark.
> With a white apron pinned around her he took her
> for a swan,
> He shot her and killed her, and it was Mollie Bond.

In many versions, even the American ones, Mollie's ghost appears in court and testifies, in her lover's behalf, that the shooting was indeed accidental. But the ballad very likely preserves echoes, misunderstood by a later generation, of an actual swan maiden and her lover. This particular ballad is certainly unusual in admitting the presence of a ghost in a court of law. But at least the apparition is a ghost, not a swan maiden, and so we get the event rationalized in terms of an unlikely but not impossible accident: he saw the apron and "took her for a swan."

Hardy's coincidences may be explained as a similar kind of substitution. He felt that the unlikely (or quasi-miraculous) element belonged in any proper story—especially a Wessex story; but he would go only so far as the late ballads and country tales went, in substituting improbabilities for supernaturalisms. Never does he concoct a pseudo-folk tale like Stephen V. Benét's "The Devil and Daniel Webster." Superstitions are used in the background of his narrative; coincidence, in the actual mechanics. Tess hears the legend of the D'Urberville phantom coach, but does not actually see it, though the moment is appropriate for its appearance. In *The Return of the Native* Susan Nonesuch pricks Eustacia Vye for a witch and later makes a waxen image of her, just before her drowning; but coincidence, not superstition, dominates the action. Henchard visits the conjurer just before his great speculation in grain, but only out of habit and in half-belief; and it is coincidence that makes Farfrae a winner just at the moment when Henchard is a loser. The supernatural, in Hardy, is allowed in the narrative, but in a subordinate position; the quasi-miraculous takes its place in the main position.

If we use a similar approach to the problem of Hardy's pessimism, it is easy to see why he was irritated by insensitive and obtuse critics. Are the ballad stories of "Edward," "Little Musgrave," and "Johnnie Armstrong" pessimistic? Were their unknown authors convinced of the fatal indifference of the Universe toward human beings? Should we, reading such stories, take the next step in the context of modern critical realism and advocate psychoanalysis for Edward's mother and social security for Johnnie Armstrong? In formal doctrine Hardy professed himself to be an "evolutionary meliorist," or almost a conventional modern. But that had nothing to do with the stories that started up in his head. The charge of pessimism has about the same relevance as the charge of indelicacy which Hardy encountered when he first began to publish. An age of polite literature, which had lost touch with the oral arts—except so far as they might survive in chit-chat, gossip, and risqué stories—could not believe that an author who embodied in his serious stories the typical seductions, rapes, murders, and lusty love-makings of the old tradition intended anything but a breach of decorum. Even today, I suppose, a group gathered for tea might be a little astonished if a respectable old gentleman in spats suddenly began to warble the outrageous ballad of Little Musgrave. But Hardy did not know he was being rough, and had no more notion than a ballad-maker of turning out a story to be either pessimistic or optimistic.

To be sure, Hardy is a little to blame, since he does moralize at times. But the passage about the President of the Immortals in *Tess* and about the persistence of the unforeseen in *The Mayor of Casterbridge* probably came to him like such ballad tags as "Better they'd never been born" or "Young men, take warning from me." He had a mistaken idea, too, that he could argue and philosophize with impunity in verse, whereas he might have to go carefully, say, in an essay or speech. "Perhaps I can express more fully in verse," he wrote in 1896, "ideas and emotions which run counter to the inert crystallized opinion . . . which the vast body of men have vested interests in supporting. . . . If Galileo had said in verse that the world moved, the Inquisition might have let him alone." The good and innocent Hardy could somehow not easily learn that a bard was no longer a bard but a social critic.

The most striking feature of Hardy's habit of mind, as traditional narrator, is in his creation of characters. The characters of the Wessex novels, with certain important exceptions, are fixed or "nondeveloping" characters. Their fortunes may change, but they do not change with their fortunes. Once fully established as characters, they move unchanged through the narrative and at the end are what they were at the beginning. They have the changelessness of the figures of traditional narrative from epic, saga, and romance to broadside balladry and its prose parallels. In this respect they differ fundamentally from the typical characters of modern literary fiction. Our story-writers have learned how to exploit the possibilities of the changing, or changeful, or "developing" character. The theory of progress has seemed to influence them to apply an analogical generalization to the heroes of their stories: to wit, the only good hero in a serious novel is one that *changes* in some important respect during the course of the narrative; and the essence of the story is the change. This has become almost an aesthetic axiom. It is assumed that a story has no merit unless it is based on a changing character. If the modern author uses the changeless character, it is only in a minor role, or as a foil; or he may appear as a caricature.

But we have forgotten a truth that Hardy must have known from the time when, as a child, he heard at the harvest home the ballad of the outlandish knight. The changeless character has as much aesthetic richness as the changeful character. Traditional narrative of every sort is built upon the changeless character. It is a defect in modern fiction that the value of the changeless character is apparently not even suspected. But since the human desire for the changeless character is after all insatiable, we do have our changeless characters—in the comic strips, the movies, the detective story. Perhaps all is not well with a literary art that leaves the role of Achilles to be filled by Pop-Eye.

At any rate Hardy made extensive use of the changeless character. The habit of his mind probably forbade him to do otherwise; or at least he could not with complete success build his stories upon the changeful character. And so his novels of manners and genteel society are failures. At the same time, Hardy was no untutored child of the folk but a great author who learned by trial and error how to utilize self-consciously the rich material which by unself-conscious habit crowded his mind. He was thinking of his problem, I believe, when he wrote: "The uncommonness must be in the events, not in the characters." He did not make the mistake of exploiting his material for its mere picturesqueness—its *special* quality. He did not write dialect poems like William Barnes or romantic reconstructions like Blackmore's *Lorna Doone*.

What Hardy did is, in its astonishing completeness and verity, a rebuke to superficial quasi-regionalists and to all who attempt to exploit "folk material" with the shallow assumption that the "folkishness" of the material is alone enough to dignify it. Hardy rationalizes the changeless characters by creating in highest circumstantiality not only the local environment in which they move, but the entire social order—the tradition itself, and the basis of the tradition—which will accommodate them. The basis of the tradition is a natural environment—a nature not very much despoiled or exploited, a town life neither wholly antique nor wholly modern, and the whole removed a little in time from the strictly contemporary, but not so far removed as to seem like a historical reconstruction. The antiquities, the local color, the folk customs are not decorative or merely picturesque; they are organic with the total scheme. They are no less essential and no more decorative than the occupations, ambitions, and interrelationships of the changeless characters. He accepts the assumptions of the society that he depicts, and neither apologizes for it nor condescends to it. The stories are stories of human beings, not of peasants or moor-dwellers as such.

The scheme is somewhat more complex than it might appear to be. The changeless characters of the Wessex world are of both minor and major order; and they are generally set in juxtaposition with one or two characters of a more changeful or modern type. The interplay between the two kinds of characters is the focus of the struggle that makes the story. Hardy is almost the only modern novelist who makes serious use of this conflict and at the same time preserves full and equal respect for both sets of characters. His great art lies in not setting up too great or obvious a distance between his changeless and his changeful characters. The difference between Hardy and other novelists will be clear if I cite a typical example. Ellen Glasgow's *Barren Ground,* a novel which seems to copy Hardy at certain points, reduces all the thoroughly rustic characters to a condition either of amusing oddity or of gross ineptitude; and the excellent Dorinda, who makes such an obviously admirable change from rustic backwardness to rural progressivism, is at all times infinitely above all the rest.

Nature, itself unchangeable and inscrutable, is the norm, the basis of Wessex life. Those who accept nature as unchangeable and passively accommodate themselves to nature in the ordered ritual of their lives, not rebelling against it or attempting rash Promethean manipulations—these are the changeless characters.

Nearest to nature, and therefore most changeless, are the rustics (all crusted characters) who throng Hardy's pages. In the rural comedies, like *Under the Greenwood Tree* and *Far from the Madding Crowd,* they dominate the scene. Only the vicar, in *Under the Greenwood Tree,* with his newfangled church organ, and perhaps in a slight way Sergeant Troy, in the other novel, foreshadow the kind of disturbance set up by the changeful character. But these novels are essentially comedy, joyful, and almost idyllic. In Hardy, tragedy does not arrive until changeless and changeful are engaged in bitter conflict.

Such a conflict is found in *The Return of the Native.* Here the rustics are Timothy Fairway, Grandfer Cantle, Christian Cantle, Susan Nonesuch and her son Johnny, and the mummers. It would be wrong to regard these persons as curiosities, or as interesting literary fossils planted in the environment for the verisimilitude that they give. They not only take part in the series of festivals that provide a symbolic chronological pattern for the novel; but they also participate in the critical action itself, as agents of destiny. Timothy carries the letter which was so fatally not delivered at last. Johnny Nonesuch is liaison agent between Eustacia and Wildeve. Christian Cantle carries the guineas, and gambles them away. Susan Nonesuch and her son intervene actively in the lives of both Eustacia and Clym. Their part is organic, not decorative; they are much more than the "Greek chorus" that they have been called. They are, in fact, the basic pattern to which other characters conform or from which they differ. Diggory Venn and Thomasin, at a slightly higher level, conform more or less; they are changeless characters who venture near the danger line of changefulness but do not pass over it. Eustacia and Clym have passed over the line, though not beyond the possibility of retraction. They are changeful characters, strongly touched by Promethean influences —as Wildeve, in a vulgar way, is also touched. Modernism has worked on Eustacia to lure her away from Egdon Heath; but Clym, who has already lived in Paris, has reached a second stage of revulsion against modernism. Yet when this native returns he brings with him a characteristically modern program of education and evangelism. Eustacia and Clym, as changeful characters, do not diverge extravagantly from the changeless pattern, but their rebellion is great enough to render their lifecourses inconstant and tragic.

Hardy has taken some pains to mark the essential nature of Clym's character. The motto for the chapter that describes Clym is: "My mind to me a kingdom is." Clym is a Renaissance, or nontraditional, man. His face, already marked with disillusionment, foreshadows "the typical countenance of the future." Jude, another changeful character, is like Clym in some ways. He too is a rebel against nature, whose rebellion is also idealistic; but it leads him away from Wessex. His story might have been entitled: "The Migration of the Native." In Jude's life the changeless and the changeful are further represented in Arabella and Sue; Arabella, the changeless but too gross; Sue Bridehead, the changeful but too refined. In *Tess* there are two changeful and ruin-wreaking characters. In Alec Stoke-D'Urberville the changeful character takes on a vulgar form. He is an imposter, who has appropriated an old country name and bought his way into Wessex; and the Stoke-D'Urberville establishment, with its preposterous chicken culture, is a fake rural establishment. Angel Clare, on the other hand, is a rarefied form of alien. He is willing, condescendingly, to accept Wessex, and dairy farming, and Tess, provided he can possess all this in an abstractly "pure," or respectable form. The tragedy arrives when he cannot adjust (the sociological term is necessary) his delicate sensibility to a gross, but, in the natural order, an understandable biological fact. It is the changeful modern character in Angel that cannot abide Tess's delinquency. The changeless characters might have found fault, but would not have been shocked, would not have sulked, would have not been too slow to pardon. A similar opposition appears in *The Woodlanders,* where changefulness appears in Fitzpiers and Mrs. Charmond; changelessness in Giles Winterborne and Marty South.

Perhaps these are dangerous simplifications. I do not offer them as definitive explanations of Hardy's fictions, but rather as possibilities not yet explored. Hardy's habit of mind, and his method of using his habit of mind in fiction, seem to me the least discussed of the aspects of his work. I have found no other approach that does not seem to impose a critical explanation from without, with an arbitrariness that often seems to do violence to the art work itself.

There is surely no other example in modern English fiction of an author who, while reaching the highest levels of sophisticated artistic performance, comes bringing his tradition with him, not only the mechanics of the tradition but the inner conception that is often lacking. The admonitions we hear so often nowadays about the relation of the artist and his tradition seem dry and academic when we look closely at Hardy's actual performance. He seems to illustrate what we might think the ideal way of realizing and activating a tradition, for he did, without admonition, what the admonishers are always claiming ought to be done; and yet for that particular achievement he got no thanks, or even a notice. The achievement is the more extraordinary when we consider that he worked (if I read his career rightly) against the dominant pattern of his day. He did what the modern critic (despite his concern about tradition) is always implying to be impossible. That is, Hardy accepted the assumptions of a society which in England was already being condemned to death, and he wrote in terms of those assumptions, almost as if Wessex, and perhaps Wessex only, would understand. From his work I get few of the meanings, pessimistic or otherwise, that are commonly ascribed to him. His purpose seems to have been to tell about human life in the terms that would present it as most recognizably, and validly, and completely human. That he succeeded best when he wrote of rural Wessex is significant. He probably had strong convictions on one point—convictions that had little to do with his official inquiries into Darwinism and the nature of Deity.

Hardy in Defense of His Art: The Aesthetic of Incongruity

by Morton Dauwen Zabel

> The first artists, in any line, are doubtless not those whose general ideas about their art are most often on their lips—those who most abound in precept, apology, and formula and can best tell us the reasons and the philosophy of things. We know the first usually by their energetic practice, the constancy with which they apply their principles, and the serenity with which they leave us to hunt for their secret in the illustration, the concrete example. None the less it often happens that a valid artist utters his mystery, flashes upon us for a moment the light by which he works, shows us the rule by which he holds it just that he should be measured. This accident is happiest, I think, when it is soonest over; the shortest explanations of the products of genius are the best, and there is many a creator of living figures whose friends, however full of faith in his inspiration, will do well to pray for him when he sallies forth into the dim wilderness of theory. The doctrine is apt to be so much less inspired than the work, the work is often so much more intelligent than the doctrine.
>
> —James on Maupassant

I

That Hardy's was a native and persistent order of genius; that he expressed it in a style and drama which he made unmistakably his own; that his work carries the stamp of a theme and vision which have impressed a large area of art and experience in the last eighty years; that he exists as a force in modern literature in spite of some of the severest critical reservation any notable writer has been subjected to—these we may take as facts which have survived excesses both of distaste and of eulogy and become part of the record of modern English literature. In

Hardy's middle years the scorn of Henry James and George Moore joined with the scandalized protests of press and pulpit to deny him aesthetic as much as public respect. In his old age and after, a reckless apotheosis has proved almost as damaging. Hardy survives them both. Virginia Woolf, when she visited him at Max Gate in 1926, was sincere in recognizing a fact of history. "I wanted him to say one word about his writings before we left and could only ask which of his books he would have chosen if, like me, he had had to choose one to read in the train. I had taken *The Mayor of Casterbridge* . . . 'And did it hold your interest?' he asked. I stammered that I could not stop reading it, which was true, but sounded wrong." Few readers have missed the spell, and few have missed feeling in some sense confused about it.

Yet the radical quality is less likely to be mistaken in Hardy's work than in most writers of his rank. It can easily be simplified to a convenient fault or virtue, according to the prejudice of the critic. It often remains crudely defined in memory. The conflicting elements that shape it may be minimized by admirers who are anxious to forget the difficulties they met in salvaging his genius from the uneven and erratic body of his work. But it is a quality as unmistakable in his prose and verse as in his personality and thought; as prominent in his style as in that reading of life which he insisted on disclaiming as a "philosophy."

It derives from the conjunction, in his temperament, of conformist and skeptical tendencies; in his humanism, of stoic acquiescence with moral protest; in his response to human character, of a kinship with gifted, rebellious, or destructive aberrations from the human norm as against his sympathy with the rudimentary types and stable humors of the folk. In his thought it appears in his leaning toward cosmic simplifications so large and unwieldly that their grandeur becomes inflexible, an impediment to critical thinking and an oppression to the imagination, and conversely in his humble loyalty to the claims of life in all its elusive and stubborn deviations—its vital struggles and appeals that protest and so make bearable the mindless negation of the universe. What this ambivalence of temper did to Hardy's style is apparent on almost every one of his pages. Their salt, tang, and sincerity are continuously accompanied by habits of rhetoric, pretension, and straining eloquence, even by astonishing repetitions and laborings of effect, that exceed those in most of the writers in a century abnormally conscious of crisis and the "urge to rhetoric."

To credit these divergences to Hardy with any special emphasis is to say that the large schemes into which he cast his problems, and the stormy dramas he made of them, make the central discordance in his work insistent, the basic clue to his talent. Obviously this discordance exists widely in modern art and thought. Hardy saw it as a primary rift or dichotomy in man which post-rationalist Europe had thrown into a new relief. His contemporaries were torn and distraught by it; it is the frame and condition of the modern man's typical agony. Nor does one distinguish Hardy particularly by saying that his style and form are inordinately marked by rough contrasts and antitheses. Such contrasts—of aesthetic logic and selection at odds with the rough justice and violence of experience, or plots shaped and contrived to the point of artifice against the disorder of life, of characters reduced to the basic patterns of human nature against the subtle divinations of modern psychologists—are apparent throughout modern fiction; they swarm through that chaotic and amorphous medium to which the courtesy title of novel is applied. The same heterogeneity exists in modern poetry, where serious purposes are offset by startling levities, where the grand manner is deflated by vulgar intrusions, where moral earnestness is scoffed by the scurrilities of cynicism, and where a sense of responsibility to the traditional dignities of the human spirit became so violently reproached by the squalor of modern society that satirists like Laforgue and Corbière wrought these jarring collisions into a critical medium that has descended to Pound, Eliot, Joyce, Auden, and the satirists and realists of contemporary poetry and fiction.

Hardy participated little in these developments and showed small interest in the artistic results of the modern man's skeptical consciousness. But he was too much a child of his time to remain unmarked by the traits of nineteenth century art. He inherited the aesthetic disorder of the age, its unresolved antipathies, its sprawling appetite for life, and the instability that reflected the surrounding distraction. That instability is deeply imbedded in his books, and if popular reverence now tends to slight its prominence there, two other factors insists on emphasizing it. For one thing, Hardy wrote and matured during a period in which aesthetic reformers in fiction and poetry were grappling with the problem of reducing the elements of the arts to a new unity and integrity, of bringing them into a harmony that might enhance their value, force, and intelligence. He was the contemporary, in other words, of Baudelaire, Flaubert, and Turgenev, of James, Moore, Yeats, Proust, Pound, Valéry, and Eliot, but a colleague of none of them. He was, secondly, conscious throughout his life of the struggle in himself of a distressing opposition of faculties—of immediate personal sympathies and large intellectual ambitions—and in the face of the critical hostility that surrounded him through two-thirds of his literary career he struggled to formulate a defense of his talent and method. Thus he shaped a personal aesthetic for himself; and though it shows something of the amateur's pedantry that is evident in his early fiction and in his metaphysical excursions, it demands attention from anyone concerned with the artistic progress of the modern novel and with the interrelations of modern fiction and poetry.

He was no adept at critical or aesthetic reasoning; he felt a life-long suspicion of its practitioners; his literary notes and prefaces sound a note of peremptory impatience toward them. Yet his methodical habit of mind exercised itself over many years in notations on structure, form, style, and aesthetic ideas and in a continuous effort to generalize these into working principles. The craft of fiction had not come to him easily. Poetry was his first ambition, and until he was sixty he was in doubt whether his real vocation had been obstructed or merely painfully slow in maturing. "I was quick to bloom; late to ripen." "I was a child till I was 16; a youth till I was 25; a young man till I was 40 or 50." [1] The groping awkwardness he showed in mastering the business of fiction-writing is equaled by the step-by-step pains he took to come into some kind of conscious knowledge of his aesthetic purposes. One of the first things he discovered about himself was a natural lack of artistic sophistication. He knew he was unequipped for competition with the rising schools of Paris and London. He felt the pull of older traditions of romance and a brotherhood with the rough-and-ready masters of Victorian fiction, the dramatic and sensation novelists of the Sixties from whom he learned his trade. The homeliness of his tastes is evident in "An Ancient to Ancients." In music his favorites, when not the hymns of Tate and Brady, were *The Bohemian Girl* and *Il Trovatore*. In painting, though he carefully studied the Dutch and Italian schools, he warmed to the Academy pictures of Etty, Mulready, and Maclise. In fiction the "throbbing romance" of Bulwer, Scott, Dumas, and Sand had made a golden age. His poetic loyalties, rooted in the romanticism of Keats, Shelley, and Tennyson, spent their last real enthusiasm on Browning and Swinburne. As early as 1873 we find him attempting to justify natural impulse and fancy as the basis of art:

> Read again Addison, Macaulay, Newman, Sterne, Defoe, Lamb, Gibbon, Burke, *Times* Leaders, in a study of style. Am more and more confirmed in an idea I have long held, as a matter of common sense, long before I thought of any old aphorism bearing on the subject: "Ars est celare artem." The whole

[1] The passages quoted from Hardy in this essay are from the prefaces as they appear in the Mellstock Edition (London, 1921-1922), in *Late Lyrics and Earlier* (London, 1922), and in *Winter Words* (London, 1928); from Hardy's essays, notes, and letters as they appear in *Life and Art*, collected by Ernest Brennecke, Jr. (New York, 1925); from his notebooks and letters as quoted by Mrs. Hardy in *The Early Life of Thomas Hardy* (New York, 1928) and *The Later Years of Thomas Hardy* (New York, 1930); from several entries quoted by Carl J. Weber in *Hardy of Wessex* (New York, 1940) and in the studies of Lionel Johnson, H. C. Duffin, Arthur McDowell, and S. C. Chew; and from unpublished correspondence. The *Early Life* and *Later Years* published by Mrs. Hardy after Hardy's death now take on an increased importance since Richard Little Purdy, in his *Thomas Hardy: A Bibliographical Study* (1954), pp. 262-67 and 268-73, has shown them to be "in reality an autobiography," prepared for posthumous publication by Hardy himself.

secret of a living style and the difference between it and a dead style, lies in not having too much style—being in fact, a little careless, or rather seeming to be, here and there. It brings wonderful life into the writing:

> A sweet disorder in the dress. . . .
> A careless shoe-string, in whose tie
> I see a wild civility,
> Do more bewitch me than when art
> Is too precise in every part.

Otherwise your style is like worn half-pence—all the fresh images rounded off by rubbing, and no crispness or movement at all.

It is, of course, simply a carrying into prose the knowledge I have acquired in poetry—that inexact rhymes and rhythms now and then are far more pleasing than correct ones.

He began to turn to nature for his justification of such defect and awkwardness:

> So, then, if Nature's defects must be looked in the face and transcribed, whence arises the *art* in poetry and novel-writing? which must certainly show art, or it becomes merely mechanical reporting. I think the art lies in making these defects the basis of a hitherto unperceived beauty, by irradiating them with "the light that never was" on their surface, but is seen to be latent in them by the spiritual eye.

"Faultlessness," he once agreed with Browning, "avails neither a man nor book anything unless it can be surmounted by care and sympathy," and when he read Henry James's *Reverberator* on its appearance in 1888 he emphatically dissociated himself from the new motives in fiction:

> After this kind of work one feels inclined to be purposely careless in detail. The great novels of the future will certainly not concern themselves with the minutiae of manners. . . . James's subjects are those one could be interested in at moments when there is nothing larger to think of.

This defense of casual vitality now appears inseparable from Hardy's emphasis on the significance of chance and accident in life. In his aesthetic morality it results in a defense of instinctive and emotional qualities above the intellectual. The purpose of great fiction is not basically critical, intellectual, dialectic, or minutely discriminative; it is to seize and embody the values of the heart, of instinct and intuitive sympathy, of the passions which Hardy shared with the Victorian moralists and humanitarians and which he saw exhausted and vitiated among the critical efforts of the modern schools. The "seemings" which he held, in the preface to *Jude* and elsewhere, to be the sum and substance of his work, as against the imputation of philosophical pessimism or negation (in 1917 he wrote: "I find I wrote in 1888 that 'Art is concerned with seemings only,' which is true"), are for him exactly those responses which are authorized by the heart as against the canceling judgments of the head. "I hold," he said late in life,

> that the mission of poetry is to record impressions, not convictions. Wordsworth in his later writings fell into the error of recording the latter. So also did Tennyson and so do many other poets when they grow old. Absit omen! . . . I believe it would be said by people who knew me well that I have a faculty (possibly not uncommon) for burying an emotion in my heart or brain for forty years, and exhuming it at the end of that time as fresh as when interred.

Hardy, recognizing the undeviating identity of his feeling and style over a space of seventy years, took that fact as a means of justifying the permanence of "impressions" above the instability of intellectual doctrines and convictions. "Poetry must feel," he maintained. "The Poet takes note of nothing that he cannot feel emotively." "There is a latent music in the sincere utterance of deep emotion, however expressed, which fills the place of the actual word-music in rhythmic phraseology on thinner emotive subjects, or on subjects with next to none at all." The translation of that emotion into style became his single assurance of success as a poet:

> Consider the Wordsworthian dictum (the more perfectly the natural object is reproduced, the more truly poetic the picture). This reproduction is achieved by seeing into the *heart of a thing* (as rain, wind, for instance), and is realism, in fact, though through being pursued by means of the imagination it is confounded with invention, which is pursued by the same means. It is, in short, reached by what M. Arnold calls "the imaginative reason."

Such a view of the matter made drudgery for Hardy of any intense technical discipline. When, in his earlier books, he was obliged to treat of modern artificial life, he particularly felt the strain. He had "mostly aimed at keeping his narratives close to natural life and as near to poetry in their subject as the conditions would allow, and had often regretted that those conditions would not let him keep them nearer still." When he reread Henry James in old age, he marveled and was perplexed that "a writer who has no grain of poetry, or humor, or spontaneity, in his productions, can yet be a good novelist. Meredith has some poetry, and yet I can read James when I cannot look at Meredith." He saw Meredith's failure in the fact "that he would not, or could not—at any rate did not—

when aiming to represent the 'Comic Spirit,' let himself discover the tragedy that always underlies Comedy if you only scratch deeply enough." "If all hearts were open and all desires known—as they would be if people showed their souls—how many gapings, sighings, clenched fists, knotted brows, broad grins, and red eyes should we see in the marketplace!"

The prejudice here is clear. Hardy saw the growth of sophistication and critical intellection in art as evils at its root. His scruples as a workman and his methodical seriousness as a student, even his systematic ambition for literary fame, were outbalanced by his sense of being an outsider to art's higher mysteries. It is no wonder that James and Stevenson, though compelled to admire, groaned over the flaws in *Tess,* or that George Moore spent his harshest invective on that book and its author, or that T. S. Eliot, in *After Strange Gods,* has set Hardy down as a "symptom of decadence," a victim of emotion run morbid, "a minor poet" whose matter of communication is not "particularly wholesome or edifying." The approach to Hardy through his artistic medium ("he was indifferent even to the prescripts of good writing," says Eliot, ". . . at times his style touches sublimity without ever having passed through the stage of being good") has often resulted in this inclusive contempt. This approach is inescapable; it is necessary; but in the case of Hardy's sharply qualified and unstable talent, the approach must be made in unusually wide and comprehensive terms. His own anti-aesthetic position committed him to a search for the timeless qualities of life and destiny, to a sense of history that shares little of the critical scrutiny of time and experience that was soon to become a major prepossession of the modern artist. Hardy stood, indeed, in an honored English line. He felt that poetry and fiction, if they bowed to the critical faculty, would ultimately meet an enervation of their strength, their native daemon and validity. He held in this with Bacon, Goldsmith, and Macaulay; he anticipated some of the fears that I. A. Richards has voiced in *Science and Poetry*. Caught between the intimacy of his physical sensations and the enveloping grandeur of his imaginative and scientific visions, he based his faith as a poet on a magical conception of man and nature. This sympathy suffuses his literal-mindedness, his prosaic tedium, his almost mawkish dissection of passionate fact. And he proposed to defend and exemplify it in his work as long as he lived.

Accordingly we find Hardy arguing that fiction must share with poetry the task of relieving the oppression of life's fact and commonplace. He opposed the naturalists, whom he saw joining forces with aesthetic rationalists in making an unbearable oppression of the actual.

> The real, if unavowed, purpose of fiction is to give pleasure by gratifying the love of the uncommon in human experience, mental or corporeal.

This is done all the more perfectly in proportion as the reader is illuded to believe the personages true and real like himself.

Solely to this latter end a work of fiction should be a precise transcript of ordinary life: but,

The uncommon would be absent and the interest lost. Hence,

The writer's problem is, how to strike the balance between the uncommon and the ordinary so as on the one hand to give interest, on the other to give reality.

In working out this problem, human nature must never be made abnormal, which is introducing incredibility. The uncommonness must be in the events, not in the characters; and the writer's art lies in shaping that uncommonness while disguising its unlikelihood, if it be unlikely.

He subscribed to Coleridge's view that the aim must be "at *illusion* in audience or readers—*i.e.,* the mental state when dreaming, intermediate between complete delusion (which the French mistakenly aim at) and a clear perception of falsity." As late as 1919, long after he had abandoned fiction, he felt a weight on his conscience that he had led the novel too much toward positive realism, and had by that means aided in stultifying the suggestive and poetic force of modern novel-writing. He would, he said, write at the beginning of each new romance: "Understand that however true this book may be in essence, in fact it is utterly untrue." Two days after completing *The Mayor of Casterbridge* in 1885 he had written, "The business of the poet and novelist is to show the sorriness underlying the grandest things, and the grandeur underlying the sorriest things." Nature, if left unprejudiced and uninterpreted, becomes a curse and burden to man, and this can be alleviated only by the imaginative penetration of her meaning which it is the function of art to supply. "Nature is an arch-dissembler. A child is deceived completely; the older members of society more or less according to their penetration; though even they seldom get to realize that *nothing* is as it appears." And again:

Nature is played out as a Beauty, but not as a Mystery. . . . I don't want to see the original realities—as optical effects, that is. I want to see the deeper reality underlying the scenic, the expression of what are sometimes called abstract imaginings.

The "simply natural" is interesting no longer. The much decried, mad, late-Turner rendering is now necessary to create my interest. The exact truth as to material fact ceases to be of importance in art—it is a student's style—the style of a period when the mind is serene and unawakened to the tragical mysteries of life; when it does not bring anything to the object that coalesces with and translates the qualities that are already there,—half hidden, it may be—, and the two are depicted as the All.

Thus he came to suspect any rationalization that pretended to account for the totality of life or reality, and any literary theory that maintained it is the purpose of art to convey a sense of such totality. "Since I discovered," he said in 1882, "that I was living in a world where nothing bears out in practice what it promises incipiently, I have troubled very little about theories. . . . Where development according to perfect reason is limited to the narrow region of pure mathematics, I am content with tentativeness from day to day." So it comes about that Hardy, whatever his connection with post-Darwinian fashions in determinism, resisted the formulation of a logic of experience or history.

> Is not the present quasi-scientific system of writing history mere charlatanism? Events and tendencies are traced as if they were rivers of voluntary activity, and courses reasoned out from the circumstances in which natures, religions, or what-not, have found themselves. But are they not in the main the outcome of *passivity*—acted upon by unconscious propensity?

Just before the War, viewing the rise of a new generation of documentary realists, he said that "they forget in their insistence on life, and nothing but life, in a plain slice, that a story *must be worth the telling,* that a good deal of life is not worth any such thing, and that they must not occupy a reader's time with what he can get at first hand anywhere around him."

What is "worth telling" is what recedes from the apparent, the external, the visible. It is the part of experience that withdraws into the private, the subjective, the subconscious, and hence into the mysterious energy of living matter.

> People who to one's-self are transient singularities are to themselves the permanent condition, the inevitable, the normal, the rest of mankind being to them the singularity. Think, that those (to us) strange phenomena, *their* personalities, are with them always, at their going to bed, at their uprising!
>
> Footsteps, cabs, etc., are continually passing our lodgings. And every echo, pit-pat, and rumble that makes up the general noise has behind it a motive, a prepossession, a hope, a fear, a fixed thought forward; perhaps more—a joy, a sorrow, a love, a revenge.
>
> London appears not to see *itself*. Each individual is conscious of *himself*, but nobody conscious of themselves collectively, except perhaps some poor gaper who stares round with a half-idiotic aspect.
>
> There is no consciousness of where anything comes from or goes to—only that it is present.
>
> In the City. The fiendish precision or mechanism of town-life is what makes it so intolerable to the sick and infirm. Like an acrobat performing on a succession of swinging trapezes, as long as you are at particular points at precise instants, everything glides as if afloat; but if you are not up to time—

When he transferred this sense of the endless dichotomy of life, its mysterious dualism of subject and object, to the problem of narrative, Hardy saw that the inherent animus of experience is something more than the double vision of which the blessed simple folk of the world are unconscious but by which the seeing intellects are eternally tormented. It is a matter of maintaining a precarious balance, in art as in intelligent life, between the necessities of personal, practical, and localized experience, and the knowledge of universals which transcend all individuality. "I do not expect much notice will be taken of these poems," he said when publishing *Moments of Vision* in 1917; "they mortify the human sense of self-importance by showing, or suggesting, that human beings are of no matter or appreciable value in this nonchalant universe." This was only an echo of what he had written during the stormy aftermath of *Tess* in 1893: "The whole secret of fiction and the drama—in the constructional part—lies in the adjustment of things unusual to things eternal and universal. The writer who knows exactly how exceptional, and how nonexceptional, his events should be made, possesses the key to the art." Upon that conviction he based his idea of tragedy. "The best tragedy—highest tragedy in short—is that of the WORTHY encompassed by the INEVITABLE. The tragedies of immoral and worthless people are not of the best." When *Jude* fell under the lash of the reviewers in 1895, he committed himself to his final patience and wrote in his notebook:

> Tragedy may be created by an opposing environment either of things inherent in the universe, or of human institutions. If the former be the means exhibited and deplored, the writer is regarded as impious; if the latter, as subversive and dangerous; when all the while he may never have questioned the necessity or urged the nonnecessity of either.

Thus he made consoling generalizations on his creative plight. But he was able to localize the tragic sense in himself. That he had reasons for doing so, especially during his first marriage, we have come to understand only lately (Mr. Carl Weber's biography makes them clear enough). Sometimes the twist of this pathos seized him with a pang almost as ludicrous as that which so frequently strikes his Clyms, Bathshebas, Judes, and Henchards. Once in middle life he found himself afflicted with toothache. "I look in the glass. Am conscious of the humiliating sorriness of my earthly tabernacle, and of the sad fact that the best of parents could do no better for me. . . . Why should a man's mind have been thrown into such close, sad, sensational, inexplicable relations with such a precarious object as his own body!"

II

Everyone has experienced certain tests of credulity and assent in reading Hardy. All lovers of his work, at one time or another, are caught up by the strain he places on belief and sympathy. Perhaps his own word best labels the pervading quality of his effects: they are "tentative." His appeal is cumulative, seldom concentrated; deliberate with a patient confidence in the latent meaning of life, not immediate and assumptive in its acceptance of cosmic justice. His reading of experience, whatever sense he conveys of implacable forces and blind principle, is groping, experimental, suspended, empirical. As is well known, he explicitly repudiated the imputation of pessimism in his thought, just as he implicitly broke with the monistic conception of life and matter. He practiced, "by the exploration of reality and [a] frank recognition stage by stage along the survey," the mode of thought which he called "evolutionary meliorism." At least three times he challenged directly the charge of his critics (Alfred Noyes on one notable occasion) that he argued from a position of dogmatic negation and that he reduced deity to nonentity and God to an "imbecile jester." The cosmic theater in which the warring nations of *The Dynasts* are mixed shows them obeying "resistlessly the purposive, unmotivated dominant Thing," but Hardy requested his reader not to make too close an inspection of his phantoms or arguments since they "are but tentative, and are advanced with little eye to systematic philosophy." *Jude* was offered to the public in 1895 as "simply an endeavor to give shape and coherence to a series of seemings, or personal impressions, the question of their consistency or their discordance, of their permanence or their transitoriness, being regarded as not of the first moment." And for the general preface of the Mellstock Edition in 1921 he wrote:

> Positive views on the Whence and the Wherefore of things have never been advanced by this pen as a consistent philosophy. Nor is it likely, indeed, that imaginative writings extending over more than forty years would exhibit a coherent scientific theory of the universe even if it had been attempted—of that universe concerning which Spencer owns to the "paralyzing thought" that possibly there exists no comprehension of it anywhere. . . . That these impressions have been condemned as "pessimistic"—as if that were a very wicked adjective—shows a curious muddle-mindedness. It must be obvious that there is a higher characteristic of philosophy than pessimism, or than meliorism, or even than the optimism of these critics—which is truth. Existence is either ordered in a certain way, or it is not so ordered, and conjectures which harmonize best with experience are removed above all comparison with other conjectures which do not so harmonize. . . . And there is another consideration. Differing natures find their tongue in the presence of differing spectacles.

Some natures become vocal at tragedy, some are made vocal by comedy, and it seems to me that to whichever of these aspects of life a writer's instinct for expression the more readily responds, to that he should allow it to respond. That before a contrasting side of things he remains undemonstrative need not be assumed to mean that he remains unperceiving.

These statements of Hardy's reduce to several conclusions. He had no inclination to see science as absolute or final; its whole appeal to him lay in its dissolution of "counters and fixities" in both experience and universal law. He inclined, with the natural leaning of his post-Romantic generation, toward the validity of individual perception. His respect for scientific thought was a respect for the goal it set for itself—a liberal, unprejudiced, and cumulative mode of truth. He was an empiric but not, as he insisted, a pragmatic. He sympathized less with the pessimistic arguments of Schopenhauer than with the creative and evolutionary motives of English thinkers. Of *The Dynasts* he said, "My pages show harmony of view with Darwin, Huxley, Spencer, Comte, Hume, Mill, and others, all of whom I used to read more than Schopenhauer." The year 1859 was always remembered as a red-letter date in his career: he was one of the first readers of *The Origin of Species* and at once sensed its epoch-making importance. It was the evolutionary or progressive principle, with its creative implications, that won his sympathy for the historical patterns defined by Comte, Spencer, and Eduard von Hartmann's *Philosophy of the Unconscious*. The closing lines of *The Dynasts* are often overworked by embarrassed apologists, but they express what Hardy repeatedly insists on; their gleam of promise and aspiration in the universal order redeems, as with a flicker of faith, the darkness that drops on Tess, Jude, and Henchard.

Hardy was, in fact, more than is generally assumed a pioneer defender, with Butler and Shaw, of the creative principle in evolution. The will to live, as he dramatizes it, persists through every apparent confusion of local and individual purposes. It is never without its consolations. Momentarily it instructs man in accepting nature as the refuge of his tormented spirit. Prophetically it lends him the hope that his life will be harmonized with the unconscious or instinctive energy of nature. It even advances to a higher plane and glimpses a victory of intelligence, a release of the higher Will from its cosmic condition of "immanence," so that it may become assimilated to the conscious energy and vision of human beings.

"The discovery of the law of evolution, which revealed that all organic creatures are of one family," he wrote to a New York correspondent in 1909, "shifted the center of altruism from humanity to the whole conscious world collectively." And he agreed with an Australian admirer that

The Dynasts offered an idea harmonious with the principle of Christian revelation: the Immanent Will, far from showing fiendish malignance, may appear blind and irresponsible, but it implies a growth into self-consciousness. One recent critic, Mr. Amiya Chakravarty, has extended this possibility in Hardy's thought by drawing the analogy of Freud's categories: the Spirit of the Years (of conscious or calculated experience) is analogous to the Freudian Ego; the Spirit of the Pities (of human purpose, identity, effort, frustration, tragedy) with the Super-ego; whereas the principle of unconscious and abiding energy, the Id, is represented by "the continuum of blind forces which unites the instincts with Nature and whose actions are the main theme of the drama." [2] These forces, basic and anterior to consciousness, may ultimately, with the arrival of a universal harmony, become lifted and approximated to the purposes of human will and aspiration. Another student, Pierre d'Exideuil, has echoed Hardy's distress that his version of Will should be regarded as an aimless one and that pessimism is the only adequate estimate of life, by going behind the Freudian analogy into the thinking of Hardy's middle years. He has proposed another affiliation: "the fundamental difference between Schopenhauer's and Hardy's outlook perhaps lies in the fact that Schopenhauer is pre-Darwinian, whereas Hardy's thought was definitely moulded by the conception of evolution." D'Exideuil sees that "between Schopenhauer and Hardy, as between Schopenhauer and Nietzsche, stands Darwin, the channel whereby meliorism, the idea of the greatest possible enriching and perfecting of life, reaches the poet of *The Dynasts* and the hero of *Zarathustra*. Life, therefore, may become its own aim, whereas Schopenhauer stopped short with the denial of any final aim." [3]

This oversimplifies Schopenhauer's thought and minimizes its contribution to the Freudian principle of energy. But it points to an important fact. Hardy may have diverged from Schopenhauer but he saw with him the dualistic character of man, his division between compulsive force, supremely embodied in sexual urge, and his attraction toward the transcendence of idea—an aspiration of intellect rendered pathetic or tragic by the warfare of passion. Sex is for Hardy what it is for Schopenhauer—the focal point of Will, the final sublimation of sincerity. Yet Hardy never advanced as far as Schopenhauer did in "his insight into the overweening power of instinct and the derogation of the one-time godlike reason, mind, and intellect to a mere tool with which to achieve security."

Hardy, as both poet and novelist, was prevented by his response to man's character and courage from a dualism so extreme. Accordingly, the

[2] Amiya Chakravarty, *The Dynasts and the Post-War Age in Poetry* (Oxford, 1938), p. 22.

[3] Pierre d'Exideuil, *The Human Pair in the Work of Thomas Hardy* (London, 1929), p. 209.

opposition of will and idea, instinct and intellect, is never absolute and rigorous with him. The two spheres interpenetrate. He conveys, by the dramatic reality of his characters and the poetic truth of his finest verse, a promise of ultimate unity among the forces that harry and destroy men which Schopenhauer, working within the frames of theory and ratiocination, stopped short of. Hardy's modest and confident temper never suffered the German's exacerbation. Yet what Thomas Mann has said of Schopenhauer is enlightening at this point: there is a fundamental connection between his pessimism and his humanism, "this combined melancholy and pride in the human race which make up Schopenhauer's philosophy."

> His pessimism—that is his humanity. His interpretation of the world by the concept of the will, his insight into the overweening power of instinct and the derogation of the one-time godlike reason, mind, and intellect to a mere tool with which to achieve security—all this is anticlassic and in its essence inhumane. But it is precisely in the pessimistic hue of his philosophy that his humanity and spirituality lie; in the fact that this great artist . . . lifts man out of the biological sphere of nature, makes his own feeling and understanding soul the theater where the will meets its reverse, and sees in the human being the savior of all creation.[4]

What Schopenhauer arrived at by something resembling a counsel of desperation, Hardy arrived at by the humane insight and compassion of a great artist. Where Schopenhauer rests on the latent form of such "artistry," Hardy succeeds by the imaginative immediacy of art. His Henchard, Tess, and Jude enter the sphere of "saviors of all creation" where Hamlet, Macbeth, and Lear stand in the ranks of the triumphant.

The transition in Hardy from doubt and negation to humanistic hope was encumbered by an amateur's crudity in handling philosophical machinery, and the clumsiness is evident in all his dramas. He contrives his defeats and frustrations as a means of reducing to its final and minimal condition the saving heroism, dignity, and integrity of his characters. His use of every known portent, accident, and coincidence of chance destinies is notoriously excessive. The impression that survives such buffetings of the reader's patience corresponds, no doubt intentionally, to the indestructible essence of human worth and dignity with which his characters manage to survive, Greek-like, their havoc of ruin and defeat. The role of man in the universe is, for Hardy, comparable to the role of will and intelligence themselves: it is a role of emergent exoneration and supremacy. The word *emergent* is important. Man's exoneration is not to be taken for granted. It is not to be rashly assumed by means of defiance, ambition,

[4] Thomas Mann, *The Living Thoughts of Schopenhauer* (New York, 1939), p. 29.

or egotism. It materializes slowly, out of blight and despair. It materializes so slowly and painfully, indeed, that one is inclined to think that Hardy saw an analogy for this painful vindication in the equally painful and agonized degrees by which modern man had suffered the loss of his traditional dignity in the teachings of Bacon, Montaigne, Galileo, Newton, Locke, Lyell, and Darwin, and yet survived to declare a new faith and worth for himself through a sublimation of his egoistic individuality into the instinctive wisdom and slowly maturing intelligence of the natural universe itself. Some such allegory is conveyed by the stories of Clym Yeobright, Michael Henchard, and Jude Fawley; it is implicit in Hardy's children of nature—Gabriel Oak, Giles Winterborne, Marty South, Diggory Venn, and John Loveday.

Hardy's "seemings" are rightly termed "a tentative metaphysic." His faith in nature and cosmic purpose is emergent. Correspondingly, the role of man—never demoted from his position of superiority to other parts of nature—must be emergent also. His dignity is arrived at by test, denial, humiliation, disillusion, and defeat—by every possible accident of fate, ironic mischance, and the apparently hostile action of nature. The vindication of man implies the vindication of purpose in the universe. It will appear by means of reserves that issue from the blind or instinctive life in order to become conscious and creative. This inspiration of personal will through violence and suffering corresponds to the gradualism whereby, in the closing chorus of *The Dynasts,*

> the rages
> Of the ages
> Shall be cancelled, and deliverance offered from the darts that were,
> Consciousness the Will informing, till It fashion all things fair!

III

Any reader of Hardy is continuously aware of difficulties exactly corresponding to Hardy's own slow, trial-and-error "impressions" of the meaning of man's place in nature and to the deliberate, trial-and-error way by which he built them into his tales. His novels, teeming with contrivance, show the cumbersome plotting, the exaggerated mountings, the devious complexity, which the whole craft of modern fiction, from Flaubert and Turgenev to James, Conrad, and Proust, has insisted on rejecting, and which even such prodigal contrivers as Dickens, Trollope, and Hugo had managed to subdue to their more relaxed and spacious versions of modern life.

Almost any tale by Hardy, on first reading at least, nettles the sympathy, offers stumbling-blocks to attention, and is likely to make the suspension of disbelief a resentful ordeal. The selling of Mrs. Henchard in the opening pages of *The Mayor of Casterbridge* is a violent instance of such assault on credulity, and others follow fast in the remainder of the book. It now takes persistence to move past these wrenchings of congruity, and one's faith in the novelist's seriousness must survive a good many tests before the gathering force of the local color, the Dorset speech, the richness of country customs, and the mounting grandeur of pathos slowly subsume the defects and crudities of Hardy's plots. The opening situation in *Tess* is relieved by the droll humor of its treatment, but minor tales like *Two on a Tower* are pitched at so violent an angle of improbability that they creak under the excesses of their romantic plots and the added burden of astronomical machinery that nearly crushes the lives out of the characters instead of rendering them tragically pitiable. Even the famous overture of *The Return of the Native* shows so exaggerated an air of portentous solemnity (and so much overwriting, dragging erudition, repetition of motives, and rhythmic orotundity) that it takes all the subsequent weight of the novel, all of its passions, rustic naïveté, and counterbalancing melodrama, to overcome the ponderous effect of the first chapters. Certainly *The Dynasts,* however it may impress many readers and however memorably it offers its flashes of historic synthesis and characterization, cannot survive as drama or history. The burden of its pretensions and the falseness they inflict on its style are too pervasive. Hardy admitted this to some degree; he told Henry Newbolt that "instead of saying to themselves 'Here is a performance hugely defective: is there anything in it notwithstanding the huge defects?' [the critics] have contented themselves with picking out bad lines, which any child could do, there are myriads of them, as I knew too well before they said so"; and he took consolation in Meredith's praise of the "panoramic" validity of the work. But even as a panoramic achievement *The Dynasts* puts our understanding of poetic integrity under a killing strain. The shorter poems are another matter; the finest are exquisite and superbly alive, and below the finest are three or four other levels of quality which one may richly enjoy; but even this leaves a considerable bulk that embarrasses Hardy's resources to a painful degree.

We are never permitted to forget the profound disparity in Hardy's taste and genius, a permanent division between his instinctive attraction toward life and his confusion by it, between his native feeling for words and character and his incurable tendency toward stiff erudition, toward ponderous generalizations on life and experience, toward grandiose symbolism and immensities of scale that wildly exceed the proportions necessary for maintaining his picture of man's atomic part in existence. There is an essential incongruity in Hardy's world. And he stretched the terms of the incongruity to such a degree that his tales often collapse under the test. It soon becomes apparent that the incongruity existed in his own temperament to a greater degree than most artists could ever hope to tolerate or justify. The imponderables of his thought and curiosity almost overwhelm the native and intimate resources of his personal character. "The machinery contrived by the Gods for reducing human possibilities of amelioration to a minimum" which he mentioned in *The Mayor Casterbridge* often becomes a machinery contrived by Hardy for reducing the artistic possibilities of imaginative conviction to a vanishing point.

Yet in that incongruity, and in what he made of it, lies the secret of Hardy's success, and his success survives some of the severest criticism that has been made against an author of his rank. He was conscious of this hostility among critics; he never became thick-skinned enough, even in his final apotheosis, to disregard it. His prefaces, which are usually devoted to disclaiming charges made against his moral or philosophical ideas, are always mildly defensive and in the one prefixed to *Late Lyrics and Earlier* in 1922 he voiced a denunciation of contemporary reviewers as Isaiahan as anything one may find in the prose of Housman. (Charles Morgan, as an Oxford student in 1920, found in this querulous resentment the one "failure of balance" in Hardy's personality.) But even when criticism is something more than the moral indignation of journalists or the snobbery of rising talents, its severity usually permits Hardy to emerge with the stature of a master. Mr. Frank Chapman, in one of the best essays yet written on the novels, comes to the conclusion that "his greatness [may be seen] as the greatness of the Victorian age, in its solidity and its sureness of what it really valued, yet Hardy is above the Victorian ethos and did not share the limitations that made tragedy impossible." And Vernon Lee, in the severest analysis ever made of Hardy's style, concluded her merciless dissection by saying that superior stylists like "Stevenson, Meredith, or Henry James would scarcely be what is wanted for such subject-matter . . . the faults of Hardy are probably an expression of his solitary and matchless grandeur of attitude. He belongs to a universe transcending such trifles as Writers and Readers and their little logical ways." [5] But here we return to Hardy's own analysis of his problem.

In 1888, in his essay on "The Profitable Reading of Fiction," he defended the novelist's right to be inconsistent and unequal.

> However numerous the writer's excellencies, he is what is called unequal; he has a specialty. This especial gift being discovered, he fixes his regard more particularly thereupon. It is frequently not that feature in an author's work which common repute has given him credit for; more often it is, while co-

[5] Frank Chapman, "Hardy the Novelist," in *Scrutiny* (Cambridge, England), Vol. III (June 1934), pp. 22-37. Vernon Lee, *The Handling of Words* (London, 1923), pp. 222-41.

existent with his popular attribute, overshadowed by it, lurking like a violet in the shade of the more obvious, possibly more vulgar, talent, but for which it might have received high attention. Behind the broad humor of one popular pen he discerns startling touches of weirdness; amid the colossal fancies of another he sees strokes of the most exquisite tenderness; and the unobtrusive quality may grow to have more charm for him than the palpable one.

This is sufficiently astonishing as self-examination and prophecy. It is exactly in his touches of weirdness and strokes of exquisite tenderness that we now see the qualities that redeem the broad humor and colossal fancies that are the bane of Hardy's work. He said something equally cogent in 1891, in the essay on "The Science of Fiction," when he maintained that "Art is science with an addition"; that while fiction must unquestionably show "that comprehensive and accurate knowledge of realities which must be sought for, or intuitively possessed, to some extent, before anything deserving the name of an artistic performance in narrative can be produced," it is in the addition that the vital and life-giving quality resides. Only when this "constructive stage is entered upon, Art—high or low—begins to exist." Accordingly Hardy takes issue with Zola's creed of the *roman expérimental* and repudiates the notion that fiction can ever be Truth, whole, consistent, and inclusive; that it can ever rely like science on the evidence of the outer senses; that it can ever rest on the logic and documentation of scientific naturalism; and that there is any possibility "of reproducing in its entirety the phantasmagoria of experience with infinite and atomic truth, without shadow, relevancy, or subordination."

The fallacy appears to owe its origin to the just perception that with our widened knowledge of the universe and its forces, and man's position therein, narrative, to be artistically convincing, must adjust itself to the new alignment, as would also artistic works in form and color, if further spectacles in their sphere could be presented. Nothing but the illusion of truth can permanently please, and when the old illusions begin to be penetrated, a more natural magic has to be supplied.

Here Hardy is not only aware of his instinctive use of the poetic method in fiction and of his impulse toward metaphorical values; he is arguing again along the line of Richards: that "the Neutralization of Nature, the transference from the Magical View of the world to the scientific," is robbing life of "a shape, a sharpness, and a coherence that no other means could so easily secure," and so deprives the artist of an "ease and adequacy with which the universe . . . could be emotionally handled, the scope offered for man's love and hatred, for his terror as well as for his hope and his despair."[6] (The proem of *The Return of the Native* sounds this same danger when it raises the question "if the exclusive reign of this orthodox beauty is not approaching its last quarter. The new Vale of Tempe may be a gaunt waste in Thule . . . and ultimately, to the commonest tourist, spots like Iceland may become what the vineyards and myrtle-gardens of South Europe are to him now.") What he is further arguing is that the meanness and inconsequence to which scientific realism is reducing human life are despoiling both poetry and fiction of their traditional moral and heroic values; that these must be maintained or substituted for; that

> what cannot be discerned by eye and ear, what may be apprehended only by the mental tactility that comes from a sympathetic appreciativeness of life in all its manifestations, this is the gift which renders its possessor a more accurate delineator of human nature than many another with twice his powers and means of external observation, but without that sympathy.

Hardy was protesting here not only against realism—the confounding logic by which the naturalists were depriving art of meaning and power—but also against the aesthetic version of this discipline which Flaubert and Pater were advocating—the "minutiae of manners" and of stylistic detail which spelled for him nothing but a revulsion to the "purposely careless." When he wrote on "The Profitable Reading of Fiction" for *The Forum* in 1888, he told his readers:

> To distinguish truths which are temporary from truths which are eternal, the accidental from the essential, accuracies as to custom and ceremony from accuracies as to the perennial procedure of humanity, is of vital importance in our attempts to read for something more than amusement. There are certain novels, both among the works of living and the works of deceased writers, which give convincing proof of much exceptional fidelity, and yet they do not rank as great productions; for what they are faithful in is life garniture and not life. . . . A living French critic goes even further concerning the novelists of social minutiae. "They are far removed," says he, "from the great imaginations which create and transform. They renounce free invention; they narrow themselves to scrupulous exactness; they paint clothes and places with endless detail."

His own precepts were even simpler, in the end, than these. "A story should be an organism." "Style . . . can only be treatment, and treatment

[6] I. A. Richards, *Science and Poetry* (New York, 1926), cf. pp. 53-63. The quotations in the last two paragraphs of the present essay are from Alice Meynell, *The Second Person Singular and Other Essays* (Oxford, 1922), p. 140; and from *Further Letters of Gerard Manley Hopkins*, edited by Claude Colleer Abbott (Oxford, 1938), pp. 222-23.

depends upon the mental attitude of the novelist." "Nothing but the illusion of truth can permanently please."

Hardy becomes in his poetics something very different from the victim of scientific determinism that the literal reading of his novels and key-phrases makes him. He never resists the limitations of materialism so eloquently as when he resents the modern effort to yoke the artist with mechanisms of technique or with the utilitarian purposes of economic or physical theory. His force as a stylist, dramatist, and allegorist is clarified by his refusal to fall in with the restrictions of naturalism, or with an aesthetic based on the rigid and obvious congruities of physical fact. He defended the salient quality of his art, and any intelligent reader must be compelled by it in the end, whether it is represented by startling properties like Stonehenge and Egdon and Knight's vision as he hangs from the cliff's edge in *A Pair of Blue Eyes,* by extreme characters like Arabella, Sue, Eustacia Vye, Gabriel Oak, and Jude, by his use of obvious choral devices like the Shakespearean rustics and the Parcae of Casterbridge, or, best of all, by those brilliant strokes of dramatic incident which illuminate and suddenly justify the wildness of his plots—the door closed against Mrs. Yeobright, the tree-planting by Marty and Winterborne, Tess's seeing the blood-stained paper as she stands ringing the bell of the empty house of Clare's parents. He now appears to us as a realist developing toward allegory—as an imaginative artist who brought the nineteenth century novel out of its slavery to fact and its dangerous reaction against popularity, and so prepared the way for some of the most original talents of a new time. He stands in a succession of novelists that includes Melville, Emily Brontë, and Hawthorne, that takes in James and Flaubert in the wider reach of their faculties, and that has arrived at the achievements of Joyce, Proust, Gide, and Kafka.

When his novels falter in that demonstration, his poetry takes it up. The shorter poems are, in fact, the spiritual center of his production. He was right in calling them "the more individual part of my literary fruitage." They reveal his rich and sympathetic humanity, alive with recognitions of spirit, alert in sensitive invention, and always correcting the arguments of human ignominy and defeat by their respect for man's capacity for passion, endurance, and sacrifice. They show at their best an originality that springs from deeply felt and tested experience in the ways of human ordeal. Their devices of stanza and rhythm, of verbal oddity and surprise, begin to lose the inhibiting effect of a personal convention and to take on the qualities of a genuine contribution to English diction and meter. In their finest development ("The Darkling Thrush," "He Abjures Love," "Voices from Things Growing," "The Schreckhorn," "To Meet or Otherwise," "The Something that Saved Him," "I Say I'll

Seek Her," the elegies of "Veteris Vestigia Flammae") they arrive at an authentic poignance and wholeness of style. This is not only a matter of their delicacy of suggestion and tone or their candor in restoring personal appeal to poetry in the face of the impediments which modern sophistication and experiment have set against that appeal. It is a matter of Hardy's gradual mastery of effects: of subtle turns and balances of phrasing, of the fine shadings he is able to put on traditional emotions, of the sure hand with which he succeeds in justifying, by the time a poem ends, its apparently faltering progress from stanza to stanza. It is a matter also of Hardy's skill in restoring to poetry some usages which had fallen into neglect since the seventeenth century: for one, his exquisite use of the negative particle:

> By briefest meeting something sure is won;
>   It will have been:
> Nor God nor Demon can undo the done,
>   Unsight the seen,
> Make muted music be as unbegun,
>   Though things terrene
> Groan in their bondage till oblivion supervene.

This is "our profound and powerful particle, in our 'undone,' 'unloved,' 'unforgiven,' " which Mrs. Meynell once named in describing the genius of English speech: "the 'un' that summons in order that it may banish, and keeps the living word present to hear sentence and denial, showing the word 'unloved' to be not less than archangel ruined." And in its homely archaism it reminds us of another description that suits Hardy's achievement in poetry almost exactly. "It is his naturalness that strikes me most," said Gerard Hopkins of Hardy's friend, the Dorset poet William Barnes, "he is like an embodiment or incarnation or manmuse of the country, of Dorset, of rustic life and humanity. He comes, like Homer and all poets of native epic, provided with epithets and images and so on which seem to have been tested and digested for a long age in their native air and circumstances and to have a *keeping* which nothing else could give; but in fact they are rather all of his own finding and first throwing off."

Hardy never shared Barnes's privilege of writing poetry undistracted by the claims and disturbance of the outer world. He divided his life between Wessex and the tumult of his age. The two worlds gave him a dramatic stage on which to meet the conflicts of modern thought, to witness the tragic hostilities of life, to study the discord that marks the divided nature of man. But he mastered the "keeping" of his art and brought to it the force of his long intellectual and moral struggle. How he harmonized these in the poetry of his last thirty years is one of the notable personal achievements of literary history. It crystallizes for us the conflicts of a great age of distress; it makes evident Hardy's success in forging, out of the baffling incongruities and discords of experience, not only an aesthetic but an art. It also emphasizes that he succeeded because he was a "man of character," and it makes unmistakable that character's central quality: its resolving sincerity.

Hardy's "Prédilection d'artiste"

by D. H. Lawrence

Looking over the Hardy novels, it is interesting to see which of the heroes one would call a distinct individuality, more or less achieved, which an unaccomplished potential individuality, and which an impure, unindividualized life, embedded in the matrix, either achieving its own lower degree of distinction, or not achieving it.

In *Desperate Remedies* there are scarcely any people at all, particularly when the plot is working. The tiresome part about Hardy is that, so often, he will neither write a morality play nor a novel. The people of the first book, as far as the plot is concerned, are not people: they are the heroine, faultless and white; the hero, with a small spot on his whiteness; the villainess, red and black, but more red than black; the villain, black and red; the Murderer, aided by the Adulteress, obtains power over the Virgin, who, rescued at the last moment by the Virgin Knight, evades the evil clutch. Then the Murderer, overtaken by vengeance, is put to death, whilst Divine Justice descends upon the Adulteress. Then the Virgin unites with the Virgin Knight, and receives Divine Blessing.

That is a morality play, and if the morality were vigorous and original, all well and good. But, between-whiles, we see that the Virgin is being played by a nice, rather ordinary girl.

In *The Laodicean,* there is all the way through a *prédilection d'artiste* for the aristocrat, and all the way through a moral condemnation of him, a substituting the middle- or lower-class personage with bourgeois virtues into his place. This was the root of Hardy's pessimism. Not until he comes to Tess and Jude does he ever sympathize with the aristocrat—unless it be in *The Mayor of Casterbridge,* and then he sympathizes only to slay. He always, always represents them the same, as having some vital weakness, some radical ineffectuality. From first to last it is the same.

Miss Aldclyffe and Manston, Elfride and the sickly lord she married,

"Hardy's 'Prédilection d'artiste.'" From *Phoenix* by D. H. Lawrence, pp. 434-440. The selection is from the critique entitled "A Study of Thomas Hardy."

Troy and Farmer Boldwood, Eustacia Vye and Wildeve, de Stancy in *The Laodicean,* Lady Constantine in *Two on a Tower,* the Mayor of Casterbridge and Lucetta, Mrs. Charmond and Dr. Fitzpiers in *The Woodlanders,* Tess and Alec d'Urberville, and, though different, Jude. There is also the blond, passionate, yielding man: Sergeant Troy, Wildeve, and, in spirit, Jude.

These are all, in their way, the aristocrat-characters of Hardy. They must every one die, every single one.

Why has Hardy this *prédilection d'artiste* for the aristocrat, and why, at the same time, this moral antagonism to him?

It is fairly obvious in *The Laodicean,* a book where, the spirit being small, the complaint is narrow. The heroine, the daughter of a famous railway engineer, lives in the castle of the old de Stancys. She sighs, wishing she were of the de Stancy line: the tombs and portraits have a spell over her. "But," says the hero to her, "have you forgotten your father's line of ancestry: Archimedes, Newcomen, Watt, Tylford, Stephenson?"—"But I have a *prédilection d'artiste* for ancestors of the other sort," sighs Paula. And the hero despairs of impressing her with the list of his architect ancestors: Phidias, Ictinus and Callicrates, Chersiphron, Vitruvius, Wilars of Cambray, William of Wykeham. He deplores her marked preference for an "animal pedigree."

But what is this "animal pedigree"? If a family pedigree of her ancestors, working-men and burghers, had been kept, Paula would not have gloried in it, animal though it were. Hers was a *prédilection d'artiste.*

And this because the aristocrat alone has occupied a position where he could afford to *be,* to be himself, to create himself, to live as himself. That is his eternal fascination. This is why the preference for him is a *prédilection d'artiste.* The preference for the architect line would be a *prédilection de savant,* the preference for the engineer pedigree would be a *prédilection d'économiste.*

The *prédilection d'artiste*—Hardy has it strongly, and it is rooted deeply in every imaginative human being. The glory of mankind has been to produce lives, to produce vivid, independent, individual men, not buildings or engineering works or even art, not even the public good. The glory of mankind is not in a host of secure, comfortable, law-abiding citizens, but in the few more fine, clear lives, beings, individuals, distinct, detached, single as may be from the public.

And these the artist of all time has chosen. Why, then, must the aristocrat always be condemned to death, in Hardy? Has the community come to consciousness in him, as in the French Revolutionaries, determined to destroy all that is not the average? Certainly in the Wessex novels, all but the average people die. But why? Is there the germ of death in these more single, distinguished people, or has the artist himself a bourgeois taint, a jealous vindictiveness that will now take revenge, now that the community, the average, has gained power over the aristocrat, the exception?

It is evident that both is true. Starting with the bourgeois morality, Hardy makes every exceptional person a villain, all exceptional or strong individual traits he holds up as weaknesses or wicked faults. So in *Desperate Remedies, Under the Greenwood Tree, Far from the Madding Crowd, The Hand of Ethelberta, The Return of the Native* (but in *The Trumpet-Major* there is an ironical dig in the ribs to this civic communal morality), *The Laodicean, Two on a Tower, The Mayor of Casterbridge,* and *Tess,* in steadily weakening degree. The blackest villain is Manston, the next, perhaps, Troy, the next Eustacia, and Wildeve, always becoming less villainous and more human. The first show of real sympathy, nearly conquering the bourgeois or commune morality, is for Eustacia, whilst the dark villain is becoming merely a weak, pitiable person in Dr. Fitzpiers. In *The Mayor of Casterbridge* the dark villain is already almost the hero. There is a lapse in the maudlin, weak but not wicked Dr. Fitzpiers, duly condemned. Alec d'Urberville is not unlikable, and Jude is a complete tragic hero, at once the old Virgin Knight and Dark Villain. The condemnation gradually shifts over from the dark villain to the blond bourgeois virgin hero, from the Alec d'Urberville to Angel Clare, till in Jude they are united and loved, though the preponderance is of a dark villain, now dark, beloved, passionate hero. The condemnation shifts over at last from the dark villain to the white virgin, the bourgeois in soul: from Arabella to Sue. Infinitely more subtle and sad is the condemnation at the end, but there it is: the virgin knight is hated with intensity, yet still loved; the white virgin, the beloved, is the arch-sinner against life at last, and the last note of hatred is against her.

It is a complete and devastating shift-over, it is a complete *volte-face* of moralities. Black does not become white, but it takes white's place as good; white remains white, but it is found bad. The old, communal morality is like a leprosy, a white sickness: the old, antisocial, individualist morality is alone on the side of life and health.

But yet, the aristocrat must die, all the way through: even Jude. Was the germ of death in him at the start? Or was he merely at outs with his times, the times of the Average in triumph? Would Manston, Troy, Farmer Boldwood, Eustacia, de Stancy, Henchard, Alec d'Urberville, Jude have been real heroes in heroic times, without tragedy? It seems as if Manston, Boldwood, Eustacia, Henchard, Alec d'Urberville, and almost Jude, might have been. In an heroic age they might have lived and more or less triumphed. But Troy, Wildeve, de Stancy, Fitzpiers, and Jude have something fatal in them. There is a rottenness at the core of them. The failure, the misfortune, or the tragedy, whichever it may be, was inherent in them: as it was in Elfride, Lady Constantine, Marty South in *The Woodlanders,* and Tess. They have all passionate natures, and in them all failure is inherent.

So that we have, of men, the noble Lord in *A Pair of Blue Eyes,* Sergeant Troy, Wildeve, de Stancy, Fitzpiers, and Jude, all passionate, aristocratic males, doomed by their very being, to tragedy, or to misfortune in the end.

Of the same class among women are Elfride, Lady Constantine, Marty South, and Tess, all aristocratic, passionate, yet necessarily unfortunate females.

We have also, of men, Manston, Farmer Boldwood, Henchard, Alec d'Urberville, and perhaps Jude, all passionate, aristocratic males, who fell before the weight of the average, the lawful crowd, but who, in more primitive times, would have formed romantic rather than tragic figures.

Of women in the same class are Miss Aldclyffe, Eustacia, Lucetta, Mrs. Charmond.

The third class, of bourgeois or average hero, whose purpose is to live and have his being in the community, contains the successful hero of *Desperate Remedies,* the unsuccessful but not very much injured two heroes of *A Pair of Blue Eyes,* the successful Gabriel Oak, the unsuccessful, left-preaching Clym, the unsuccessful but not very much injured astronomer of *Two on a Tower,* the successful Scotchman of Casterbridge, the unsuccessful and expired Giles Winterborne of *The Woodlanders,* the arch-type, Angel Clare, and perhaps a little of Jude.

The companion women to these men are: the heroine of *Desperate Remedies,* Bathsheba, Thomasin, Paula, Henchard's daughter, Grace in *The Woodlanders,* and Sue.

This, then, is the moral conclusion drawn from the novels:

1. The physical individual is in the end an inferior thing which must fall before the community: Manston, Henchard, etc.

2. The physical and spiritual individualist is a fine thing which must fall because of its own isolation, because it is a sport, not in the true line of life: Jude, Tess, Lady Constantine.

3. The physical individualist and spiritual bourgeois or communist is a thing, finally, of ugly, undeveloped, nondistinguished or perverted physical instinct, and must fall physically. Sue, Angel Clare, Clym, Knight. It remains, however, fitted into the community.

4. The undistinguished, bourgeois or average being with average or civic virtues usually succeeds in the end. If he fails, he is left practically uninjured. If he expire during probation, he has flowers on his grave.

By individualist is meant, not a selfish or greedy person, anxious to satisfy appetites, but a man of distinct being, who must act in his own particular way to fulfill his own individual nature. He is a man who, being beyond the average, chooses to rule his own life to his own completion, and as such is an aristocrat.

The artist always has a predilection for him. But Hardy, like Tolstoi, is forced in the issue always to stand with the community in condemnation of the aristocrat. He cannot help himself, but must stand with the average against the exception, he must, in his ultimate judgment, represent the interests of humanity, or the community as a whole, and rule out the individual interest.

To do this, however, he must go against himself. His private sympathy is always with the individual against the community: as is the case with the artist. Therefore he will create a more or less blameless individual and, making him seek his own fulfillment, his highest aim, will show him destroyed by the community, or by that in himself which represents the community, or by some close embodiment of the civic idea. Hence the pessimism. To do this, however, he must select his individual with a definite weakness, a certain coldness of temper, inelastic, a certain inevitable and inconquerable adhesion to the community.

This is obvious in Troy, Clym, Tess, and Jude. They have naturally distinct individuality but, as it were, a weak life-flow, so that they cannot break away from the old adhesion, they cannot separate themselves from the mass which bore them, they cannot detach themselves from the common. Therefore they are pathetic rather than tragic figures. They have not the necessary strength: the question of their unfortunate end is begged in the beginning.

Whereas Œdipus or Agamemnon or Clytemnestra or Orestes, or Macbeth or Hamlet or Lear, these are destroyed by their own conflicting passions. Out of greed for adventure, a desire to be off, Agamemnon sacrifices Iphigenia: moreover he has his love affairs outside Troy: and this brings on him death from the mother of his daughter, and from his pledged wife. Which is the working of the natural law. Hamlet, a later Orestes, is commanded by the Erinyes of his father to kill his mother and his uncle: but his maternal filial feeling tears him. It is almost the same tragedy as Orestes, without any goddess or god to grant peace.

In these plays, conventional morality is transcended. The action is between the great, single, individual forces in the nature of Man, not between the dictates of the community and the original passion. The Commandment says: "Thou shalt not kill." But doubtless Macbeth had killed many a man who was in his way. Certainly Hamlet suffered no qualms about killing the old man behind the curtain. Why should he? But when Macbeth killed Duncan, he divided himself in twain, into two hostile parts. It was all in his own soul and blood: it was nothing outside himself: as it was, really, with Clym, Troy, Tess, Jude. Troy would probably have been faithful to his little unfortunate person, had she been a lady, and had he not felt himself cut off from society in his very being, whilst all the time he cleaved to it. Tess allowed herself to be condemned, and asked for punishment from Angel Clare. Why? She had done nothing particularly, or at least irrevocably, unnatural, were her life young and strong. But she sided with the community's condemnation of her. And almost the bitterest, most pathetic, deepest part of Jude's misfortune was his failure to obtain admission to Oxford, his failure to gain his place and standing in the world's knowledge, in the world's work.

There is a lack of sternness, there is a hesitating betwixt life and public opinion, which diminishes the Wessex novels from the rank of pure tragedy. It is not so much the eternal, immutable laws of being which are transgressed, it is not that vital life-forces are set in conflict with each other, bringing almost inevitable tragedy—yet not necessarily death, as we see in the most splendid Aeschylus. It is, in Wessex, that the individual succumbs to what is in its shallowest, public opinion, in its deepest, the human compact by which we live together, to form a community.

Hardy's Major Fiction

by John Holloway

The deepening and harshening pessimism of Hardy's later novels has been stressed often enough in the past. All that need be done here is to remind readers of how it is usually located in two particular aspects of his work: first, his "philosophical" asides ("the President of the Immortals, in Aeschylean phrase, had ended his sport with Tess" will be enough in illustration of this familiar story; the phrase itself will need re-examination later); and second, his apparently growing preoccupation with problems of marriage. One should perhaps add that to see this second issue as the product of difficulties in Hardy's own married life is very uninformative. Much more to the point are the divorce cases (the Parnell case being the best known) which became national sensations in the later 1880's and early 1890's; and besides this, the important influence of Ibsen, at least in the case of *Jude the Obscure*.

Recent criticism of Hardy has also emphasized something else: a special part of his connection with the southwest of England. An earlier generation of writers on Hardy underestimated this. Amiably if innocently equipped with haversack and large-scale map, they cycled over Wessex and noted Hardy's faithful geography, or his intimate and affectionate knowledge of rural occupations and customs. More recently, the stress has fallen on Hardy as one who registered the impact upon rural England of a great historical change, which went to the very roots of life. One cause of this was the swift and decisive decline in British agriculture which followed almost instantaneously on the completion of the railroad links to the American Middle West in about 1870. The other, less spectacular but in the long run much more far-reaching, was the industrial revolution in agriculture. This was progressing steadily in the later years of the century, and has even now far from completed its radical transforming work. As symbol of this second force, one might take a pair of

"Hardy's Major Fiction" by John Holloway. From *Jane Austen to Joseph Conrad* (Minneapolis: University of Minnesota Press, 1959) edited by Robert Rathburn and Martin Steinmann, Jr.

incidents from Hardy's own work. In *The Mayor of Casterbridge* (1886) the new mechanical seed-drill which is to replace the methods in use since the time of the Anglo-Saxons is for sale in the market place. Someone has still to buy and use it. In *Tess of the D'Urbervilles,* only five years later, the mechanical harvester dominates and controls the whole scene of the cornstacking (Chapter 48) and reduces the tired, dazed human beings who serve it to mere automatons. The contrast is no proof of how rural life was changing; but as an illustration it is vivid.

Modern criticism of fiction often seems at its weakest in trying (or failing) to consider the forces in a book which unify it from beginning to end. This weakness is perhaps the result of a certain uneasiness which (for reasons obvious enough) often shows itself when the critic turns his attention to the plot. Yet such attention is necessary if the pervasive unifying drives of the work are to be located; and certainly the full seriousness and import of Hardy's major novels will be concealed from the reader who fails to apprehend their plots: plots, that is, not as mere summarizable sequences of events, but as the central unifying and significating forces of the books. These I hope now to approach.

The first step in that approach is not difficult, for it is taken simply by combining the two more or less familiar points from which this discussion started; by seeing Hardy's deepening and harshening gloom as not a mere self-ingraining philosophical bias, but rather as something in most intimate relation to his vision of the passing of the old rhythmic order of rural England. Once the novels are seen from this point of view, they suggest a surprising development in Hardy's thought. They suggest not just a growing preoccupation with the rural problem, nor even a growing sense that an earlier way of life was inevitably vanishing. They suggest something more disquieting: a gathering realization that that earlier way did not possess the inner resources upon which to make a real fight for its existence. The old order was not just a less powerful mode of life than the new, but ultimately helpless before it through inner defect.

When one is arguing that a thought or an attitude comes increasingly into focus in a writer's work, it is always easy to claim too much and hide too much; yet in the present case the change looks convincingly steady. *The Return of the Native* (1878) has a half-tragic ending in its present form; and Hardy's original intention seems to have been to have made it more tragic rather than less so. Yet throughout the book, the stress falls on the revitalizing power of rural life, and on how its vitality is intrinsically greater than that of modernity. Eustacia and Wildeve, and at first Clym too, are alienated from it: indeed, this very alienation lies behind their ostensible successes (the marriages, for example). But because of the alienation, the successes are ill-placed and precarious, they are the successes of those who have lost the soundness, the inner strength, the power to choose and to achieve wisely which belongs to men whose life is in harmony with their world. By contrast, Venn the reddleman suffers reverses, but they do not impair his integrity; his vitality runs submerged, but it runs with the tide of life. The gambling scene on the heath is fantastic enough, but it tellingly conveys this. Moreover, the whole rural ambience can ultimately assert a greater vitality than the city life from which Clym has come. As he gives himself to it, he is regenerated from a basic source. By the end, Egdon has triumphed, even if on its own stern terms. The renegades have been destroyed or won over: even if Venn had never married Thomasin, the faithful would have been in possession. The novel resolves in an assertion of the old order, its regenerative austerity, its rewarding unrewardingness.

The next novel is very different. Henchard is the only major figure in *The Mayor of Casterbridge* (1886) who stands integrally for the traditional qualities. Farfrae is an agriculturalist, but of the new kind: he prospers by chemistry, machinery, and bookkeeping and elementary economics. His traditional songs are partly a social accomplishment, neither sincere nor insincere; his kindliness and even his amorousness are conventional. Henchard's daughter Elizabeth-Jane is turning into a cultivated young lady (I would sooner overrate than underrate Hardy's own educatedness, but I cannot help seeing something of importance in his seeming assurance here that education could without loss be self-education). Lucetta is entirely *déraciné*. On these premises, contrast with *The Return of the Native* is vivid. From beginning to end Henchard's course is downward. Whenever his older way of life meets the new, it is defeated. Step by step, he comes to work for the man whom he once employed, and in the end he feels himself driven away to his death; while those who were once his laborers work the new, harder (and easier) way, for a shilling a week less than they had had from him.

Yet, although this relentless decline of Henchard's is (as we take its meaning) what unifies the book, Henchard still stands above the others in what might be called psychic virtue. In the conventional sense, he is both less moral than they, and more so. He is violent and a liar and in one sense intensely selfish, but his generosity is true magnanimity, and he has reserves of affection and humility that they quite lack. The essential is something else, though: that his whole nature, good or bad, is centered upon a deep source of vital energy. The rich stream of life still issues from life's traditional order. It does not bring success, but it brings greatness and in a sense goodness. Farfrae prospers through *skill* which the new mode of life has impersonally taught him; Henchard is able to struggle on, though defeated, not because of what he has learned but because of what he *is*. He blocks out something like the full contour of the human being.

That Henchard should stand out as a human rather than a man was surely part of Hardy's intention. His lack of interest in "womankind" is stressed more than once, and we are reminded of how Marty South is also in a sense made sexless at the end of *The Woodlanders* (1887). But to turn to *The Woodlanders* is to find that Hardy has now moved further still. Marty South and Giles Winterborne do not display, like Henchard, a defeated strength. On the contrary, they leave the impression of debility. So far as goodness itself goes, they are, to be sure, alone in having contact with it: "you was a good man, and did good things." But the springs of goodness are now no longer the springs of strength. Rather the opposite. Such vitality as there is lies on the other side, in the self-assurance and plausible fluency of Fitzpiers, or the passionate sensuousness of Felice. Grace Melbury has a thwarted contact, anyhow, with the traditional order: but what it does is chiefly to make her impassive and acceptant.

In *Tess of the D'Urbervilles* (1891), Hardy moves further. Tess is "a pure woman," admittedly; but this is not the feminine counterpart to Henchard's "A Man of Character." It is not Tess's sexual misadventures which impugn her as a woman of character, and Hardy is indeed at pains to show, in the later part of the book when she resists the now twice-reprobate Alec, that she is comparatively faithful and steadfast. But she has a weakness nearer her center: an alienation, a dreaminess which Hardy depicts unsuccessfully in the ride at night when she tells her young brother that we live on a "blighted" planet (and becomes so engrossed that she causes a fatal injury to the horse), and which he depicts again, this time with brilliant success, at Talbothay's dairy when she tells Dairyman Crick how "our souls can be made to go outside our bodies when we are alive" (Chapters 4 and 18). Again, this incident is nodal in the book, and I must return to it. For the present it is enough to say that its nodality is stressed by Hardy, in that he makes this the moment when Angel Clare first gives Tess any special notice.

This dreamy unreality in Tess is no personal quirk. It results from her heredity, and is reflected in both her parents. Moreover, Hardy is at pains to stress that among country folk, degeneration of an old stock is common enough. The stock is in decline. It seems a positive disparagement of the old order. The contrast with Henchard is revealing. Quietly but clearly, Hardy indicates that in Tess there is something self-destroying. So there was, in a sense, in Henchard. Yet how differently does the stress fall, provided that the reader follows only the contours created by the author!

Tess of the D'Urbervilles also dwells, quite for the first time, upon another unattractive side of rural life. This is what appears in the barrenness and crippling toil of life on the upland farm of Flintcomb-Ash. Hardy links his picture to contemporary agricultural realities—the farm belongs to an absentee landlord—but the essential things which make life hard on it are those which have made the rural life hard since the beginning: stony soil, cold wind, rain, snow, callous masters—things that can be found in the Wakefield *Second Shepherds' Play* as easily as in *Tess*. Should this be in doubt, it may be confirmed from *Jude the Obscure* (1895). In fact, there is something like a parallel here to the double indictment of *Tess*. Jude Fawley is "crazy for books. . . . It runs in our family. . . ." Later, when the now adult Jude sees a stone-mason's yard and glimpses for a moment that happiness for him lay only in a life like that, Hardy passes decisive judgment upon bookish tastes in laborers' families. A still clearer parallel with *Tess,* however, is Hardy's insistence in this novel upon the essential harshness of rural life. "How ugly it is here," thinks Jude, as he drives off the rooks from the brown, featureless arable of the upland. This is in part an ironical judgment upon Jude. Hardy is at pains to stress the rich human associations of the scene. Yet some of these associations are themselves associations of human unhappiness; and the whole chapter goes far to endorse Jude's revulsion from the drab landscape and the inevitable greed and callousness of the farmer. Nor are this revulsion, and the inescapable grounds tending to justify it, incidentals. They initiate the whole train of events. Jude's quest for learning is to escape from a life of grinding toil that he could not but wish to escape. And what are the compensations of rurality, as they now appear? Only Arabella, whose work is to wash the innards of the newly slaughtered pig, and whose attractions take their force from brutal humor, coarse sensuality, and a rooted tradition of deceit.

This discussion of the later novels is not by itself, of course, anything like the whole truth about them. It virtually ignores Hardy's rich and intimate contact with the rural tradition in every book before *Jude,* and his profound dependence upon, and loyalty to, its characteristic virtues. It ignores these matters because they have often been discussed elsewhere, and its concentration upon Hardy's growing sense of weakness in the country world must be taken in the context of Hardy criticism as it now stands. Yet it remains true that in these later works the essence of plot, the distinctive trajectory of the narrative, is the steadily developed decline of a protagonist who incarnates the older order, and whose decline is linked, more and more clearly, with an inner misdirection, an inner weakness.

Two of the novels stand out as inviting a closer scrutiny, if we wish to see how this kind of movement lies at the heart of unity and meaning. These are *The Mayor of Casterbridge,* and *Tess of the D'Urbervilles.*

Jude the Obscure clearly has another kind of concern; and *The Woodlanders,* surprisingly enough, proves largely to have it as well. Indeed, there is a sense in which this novel has a much looser organization than the other late ones. Deep and powerful as its awareness of rural life undoubtedly is (one cannot keep from mind the pictures of Giles spattered all over with his apples and their juice), yet much at the center of this work pursues another concern. Grace's response to Fitzpiers' infidelity, and the gradual rebirth of her affection for him, are not Wessex products. The novel resolves itself by amiably decanting these two characters into the middle-class urban life of the Midlands. The psychological change that we see in Grace is barely connected with Hardy's rural interest; and that, I think, is why the whole episode of their reconciliation is treated with a lightness and even something of a gentle half-ironical detachment that distinguishes the book clearly from *Tess.* At one point Hardy brings the difference out starkly through a metaphor. This occurs when Grace, running swiftly through the wood to meet Fitzpiers, just misses the man-trap (which is in itself, by the way, another scrap of evidence for the view that Hardy was beginning to dwell on the harsher side of country life). Her destiny is to evade, though barely, the issues of life in their brutal sharpness. All the man-trap does is whisk her skirt off: in Hardy's making this the occasion of her being reconciled to Fitzpiers we are to see, I think, that the whole sequence has about it something of the essentially trivial. Tess turns back to Angel over her rush-drawing labor in the snow-laden barn, as she comes to grasp her case, and Angel's, in terms of the plainest, the essential relations between women and men as human animals. We are in a much different world, a world that has not skipped over the waiting man-trap. For these reasons, among others, it is *The Mayor of Casterbridge* and *Tess* that best warrant further questioning. They are the novels which have a single-minded organization along our present line of thought.

The word "theme," now the most hackneyed of clichés in criticism, is also one of its bugbears. An essay, a philosophical discourse, even a collection of different pieces, all these may equally well have a theme, or several themes. The word has no necessary connection even with imaginative literature, let alone with the narrative forms of it, and is therefore a standing temptation to the critic to overlook the whole narrative dimension. But almost always, the narrative trajectory is what makes a novel a novel and what makes any particular novel the novel it is. Only within the framework of this central drive can the real significance of the detail (incident, imagery, metaphor, local contrast) be grasped at all. Examples may be needed here; let us revert to *The Woodlanders.* To connect, say, Giles Winterborne's meeting with Grace while he holds up his apple tree in the market-place merely with "the theme of rural fertility," or Marty South's selling her hair with "the commercial theme," would be grotesquely uninformative. The significance of both these incidents, prominently placed at the outset of the narrative, is that the two characters are made to carry out, at the start, ritual gestures by which they formally (though unwittingly) surrender their essential strength. From this point out, we know what kind of character we are to watch, we are put on the track of the path their lives must take.

A tree also embodies the essential strength of Marty's father. In an aberration from his proper rural life, he wants it cut down. When this is done, he dies. As for Marty's hair, Hardy invests this with almost talismanic virtue. While Felice wears it as her own, her luck prospers. Toward the end of the book, her secret comes out. At once she loses her power over Fitzpiers, and almost immediately after she meets her death. Similarly with the contrast between how Grace meets Winterborne (under the flowering apple tree in his hand) and how she first meets Fitzpiers (he has bought the right to dissect her old nurse's body after she is dead, and Grace goes to buy it back). These meetings are no mere specimens of a theme, but exact pointers to a narrative movement; and they come at the start of the relation and show what its significance is, and what (if pursued) it will bring. For Grace to progress with one is to pursue the forces of life, with the other to pursue those of death. Similarly with the incident where Marty helps Giles to plant the young trees (Chapter 8). This does not merely take up the theme of rural order; it exactly indicates how Marty is Giles's proper strength and counterpart. His trees will flourish if he chooses her to help. When he turns elsewhere, we know what he has done. But all these details have significance within the frame of the basic narrative movement of the book, a movement which, as it takes its shape out of them, reciprocally determines what meaning they shall have.

"From beginning to end," it was suggested above, "Henchard's course is downward. Whenever his older way of life meets the new, it is defeated." It is this narrative movement in the book which embodies Hardy's deepest interest and the essence of his moral insight. But there is more to be said about the exact nature of the struggle and the downward movement, as he envisages it; and it is at this point that such matters as incident and imagery can take their proper and proportionate place in our awareness of the whole work. For it seems that Hardy has employed a single basic metaphor through which to embody the war between Farfrae and Henchard; local incidents and metaphors have their allotted place within it; and in spite of the recurrent suggestions that Henchard (like Old Hamlet) is "a man, take him for all in all," the basic metaphor through which Hardy sees the struggle between Farfrae and him, is that of a struggle between a man and an animal. This begins with the animal in possession of its territory. Henchard arrived on the scene during, as it were, the prehistory of the narrative. Now he is in occupation at Casterbridge. Farfrae is passing through on his way to emigrate. As the novel pursues its course, Farfrae takes possession. It is his rival who thinks to emigrate. But instead he is persuaded to live in his own old home, now occupied by Farfrae; and like an animal, he becomes domesticated. "Henchard had become in a measure broken in, he came to work daily on the home premises like the rest." Later he is likened to a "netted lion," or to a lion whose fangs have been drawn. When he describes how Farfrae, now mayor, as he himself once was, forced him away on the occasion of the royal visit, he says, ". . . how angry he looked. He drove me back as if I were a bull breaking fence. . . ."

Several of the incidents of the book enter into this sustained metaphor. Henchard and Farfrae fighting in the cornstore is, in a sense, animal against man: it is very like the earlier fight in the barn between Henchard and the bull. The parallel extends even to Farfrae's "wrenching Henchard's arm . . . causing him sharp pain, as could be seen from the twitching of his face," and Henchard when he "wrenched the animal's head as if he would snap it off. . . . The premeditated human contrivance of the nose-ring was too cunning for impulsive brute force, and the creature flinched." Finally, at the end of the novel, Henchard crawls away, like a wounded beast, to die in an empty hovel that is more like an animal's hole than a place for men. His final instructions for how he is to be buried are not appropriate for *felo-de-se*: they are appropriate for the burial of an animal.

Henchard's character, moreover, is that of a beast; in the true, not the townee, sense of that word. His immense natural energy, his simplicity, his having no skill of any kind save that of hay-cutting, and his liability to enslavement above all through a disabling, yearning, dog-like need for human affection, all these features of his nature make their contribution. There is no need to remind readers that Henchard is not *simply* an animal. Far from it. At no point does metaphor become literal truth. But it is through this metaphor that we must see the struggle which constitutes the narrative and the unity of the book, and which predominantly defines its significance. Indeed, nothing but awareness of this metaphor will fully bring out the issues between old and new that are involved, or the length to which Hardy pursues them. "My furniture too! Surely he'll buy my body and soul likewise!" Henchard says at one point. (One cannot but—though it is an unhappy touch—see the caged singing-bird which Henchard brings Elizabeth-Jane at the end as a wedding present, and which he leaves behind when he goes away to die, as linking with this idea of his giving up "body and soul" together.) Yet even this is insufficient to bring out the lengths to which Hardy pursues his central conflict. Henchard is more than enslaved, he is *tamed.* That is something far more thoroughgoing. It is the measure of what Hardy sees as at issue.

Tess of the D'Urbervilles also has unity through a total movement; and the nature of this may also largely be grasped through a single metaphor. It is not the taming of an animal. Rather (at least for a start) it is the hunting of one. Several remarks and incidents in the book make this explicit, notably Tess's letter to her absent husband when he has deserted her: "I must cry out to you in my trouble—I have no one else . . . if I break down by falling into some dreadful snare, my last state will be worse than my first." So does the night she spends in the wood with the wounded pheasants: strongly reminiscent, of course, of her earlier night in a wood, when she fell into the snare set for her by Alec. Throughout, Tess is harried from place to place at what seems like gradually increasing speed. Even the very start of her relation with Alec is relevant: "the handsome, horsey young buck" drove up early in the morning in his gig to fetch her. At the end, it is especially clear. When the hunt is over, Tess is captured on the sacrificial stone at Stonehenge, the stone where once, like the hart at bay, the victim's throat was slit with the knife. With these things in mind, Hardy's much-abused quotation from Aeschylus ("the President of the Immortals, in Aeschylean phrase, had ended his sport with Tess") takes on a new meaning and aptness.

Yet Tess's career represents more than a hunt. What this is, can again be summed up in a metaphor, one to which we are almost inadvertently led, if we attempt to summarize. That Hardy should have divided his book into "phases" is itself, perhaps, an indication of the field in which his mind was partly working: the word was good nineteenth century currency in history and natural history, and Carlyle was fond of it. "Phase Three" is entitled "The Rally." In it, Tess strikes out for new country. She leaves the snug and familiar environment of the "Vale of the Little Dairies," surmounts the challenge of barren Egdon Heath which lies across her path, and enters a new territory, the "Vale of the Great Dairies," where life runs upon a basically different pattern. To this she almost completely adapts herself: so much so, that she finds a mate in Angel Clare, and almost succeeds in—there is only one word to use—in germinating. This word is less odd than it seems at first. Hardy lays great stress on the rich, blossoming fertility of Tess's whole environment during this period, and also stresses, discreetly but with great force, her own richly sensuous nubility, her genuine bond, in the truest sense, with the milch cows and the lush blossoms where the fruit is setting.

The rally fails. Tess has to abandon her favorable environment, and is forced on to a harsh upland soil where existence is more difficult. She struggles not at the level of reproduction, but for mere survival. She is resistant, though, and for a long time she does survive. But her strength is shaken when her family is finally driven off the soil; and in the end, what Darwin called sexual selection begins to work contrariwise to natural selection. Tess gives up the struggle. She is driven out of her natural habitat altogether, and goes to live, kept like a pet, with Alec in Sandbourne.

Here, I think, is the second, bigger metaphor, embracing the first, through which Hardy embodies his central fictional movement. The central train of events demands description in Darwinian terms: organism, environment, struggle, adaptation, fertility, survival, resistant—and one more: Hardy has envisaged an individual life at the depth of, and to the length of, the ultimates for a species—establishment at one end, and at the other, extinction.

Many of the incidents in the book bring this total movement into focus. For example, Hardy provides the reader with an index to it by two scenes, one at the beginning and one at the end. In the first, Angel looks back down the road and sees the village girls in white, dancing in springtime on the green: Tess, still integrated with them, stands by the hedge. In the other, he looks back after what he thinks is their final parting, over bare, open countryside and an empty road: "and as he gazed a moving spot intruded on the white vacuity of its perspective. It was a human figure running." It is Tess, now alienated and isolated. Tess and her family take refuge in the family vault (Chapter 52). In terms of the hunt metaphor, they have been run to earth; and this parallels the sleepwalking scene (Chapter 37) when Angel lays Tess in the open tomb: within the larger movement there is a recurrent smaller pattern. Tess at the dairy says that "our souls can be made to go outside our bodies" if we "lie on the grass at night and look straight up at some big bright star." (This is exactly what she does at the end of the book, on her fatal last night on Salisbury Plain.) Meanwhile, Dairyman Crick was balancing his knife and fork together "like the beginning of a gallows." Most striking of all, Hardy reinvites us to register the total movement of Tess's career, in all its integration, by an ingenious and vivid résumé of it, toward the close of the book. He does this through the final days that Tess and Angel spend together—partly a psychological fugue, partly a kind of total recall, partly both. Leaving her sin with Alec behind her, she rejoins Angel, and the rich woodland of the first two days together corresponds to the rich vale of the dairies. The empty manor house they sleep in corresponds to the ancient house where their marriage was so nearly consummated before. Barren Salisbury Plain corresponds to the uplands of Flintcomb-Ash. The scene at Stonehenge corresponds both to Tess in the vault, and to the moment when she hung on the wayside cross to rest and looked like a sacrificial victim. Her whole tragic life is mirrored in little at its close.

To notice things of this order is to realize, in effect, that Hardy's novels (like many others) need a special mode of reading. The incidents in them which strike us as improbable or strained or grotesque invite (this is not to say that they always deserve) the kind of response that we are accustomed to give, say, to the Dover Cliff scene in *Lear*. Admittedly, Hardy has local failures; but incidents like these are intrinsically at one remove from the probable and the realistic. Almost, it is necessary for them to be unrealistic in order that their other dimension of meaning, their relevance to the larger rhythms of the work, shall transpire. Again and again, it is those larger rhythms which finally expand into the total movement of the novel, transmitting the author's sense of life, the forces that operate through it, the values that chart it out and make it what it is.

From what has so far been said, a new reason may perhaps be advanced as to why Hardy gave up fiction. It is both the strength (because of the integrity that it brought) and the limit of his achievement, to have seen the source of life-creating strength for human beings as connected always with a certain limited context, the traditional rural order. As time passed, he lost confidence in the strength of this order to resist and survive, and in part, even seems more and more to have regarded the element of drabness and harshness in rural life as not a product of change and modernity, but intrinsic. This being so, he had no position to which to retreat. He does not seem ever to have viewed human nature as itself ineradicably vital, as possessing an innate power to transform, from its own resources, its waste land into a fertile one. To say this is not necessarily to make a point against him. He may very well have been right in thinking that the human species, like others, wilts out of its natural habitat and communal order. It is merely to recognize that by the middle 1890's, Hardy's course in fiction had become one that he could neither retrace, nor pursue.

The Women of the Novels

by Albert J. Guerard

Hardy's first and second novels showed surprising knowledge of girlish coquetries and mannerisms; much later novels would show insight as surprising into feminine motives and feelings. *A Pair of Blue Eyes* offers, however, a curious midpoint of knowledge, which one can only call a knowledge of the feminine nervous temperament. Toward the end of the novel Hardy himself discriminates between Elfride's nature (gentle, confiding, and innocent) and her personality (vain, evasive, and ambiguous). Hardy was often tempted to generalize about all women from the particular woman at hand, as Conrad to generalize about all men. "Woman's ruling passion—to fascinate those more powerful than she—though operant in Elfride, was decidedly purposeless." As we re-examine each crisis from the vantage point of Hardy's final sympathy, the "purposeless" character of Elfride's betrayals becomes evident enough. It is a trick of excited nerves that throws her into Knight's arms a moment after she has saved his life; later she shows a nervous rather than moral inability to confess her sins. Much earlier the mere "act of alighting upon strange ground" in London was sufficient to induce a *crise de nerfs* and send her back to Endelstow unmarried. Paddington has disillusioned many a traveler both before Elfride and since. But few novelists have caught so well, in dialogue, the sheer revolt of nerves which so many women feel at the threshold of a new life. In three compact pages we have a first sketch of a situation which would be complicated and subtilized in *Jude the Obscure* and charged not with pathos but horror.

Was this already, rather than Knight's cross-examination, the turning point of Hardy's sympathy? The characterization of Elfride is an incomplete one, since the true origin of the sympathy seems to exist somewhere outside the book itself. The reader, in any event, can hardly share that sympathy. But sympathy—something more, that is, than the cool observation of women as fascinating objects—would be necessary to the later and universally praised portraits of Eustacia Vye and Tess Durbeyfield. Hardy's sympathy, however unmotivated in *A Pair of Blue Eyes,* is justified in *Far from the Madding Crowd.* Bathsheba Everdene, at first another Fancy Day, a vain and highly amusing tease, becomes almost a symbolic figure of resourcefulness and endurance. Less obviously striking than Cytherea, Fancy, and Elfride, and perhaps even less alive than they, she is the first of Hardy's heroines to face her life at all squarely. She is the first of his women to show more character than personality. In the most interesting women, in Sue Bridehead for instance, personality and character coincide. Sue's bird-like mannerisms and mobile features are a true index to her nervous disorders, which in turn *are* her character to a very considerable degree.

The conflict between the impulse to create personality and the impulse to create character appears for the last time in the portrait of Eustacia Vye, who is also the first of Hardy's irresponsible and mildly neurotic hedonists. A great deal that is obviously successful in the portrait no longer need be discussed: the sense that it gives of a presence brooding dangerously over the fortunes of more docile persons in the valley below —a presence equipped with bonfire and telescope; the impression of unused baffled energies and a recklessly masculine intellect; the conveyed despair and loneliness that will make any bargain to escape the heath; the desperate clawing for love as the only form of pleasure known; the pride, which refuses to explain away misleading appearances; the harsh honesty, finally, of a direct appraisal of self. The famous seventh chapter, "Queen of Night," will still repay the attention of any student of Hardy's development, however, for it is not merely an attempt to create character through personality but also an attempt to create personality through grandiose impressionism. Could the large methods which had been used to evoke the totality of Egdon Heath be applied to a mere nineteen-year-old girl—still a girl, though she might someday sit between the Héloïses and the Cleopatras? The impressionism, which leaps daringly from pedantic meditations on the gods to minute descriptions of hair fillets and hair, reminds one of Pater's prose poem on the Gioconda, published five years before. Hardy's prose poem created its desired and dark effect, however obvious its methods may seem on a third or fourth reading. The wonder is rather that the subsequent and more orthodox portrait should have been able to survive such an overwhelming first impression. The eight seemingly diffuse but in fact very close pages dwell on Eustacia's appearance, moral isolation, and larger "nocturnal mysteries." But they also manage to take in, almost parenthetically, the important facts of her childhood and heredity, of her daily way of life, of her idealizing love for Wildeve. The statement is so full as to threaten any further appearance of Eustacia with commonplaceness and redundancy. But the portrait does survive—and not least in its curious ability to suggest savage and even immoral feeling without recourse to much unconventional behavior. It required unusual tact, for instance, to make Eustacia's giving of her hand to Charley to kiss, for a certain number of minutes, the sleaziest of bargains. The general impression of darkness achieved apart from particular dark deeds is so strong that Hardy feels obliged to summarize it explicitly only once: "As far as social ethics were concerned Eustacia approached the savage state, though in emotion she was all the while an epicure. She had advanced to the secret recesses of sensuousness, yet had hardly crossed the threshold of conventionality."

Hardy's characterizations of young women are rarely ambiguous and with the single exception of Sue Bridehead require no interpretation. There is little to say about them individually that has not already been said abundantly and often. These women do, on the other hand, fall into fairly distinct groups—the sweet ingénues, the restless hedonists, the patient and enduring sufferers, and so forth—and the relationships among and within these groups are worth some attention. To chart these groupings is to observe at once how steadily Hardy progressed toward a dramatization of character rather than personality; and toward frankness as well as charity (see chart, below). All novelists tend to borrow from their earlier works, though as a rule unconsciously. Hardy's tendency to do this was particularly strong. One could almost say, given the degree to which women dominate his stories, that nearly every novel had its source in some trait, perhaps unemphasized or undeveloped, of the preceding novel's heroine. Thus Cytherea Graye's inability to choose the right man becomes in Fancy Day a rather astounding fickleness. Fancy, far more vain than Cytherea, passes on both her fickleness and her still fairly innocent pride to Elfride Swancourt, in whom evasiveness becomes systematic, somber, and at last of tragic consequence. Elfride in turn is not merely vain, proud, and vacillating, but is also intelligent and in a sense irrepressible; she almost survives the holocaust. Bathsheba Everdene of the early chapters inherits all Elfride's qualities, and her teasing dismissal of Oak's first proposal marks the farthest point Hardy would go in this single and amusing but rather conventional direction of satire. There was no more to be said about mere girlish vanity, but there was much else about women that had not been said. What would the intelligence and even strength of Elfride have amounted to had they overcome her youthful inconsequence? What would *she* have amounted to, had she been thrown on her own resources and forced to make a living? These questions take us at once into the later chapters of *Far from the Madding Crowd.* The matured Bathsheba may have to depend on Oak at critical hours, but she is a courageous figure in her own right. She

THE GENEALOGY OF HARDY'S YOUNGER WOMEN

An illustration of the way in which many of Hardy's women characters draw on their predecessors and even derive directly from them

NOVELS	THE VAIN AND FICKLE	THE INGÉNUES	THE AVERAGE INTELLIGENT WOMEN	THE HEDONISTS TENDING TO NEUROSIS	THE HIGHLY SEXED	THE RESOURCEFUL AND ENDURING	TWO PURE WOMEN
Desperate Remedies, '71	Cytherea		Cytherea				
Greenwood Tree, '72	Fancy Day						
Blue Eyes, '73	Elfride						
Madding Crowd, '74	The early Bathsheba					The later Bathsheba	
Ethelberta, '76	The early Ethelberta	Picotee				The later Ethelberta	
Return, '78		Thomasin		Eustacia	Eustacia		
Trumpet-Major, '80		Anne					
Laodicean, '81			Paula				
Two on a Tower, '82		Tabitha	Viviette				
Milkmaid, '83		Margery					
Mayor, '86			Elizabeth	Lucetta			
Woodlanders, '87			Grace	Felice	Suke	Marty	Marty
Tess, '91					Tess	Tess	Tess
Well-Beloved, '92,'97	Avice II	Avice I	Avice III	Marcia			
Jude, '95				Sue	Arabella	Arabella	

has been changed by responsibility and disaster. She passes on much of her courage, resourcefulness, and determination to survive to the grasping and harsh Ethelberta; but passes on very little of her honesty and none of her early charm. Did Ethelberta's unmoral pursuit of power and wealth suggest, finally, Eustacia's unmoral pursuit of pleasure?

There are other links between the various books as curious as these, and to list Hardy's women is to construct a more than figurative genealogy. Felice Charmond not merely follows Lucetta Le Sueur, but is descended directly from her, inheriting her bored restlessness, her aura of foreign and unmoral glamor, her slightly faded vivacity, and even her French-sounding name. She does not inherit, however, Lucetta's status as a victim, and so receives much less sympathy than she. Did Hardy ask himself what kind of mischief such a person as Lucetta might cause if thrust into an even more cloistered environment than Casterbridge? A novelist rarely asks himself such direct questions, but he does work under direct though subconscious obligations: to pursue the ideas he has only half explored, the feelings only half expressed, the characters only half realized and *tested*.

A novel may be in direct reaction against the preceding one, but it nearly always proceeds out of it in some discernible way—especially since a true novelist can hardly exhaust his intentions in a single book. The connections between *The Woodlanders* and *Tess of the D'Urbervilles,* for instance, may at first glance seem fairly tenuous, fining down to nothing more specific than the contrast between urban corruptness and rural innocence and the close common dependence of the characters on physical nature for their living. Yet Tess herself is directly descended from Marty South, and even perhaps from Suke Damson. Suke merely stands on the squalid fringes of the story, a highly sexed and unreflective hoyden who casually gives herself to the rakish Dr. Fitzpiers. Marty, on the other hand, is a "pure woman" as well as a hard-working and unselfish child of the soil; she is betrayed only in the sense that Giles never appreciates her solid worth and fidelity. But what would have happened had Marty been endowed with Suke's sensuous nature as well as her own purity and faithfulness? What would have happened had *she* been seduced by an intruding Dr. Fitzpiers? And what, finally, must have been the inner life of such a simple and pure child of the soil, seduced or unseduced? To answer these questions about Marty South, consciously or unconsciously, is to conceive of Tess Durbeyfield.

All groupings are to a degree arbitrary, however, and must be looked on with unremittent distrust. Both Tess and Arabella, for instance, are simple, uneducated, and sensuously ample women, and both show astounding endurance. But it would be manifestly absurd to argue that one character suggested the other. The significance of their close juxtaposition (the two least epicene of Hardy's women) consists rather in the changing public attitude toward the treatment of sexual impulses in fiction. It could be argued at last that ethics went beyond the single problem of chastity; that the devirginated could be pure or impure. The only other possible connection between the two characters may lie in a possible desire to correct an exaggerated impression. Hardy (who had once argued the innocence of all rustics, servant girls, etc.) may have wanted to acknowledge, however belatedly, that it takes all kinds to make even a Wessex world. He could not in all conscience let Tess and her dairymaid friends stand as his final portraits of female rural character.

The groupings nevertheless remain valid and useful even after a detailed surview of Hardy's women had been taken; certain traits and types unmistakably recur. The obvious progress was from an assumption that all young women are unpredictable in the same amusing way to an understanding that women may differ one from the other as much as men do and may even be as purposeful and idealistic as they. To the last Hardy's women never lose their feminine mannerisms and may revert to startling inconsequence; even Marty South and Tess can never become as stolid as Gabriel Oak or as colorlessly passive as Stephen Smith. But the heroine who is above all vain and fickle disappears almost completely from the novels—though she makes a few last and perverse appearances in *A Group of Noble Dames*. The group of sweet, passive ingénues is the most distinct and the least interesting of all. Like all women they are incapable of making unsexed judgments and so usually choose the wrong men. They are rather unintelligent but neither selfish nor perverse; they might all have been the parson's younger daughter who did not write a novel. They are victims when exposed to the rakes, but make the unaggressive Diggory Venns and John Lovedays their unintentional victims. What of any significance distinguishes Picotee from Thomasin or Thomasin from Anne Garland? Tabitha Lark, a mere pert and blooming presence bounding healthfully across a field, might well be considered the reduction to nonentity of the conventional ingénue.

To describe Paula Power, Viviette Constantine, Elizabeth-Jane Newson, and Grace Melbury as average intelligent women is to beg the one interesting question of their everyday realism. Yet it would be still more misleading to call them average women or intelligent women. They belong to the class of the unclassified not because they are highly individualized, which they are not, but because they have no very prominent traits. They are neither selfish nor exceptionally generous, neither stupid nor remarkably intelligent, neither highly sexed nor epicene. They are ordinary English women, examined with quiet ordinary realism, and their interest thus depends almost exclusively on the mishaps that befall them. With luck as commonplace as her own character was commonplace, Baptista Trewthen of "A Mere Interlude" might have drifted through the most uneventful of cloistered lives. As it is, her indifferent drifting character provokes one of Hardy's finest comedies: a long short story which deserves a much wider audience than it has ever won. On the way to marry one man she drifts into marriage with another, and accepts the fact of his drowning a few hours later with a rather astounding calm. She does the calm sensible thing, which is to go ahead with her original plan. It is mere mischance that brings her, on her second wedding night, to the room from which the body of her first husband had just been removed and where his hat was still to be found. In the end she does confess, sensibly enough. Her husband in turn makes his own confession: he has by an earlier wife four termagant daughters, whom Baptista will be obliged to raise.

As a rule the women of the short stories and novelettes resist obvious classification more often than do those of the novels. It is hard to see why this should be so, unless a brief glance fixes on obvious individuality, while full exploration goes beyond it to the type: to what has already been observed and often. The homesick Sophy of "The Son's Veto," the frustrated Mrs. Harnham of "On the Western Circuit," the independent Mrs. Frankland of "For Conscience' Sake," the hysterical Car'line of "The Fiddler of the Reels"—these and many others refuse to fit any of the broad categories. Lizzy Newberry of "The Distracted Preacher" (1879, *Wessex Tales*) makes that novelette one of Hardy's most successful comedies. She is certainly more independent than any of her contemporaries in the novels, with the exception of Eustacia Vye; she is a very unmoral young lady who smuggles rum for fun rather than profit and who takes in the new Methodist preacher as a boarder. Do we not have here, once again, Hardy's inevitable contrast between the lively engaging heroine and the dull moralizing hero? When her preacher catches cold, Lizzy has only to broach one of the tubs of rum hidden in the cellar of the church and refill it with water. The real Lizzy, according to a note of 1912, did not reform and did not marry the minister. Hardy regretted that the conventional ending had been "almost *de rigueur* in an English magazine at the time of writing." Lizzy has this only in common with Hardy's other heroines: she is more interesting than the man who loves her.

The women, whatever their perverse absurdities, are also more plausible than the men. Hardy's was a world of young women and girls, but even the older women hovering in the background of his achievement are convincing and individualized: the severe and haunted Miss Aldclyffe; the superstitious Rhoda Brook; the faded and naïve Susan Henchard; Mrs. Yeobright, grasping her son's affection. Hardy's women, young or old, unfailingly betray themselves by some radically feminine impulse which another novelist would have ignored; by some characteristic gesture or unguarded word. They blunder ahead, creating the circumstances that trap them—while the men go through their dull and predetermined paces. Hardy missed his chance more than once with potentially great characters; most notably with Ethelberta. But the foreground of the achievement is impressive enough. None of Hardy's women are unalive, and very few of them are wholly uninteresting; even the innocent ingénues are capable of occasional violent flare-ups. Can we approve, finally, such a marked tendency to assign women to types; to present a few similar heroines again and again? For one thing, there are always important differences. The woman deemed to be of a certain temperament is also seen as an individual; Elfride is by no means Fancy Day. More importantly, Hardy's six greatest women characters differ radically among themselves: Elfride, nervous and evasive; Bathsheba, curiously masculine and feminine; the wild, proud, and unreconciled Eustacia; the tender and "pure" Tess; the tormented yet fun-loving Sue; and Arabella, the female animal. Against these six major characters and a host of convincing minor ones, Hardy offers only two men of more than average interest and vitality: Michael Henchard and Jude Fawley.

Sue Bridehead

by D. H. Lawrence

Sue is the production of the long selection by man of the woman in whom the female is subordinated to the male principle. A long line of Amelias and Agneses, those women who submitted to the man-idea, flattered the man, and bored him, the Gretchens and the Turgenev heroines, those who have betrayed the female and who therefore only seem to exist to be betrayed by their men, these have produced at length a Sue, the pure thing. And as soon as she is produced she is execrated.

What Cassandra and Aspasia became to the Greeks, Sue has become to the northern civilization. But the Greeks never pitied Woman. They did not show her that highest impertinence—not even Euripides.

But Sue is scarcely a woman at all, though she is feminine enough. Cassandra submitted to Apollo, and gave him the Word of affiance, brought forth prophecy to him, not children. She received the embrace of the spirit, He breathed His Grace upon her: and she conceived and brought forth a prophecy. It was still a marriage. Not the marriage of the Virgin with the Spirit, but the marriage of the female spirit with the male spirit, bodiless.

With Sue, however, the marriage was no marriage, but a submission, a service, a slavery. Her female spirit did not wed with the male spirit: she could not prophesy. Her spirit submitted to the male spirit, owned the priority of the male spirit, wished to become the male spirit. That which was female in her, resistant, gave her only her critical faculty. When she sought out the physical quality in the Greeks, that was her effort to make even the unknowable physique a part of knowledge, to contain the body within the mind.

One of the supremest products of our civilization is Sue, and a product that well frightens us. It is quite natural that, with all her mental alertness, she married Phillotson without ever considering the physical quality of marriage. Deep instinct made her avoid the consideration. And the duality of her nature made her extremely liable to self-destruction. The suppressed, atrophied female in her, like a potent fury, was always there, suggesting to her to make the fatal mistake. She contained always the rarest, most deadly anarchy in her own being.

It needed that she should have some place in society where the clarity of her mental being, which was in itself a form of death, could shine out without attracting any desire for her body. She needed a refinement on Angel Clare. For she herself was a more specialized, more highly civilized product on the female side, than Angel Clare on the male. Yet the atrophied female in her would still want the bodily male.

She attracted to herself Jude. His experience with Arabella had for the time being diverted his attention altogether from the female. His attitude was that of service to the pure male spirit. But the physical male in him, that which knew and belonged to the female, was potent, and roused the female in Sue as much as she wanted it roused, so much that it was a stimulant to her, making her mind the brighter.

It was a cruelly difficult position. She must, by the constitution of her nature, remain quite physically intact, for the female was atrophied in her, to the enlargement of the male activity. Yet she wanted some quickening for this atrophied female. She wanted even kisses. That the new rousing might give her a sense of life. But she could only *live* in the mind.

Then, where could she find a man who would be able to feed her with his male vitality, through kisses, proximity, without demanding the female return? For she was such that she could only receive quickening from a strong male, for she was herself no small thing. Could she then find a man, a strong, passionate male, who would devote himself entirely to the production of the mind in her, to the production of male activity, or of female activity critical to the male?

She could only receive the highest stimulus, which she must inevitably seek, from a man who put her in constant jeopardy. Her essentiality rested upon her remaining intact. Any suggestion of the physical was utter confusion to her. Her principle was the ultra-Christian principle—of living entirely according to the Spirit, to the One, male spirit, which knows and utters, and shines, but exists beyond feeling, beyond joy or sorrow, or pain, exists only in Knowing. In tune with this, she was herself. Let her, however, be turned under the influence of the other dark, silent, strong principle, of the female, and she would break like a fine instrument under discord.

Yet, to live at all in tune with the male spirit, she must receive the male stimulus from a man. Otherwise she was as an instrument without a player. She must feel the hands of a man upon her, she must be infused with his male vitality, or she was not alive.

Here then was her difficulty: to find a man whose vitality could infuse her and make her live, and who would not, at the same time, demand of her a return, the return of the female impulse into him. What man could receive this drainage, receiving nothing back again? He must either die, or revolt.

One man had died. She knew it well enough. She knew her own fatality. She knew she drained the vital, male stimulus out of a man, producing in him only knowledge of the mind, only mental clarity: which man must always strive to attain, but which is not life in him, rather the product of life.

Just as Alec d'Urberville, on the other hand, drained the female vitality out of a woman, and gave her only sensation, only experience in the senses, a sense of herself, nothing to the soul or spirit, thereby exhausting her.

Now Jude, after Arabella, and following his own *idée fixe,* haunted this mental clarity, this knowing, above all. What he contained in himself, of male and female impulse, he wanted to bring forth, to draw into his mind, to resolve into understanding, as a plant resolves that which it contains into flower.

This Sue could do for him. By creating a vacuum, she could cause the vivid flow which clarified him. By rousing him, by drawing from him his turgid vitality, made thick and heavy and physical with Arabella, she could bring into consciousness that which he contained. For he was heavy and full of unrealized life, clogged with untransmuted knowledge, with accretion of his senses. His whole life had been till now an indrawing, ingestion. Arabella had been a vital experience for him, received into his blood. And how was he to bring out all this fullness into knowledge or utterance? For all the time he was being roused to new physical desire, new life-experience, new sense-enrichening, and he could not perform his male function of transmitting this into expression, or action. The particular form his flowering should take, he could not find. So he hunted and studied, to find the call, the appeal which should call out of him that which was in him.

And great was his transport when the appeal came from Sue. She wanted, at first, only his words. That of him which could come to her through speech, through his consciousness, her mind, like a bottomless gulf, cried out for. She wanted satisfaction through the mind, and cried out for him to satisfy her through the mind.

Great, then, was his joy at giving himself out to her. He gave, for it was more blessed to give than to receive. He gave, and she received some satisfaction. But where she was not satisfied, there he must try still to satisfy her. He struggled to bring it all forth. She was, as himself, asking himself what he was. And he strove to answer, in a transport.

And he answered in a great measure. He singled himself out from the old matrix of the accepted idea, he produced an individual flower of his own.

It was for this he loved Sue. She did for him quickly what he would have done for himself slowly, through study. By patient, diligent study, he would have used up the surplus of that turgid energy in him, and would, by long contact with old truth, have arrived at the form of truth which was in him. What he indeed wanted to get from study was, not a store of learning, nor the vanity of education, a sort of superiority of educational wealth, though this also gave him pleasure. He wanted, through familiarity with the true thinkers and poets, particularly with the classic and theological thinkers, because of their comparative sensuousness, to find conscious expression for that which he held in his blood. And to do this, it was necessary for him to resolve and to reduce his blood, to overcome the female sensuousness in himself, to transmute his sensuous being into another state, a state of clarity, of consciousness. Slowly, laboriously, struggling with the Greek and the Latin, he would have burned down his thick blood as fuel, and have come to the true light of himself.

This Sue did for him. In marriage, each party fulfills a dual function with regard to the other: exhaustive and enrichening. The female at the same time exhausts and invigorates the male, the male at the same time exhausts and invigorates the female. The exhaustion and invigoration are both temporary and relative. The male, making the effort to penetrate into the female, exhausts himself and invigorates her. But that which, at the end, he discovers and carries off from her, some seed of being, enrichens him and exhausts her. Arabella, in taking Jude, accepted very little from him. She absorbed very little of his strength and vitality into herself. For she only wanted to be aware of herself in contact with him, she did not want him to penetrate into her very being, till he moved her to her very depth, till she loosened to him some of her very self for his enrichening. She was intrinsically impotent, as was Alec d'Urberville.

So that in her Jude went very little further in Knowledge, or in Self-Knowledge. He took only the first steps: of knowing himself sexually, as a sexual male. That is only the first, the first necessary, but rudimentary, step.

When he came to Sue, he found her physically impotent, but spiritually potent. That was what he wanted. Of Knowledge in the blood he had a rich enough store: more than he knew what to do with. He wished for the further step, of reduction, of essentializing into Knowledge. Which Sue gave to him.

So that his experience with Arabella, plus his first experience of trembling intimacy and incandescent realization with Sue made one complete marriage: that is, the two women added together made One Bride.

When Jude had exhausted his surplus self, in spiritual intimacy with Sue, when he had gained through her all the wonderful understanding she could evoke in him, when he was clarified to himself, then his marriage with Sue was over. Jude's marriage with Sue was over before he knew her physically. She had, physically, nothing to give him.

Which, in her deepest instinct, she knew. She made no mistake in marrying Phillotson. She acted according to the pure logic of her nature. Phillotson was a man who wanted no marriage whatsoever with the female. Sexually, he wanted her as an instrument through which he obtained relief, and some gratification: but, really, relief. Spiritually, he wanted her as a thing to be wondered over and delighted in, but quite separately from himself. He knew quite well he could never marry her. He was a human being as near to mechanical function as a human being can be. The whole process of digestion, masticating, swallowing, digesting, excretion, is a sort of super-mechanical process. And Phillotson was like this. He was an organ, a function-fulfilling organ, he had no separate existence. He could not create a single new movement or thought or expression. Everything he did was a repetition of what had been. All his study was a study of what had been. It was a mechanical, functional process. He was a true, if small, form of the *Savant*. He could understand only the functional laws of living, but these he understood honestly. He was true to himself, he was not overcome by any cant or sentimentalizing. So that in this he was splendid. But it is a cruel thing for a complete, or a spiritual, individuality to be submitted to a functional organism.

The Widow Edlin said that there are some men no woman of any feeling could touch, and Phillotson was one of them. If the Widow knew this, why was Sue's instinct so short?

But Mrs. Edlin was a full human being, creating life in a new form through her personality. She must have known Sue's deficiency. It was natural for Sue to read and to turn again to:

> Thou hast conquered, O pale Galilean!
> The world has grown grey from Thy breath.

In her the pale Galilean had indeed triumphed. Her body was as insentient as hoar-frost. She knew well enough that she was not alive in the ordinary human sense. She did not, like an ordinary woman, receive all she knew through her senes, her instincts, but through her consciousness. The pale Galilean had a pure disciple in her: in her He was fulfilled. For the senses, the body, did not exist in her; she existed as a consciousness. And this is so much so, that she was almost an Apostate. She turned to look at Venus and Apollo. As if she could know either Venus or Apollo, save as ideas. Nor Venus nor Aphrodite had anything to do with her, but only Pallas and Christ.

She was unhappy every moment of her life, poor Sue, with the knowledge of her own nonexistence within life. She felt all the time the ghastly sickness of dissolution upon her, she was as a void unto herself.

So she married Phillotson, the only man she could, in reality, marry. . . .

On *Tess of the D'Urbervilles*

by Dorothy Van Ghent

It was Hardy who said of Meredith that "he would not, or could not—at any rate did not—when aiming to represent the 'Comic Spirit,' let himself discover the tragedy that always underlies comedy if you only scratch deeply enough." Hardy's statement does not really suggest that comedy is somehow tragedy *manqué,* that writers of comedy would write tragedies if they only "scratched deeply enough." What he says is what Socrates said to Aristophanes and Agathon at the end of the *Symposium* —that the genius of tragedy is the same as that of comedy. It is what Cervantes knew, whose great comic hero, Quixote, walks in the same shades with Orestes and Oedipus, Hamlet and Lear. It is what Molière knew. Even Jane Austen knew it. The precariousness of moral consciousness in its brute instinctual and physical circumstances, its fragility as an instrument for the regeneration of the will: this generic disproportion in the human condition comedy develops by grotesque enlargement of one or another aberrated faculty; tragedy, by grotesque enlargement of the imbalance between human motive and the effect of action. The special point to our purpose is, however, another: neither tragic figure nor comic figure is merely phenomenal and spectacular if it truly serves the function common to both genres—the catharsis; acting as scapegoats for the absurdity of the human dilemma, they are humanity's thoughtful or intuitive comment on itself. We return, thus, deviously by way of the kinship of tragedy and comedy, to the matter of "internal relations." The human condition, whether in the "drawing-room of civilized men and women" or on a wild heath in ancient Britain, shows, if scratched deeply enough, the binding ironies that bind the spectacular destiny of the hero with the unspectacular common destiny; and it is in the internal relations of the art form, the aesthetic structure, that these bonds have symbolic representation. The aesthetic failure of the *The Egoist* is thus a diagnostic mark of a crucial failure of vision, a weakness and withdrawal of vision before the common dilemma and the common destiny.

To turn to one of Hardy's great tragic novels is to put "internal relations" in the novel to peculiar test, for there is perhaps no other novelist, of a stature equal to Hardy's, who so stubbornly and flagrantly foisted upon the novel elements resistant to aesthetic cohesion. We shall want to speak of these elements first, simply to clear away and free ourselves from the temptation to appraise Hardy by his "philosophy"—that is, the temptation to mistake bits of philosophic adhesive tape, rather dampened and rumpled by time, for the deeply animated vision of experience which our novel, *Tess,* holds. We can quickly summon examples, for they crop out obviously enough. Before one has got beyond twenty pages one finds this paragraph on the ignominy and helplessness of the human estate:

> All these young souls were passengers in the Durbeyfield ship—entirely dependent on the judgment of the two Durbeyfield adults for their pleasures, their necessities, their health, even their existence. If the heads of the Durbeyfield household chose to sail into difficulty, disaster, starvation, disease, degradation, death, thither were these half-dozen little captives under hatches compelled to sail with them—six helpless creatures, who had never been asked if they wished for life on any terms, much less if they wished for it on such hard conditions as were involved in being of the shiftless house of Durbeyfield. Some people would like to know whence the poet whose philosophy is in these days deemed as profound and trustworthy as his song is sweet and pure, gets his authority for speaking of "Nature's holy plan."

Whenever, in this book, Hardy finds either a butt or a sanction in a poet, one can expect the inevitable intrusion of a form of discourse that infers proofs and opinions and competition in "truth" that belongs to an intellectual battlefield alien from the novel's imaginative concretions. On the eve of the Durbeyfield family's forced deracination and migration, we are told that

> to Tess, as to some few millions of others, there was ghastly satire in the poet's lines:
>
> Not in utter nakedness
> But trailing clouds of glory do we come.
>
> To her and her like, birth itself was an ordeal of degrading personal compulsion, whose gratuitousness nothing in the result seemed to justify, and at best could only palliate.

Aside from the fact that no circumstances have been suggested in which Tess could have had time or opportunity or the requisite development of critical aptitudes to brood so formidably on Wordsworth's lines, who are those "few millions" who are the "like" of Tess? as, who are the "some people" in the previous quotation? and in what way do these statistical generalizations add to the already sufficient meaning of Tess's situation? At the end of the book, with the "Aeschylean phrase" on the sport of the gods, we feel again that intrusion of a commentary which belongs to another order of discourse. The gibbet is enough. The vision is deep and clear and can only be marred by any exploitation of it as a datum in support of abstraction. We could even do without the note of "ameliorism" in the joined hands of Clare and Tess's younger sister at the end: the philosophy of an evolutionary hope has nothing essential to do with Tess's fate and her common meaning; she is too humanly adequate for evolutionary ethics to comment upon, and furthermore we do not believe that young girls make ameliorated lives out of witness of a sister's hanging.

What philosophical vision honestly inheres in a novel inheres as the signifying form of a certain concrete body of experience; it is what the experience "means" because it is what, structurally, the experience *is*. When it can be loosened away from the novel to compete in the general field of abstract truth—as frequently in Hardy—it has the weakness of any abstraction that statistics and history and science may be allowed to criticize; whether true or false for one generation or another, or for one reader or another, or even for one personal mood or another, its status as truth is relative to conditions of evidence and belief existing outside the novel and existing there quite irrelevant to whatever body of particularized life the novel itself might contain. But as a structural principle active within the particulars of the novel, local and inherent there through a maximum of organic dependencies, the philosophical vision has the unassailable truth of living form.

We wish to press this difference a bit further by considering—deliberately in a few minor instances, for in the minor notation is the furthest reach of form—the internality and essentiality of Hardy's vision, just as we have previously considered instances of its externalization and devitalization. Significantly, his "ideas" remain the same in either case. They are abruptly articulated in incident, early in the book, with the death of Prince, appearing here with almost ideographical simplicity.

> The morning mail-cart, with its two noiseless wheels, speeding along these lanes like an arrow, as it always did, had driven into [Tess's] slow and unlighted equipage. The pointed shaft of the cart had entered the breast of the unhappy Prince like a sword, and from the wound his life's blood was spouting in a stream, and falling with a hiss into the road.
>
> In her despair Tess sprang forward and put her hand upon the hole, with the only result that she became splashed from face to skirt with the crimson drops . . .

The mail cart leaves, and she remains alone on the road with the ruin.

> The atmosphere turned pale; the birds shook themselves in the hedges, arose, and twittered; the lane showed all its white features, and Tess showed hers, still whiter. The huge pool of blood in front of her was already assuming the iridescence of coagulation; and when the sun rose, a million prismatic hues were reflected in it. Prince lay alongside still and stark, his eyes half open, the hole in his chest looking scarcely large enough to have let out all that had animated him.

With this accident are concatenated in fatal union Tess's going to "claim kin" of the D'Urbervilles and all the other links in her tragedy down to the murder of Alec. The symbolism of the detail is naïve and forthright to the point of temerity: the accident occurs in darkness and Tess has fallen asleep—just as the whole system of mischances and cross-purposes in the novel is a function of psychic and cosmic blindness; she "put her hand upon the hole"—and the gesture is as absurdly ineffectual as all her effort will be; the only result is that she becomes splashed with blood—as she will be at the end; the shaft pierces Prince's breast "like a sword"—Alec is stabbed in the heart with a knife; with the arousal and twittering of the birds we are aware of the oblivious manifold of nature stretching infinite and detached beyond the isolated human figure; the iridescence of the coagulating blood is, in its incongruity with the dark human trouble, a note of the same indifferent cosmic chemistry that has brought about the accident; and the smallness of the hole in Prince's chest, that looked "scarcely large enough to have let out all that had animated him," is the minor remark of that irony by which Tess's great cruel trial appears as a vanishing incidental in the blind waste of time and space and biological repetition. Nevertheless, there is nothing in this event that has not the natural "grain" of concrete fact; and what it signifies—of the complicity of doom with the most random occurrence, of the cross-purposing of purpose in a multiple world, of cosmic indifference and of moral desolation—is a local truth of a particular experience and irrefutable as the experience itself.

In the second chapter of *Tess* the gathering for the May-day "club-walking" is described, a debased "local Cerealia" that has lost its ancient motive as fertility rite and that subsists as a social habit among the village young people. Here Clare sees Tess for the first time, in white dress, with peeled willow wand and bunch of white flowers. But it is too late for him to stop, the clock has struck, he must be on his way to join his companions. Later, when he wants to marry Tess, he will tell his parents of the "pure and virtuous" bride he has chosen, when her robe is no longer the white robe of the May-walking but the chameleon robe of Queen Guinevere,

> That never would become that wife
> That had once done amiss.

In the scene of the May-walking, the lovers are "star-crossed" not by obscure celestial intent but by ordinary multiplicity of purposes and suitabilities; but in the submerged and debased fertility ritual—ironically doubled here with the symbolism of the white dress (a symbolism which Clare himself will later debase by his prudish perversity)—is shadowed a more savage doom brought about by a more violent potency, that of sexual instinct, by which Tess will be victimized. Owing its form entirely to the vision that shapes the whole of Tess's tragedy, the minor incident of the May-walking has the assurance of particularized reality and the truth of the naturally given.

Nothing could be more brutally factual than the description of the swede field at Flintcomb-Ash, nor convey more economically and transparently Hardy's vision of human abandonment in the dissevering earth.

> The upper half of each turnip had been eaten off by the live-stock, and it was the business of the two women to grub out the lower or earthy half of the root with a hooked fork called a hacker, that this might be eaten also. Every leaf of the vegetable having previously been consumed, the whole field was in color a desolate drab; it was a complexion without features, as if a face, from chin to brow, should be only an expanse of skin. The sky wore, in another color, the same likeness; a white vacuity of expression with the lineaments gone.

The visitation of the winter birds has the same grain of local reality, and yet all the signifying and representative disaster of Tess's situation—its loneliness, its bleak triviality, its irrelevance in the dumb digestion of earth—is focused in the mirroring eyes of the birds.

> . . . strange birds from behind the North Pole began to arrive silently . . . gaunt spectral creatures with tragical eyes—eyes which had witnessed scenes of cataclysmal horror in inaccessible polar regions, of a magnitude such as no human being had ever conceived, in curdling temperatures that no man could endure; which had beheld the crash of icebergs and the slide of snow-hills by the shooting light of the Aurora; been half blinded by the whirl of colossal storms and terraqueous distortions; and retained the expression of feature that such scenes had engendered. These nameless birds came quite near to Tess and Marian, but of all they had seen which humanity would never see they brought no account. The traveller's ambition to tell was not theirs, and, with dumb impassivity, they dismissed experiences which they did

> not value for the immediate incidents of this upland—the trivial movements of the two girls in disturbing the clods with their fragile hackers so as to uncover something or other that these visitants relished as food.

There is the same sensitive honesty to the detail and expression of fact, the same inherence of vision in the particulars of experience, in the description of the weeds where Tess hears Clare thrumming his harp.

> The outskirt of the garden in which Tess found herself had been left uncultivated for some years, and was now damp and rank with juicy grass which sent up mists of pollen; and tall blooming weeds, emitting offensive smells—weeds whose red and yellow and purple hues formed a polychrome as dazzling as that of cultivated flowers. She went stealthily as a cat through this profusion of growth, gathering cuckoo-spittle on her skirts, brushing off snails that were climbing the apple-tree stems, staining her hands with thistle-milk and slug-slime, and rubbing off upon her naked arms sticky blights that, though snow-white on the tree-trunks, made blood-red stains on her skin; thus she drew quite near to Clare, though still unobserved of him.

The weeds, circumstantial as they are, have an astonishingly cunning and bold metaphorical function. They grow at Talbothays, in that healing procreative idyl of milk and mist and passive biology, and they too are bountiful with life, but they stain and slime and blight; and it is in this part of Paradise (an "outskirt of the garden"—there are even apple trees here) that the minister's son is hidden, who, in his conceited impotence, will violate Tess more nastily than her sensual seducer: who but Hardy would have dared to give him the name Angel, and a harp too? It is Hardy's incorruptible feeling for the actual that allows his symbolism its amazingly blunt privileges and that at the same time subdues it to and absorbs it into the concrete circumstance of experience, real as touch.

The dilemma of Tess is the dilemma of morally individualizing consciousness in its earthy mixture. The subject is mythological, for it places the human protagonist in dramatic relationship with the nonhuman and orients his destiny among preternatural powers. The most primitive antagonist of consciousness is, on the simplest premise, the earth itself. It acts so in *Tess,* clogging action and defying conscious motive; or, in the long dream of Talbothays, conspiring with its ancient sensuality to provoke instinct; or, on the farm at Flintcomb-Ash, demoralizing consciousness by its mere geological flintiness. But the earth is "natural," while, dramatically visualized as antagonist, it transcends the natural. The integrity of the myth thus depends, paradoxically, upon naturalism; and it is because of that intimate dependence between the natural and the mythological, a dependence that is organic to the subject, that Hardy's vision is able to impregnate so deeply and shape so unobtrusively the naturalistic particulars of the story.

In *Tess,* of all his novels, the earth is most actual as a dramatic factor —that is, as a factor of causation; and by this we refer simply to the long stretches of earth that have to be trudged in order that a person may get from one place to another, the slowness of the business, the irreducible reality of it (for one has only one's feet), its grimness of soul-wearying fatigue and shelterlessness and doubtful issue at the other end of the journey where nobody may be at home. One thinks, in immediate comparison, of Egdon Heath in *The Return of the Native.* Except for one instance—when Mrs. Yeobright has a far walk to Clym's cottage, and Clym, unforewarned, fails to meet her, and she turns away—the heath in *The Return* exists peripherally and gratuitously in relation to the action, on the one hand as the place where the action happens to happen (an action has to happen somewhere), and on the other, as a metaphor—a metaphorical reflection of the loneliness of human motive, of the inertia of unconscious life, of the mystery of the enfolding darkness; but it is not a dramatically causative agent and its particular quality is not *dramatically* necessary. In *The Mayor of Casterbridge,* the Roman ruins round about the town of Casterbridge are a rather more complicated metaphor, for they are works of man that have fallen into earth; they speak mutely of the anonymity of human effort in historical as well as in geological time; their presence suggests also the classic pattern of the Mayor's tragedy, the ancient repetitiveness of self-destruction; and they provide thus a kind of guarantee or confirming signature of the heroism of the doomed human enterprise. But the Mayor could have had his tragedy in a town with no Roman ruins about it at all; they are, even more than Egdon Heath, gratuitous, and their gratuitousness leads Hardy into some pedantry of documentation to support their metaphorical standing in the story. In *Tess* the earth is *primarily not a metaphor but a real thing* that one has to move on in order to get anywhere or do anything, and it constantly acts in its own motivating, causational substantiality by being there in the way of human purposes to encounter, to harass them, detour them, seduce them, defeat them.

In the accident of Prince's death, the road itself is, in a manner of speaking, responsible, merely by being the same road that the mail cart travels. The seduction of Tess is as closely related, causally, to the distance between Trantridge and Chaseborough as it is to Tess's naïveté and to Alec's egoism; the physical distance itself causes Tess's fatigue and provides Alec's opportunity. The insidiously demoralizing effect of Tess's desolate journeys on foot as she seeks dairy work and field work here and there after the collapse of her marriage, brutal months that are foreshortened to the plodding trip over the chalk uplands to Flintcomb-Ash, is, again, as directly as anything, an effect of the irreducible *thereness* of the territory she has to cover. There are other fatal elements in her ineffectual trip from the farm to Emminster to see Clare's parents, but fatal above all is the distance she must walk to see people who can have no foreknowledge of her coming and who are not at home when she gets there. Finally, with the uprooting and migration of the Durbeyfield family on Old Lady Day, the simple fatality of the earth as earth, in its measurelessness and anonymousness, with people having to move over it with no place to go, is decisive in the final event of Tess's tragedy—her return to Alec, for Alec provides at least a place to go.

The dramatic motivation provided by natural earth is central to every aspect of the book. It controls the style: page by page *Tess* has a wrought density of texture that is fairly unique in Hardy; symbolic depth is communicated by the physical surface of things with unhampered transparency while the homeliest conviction of fact is preserved ("The upper half of each turnip had been eaten off by the live-stock"); and one is aware of style not as a specifically verbal quality but as a quality of observation and intuition that are here—very often—wonderfully identical with each other, a quality of lucidity. Again, it is because of the *actual* motivational impact of the earth that Hardy is able to use setting and atmosphere for a symbolism that, considered in itself, is so astonishingly blunt and rudimentary. The green vale of Blackmoor, fertile, small, enclosed by hills, lying under a blue haze—the vale of birth, the cradle of innocence. The wide misty setting of Talbothays dairy, "oozing fatness and warm ferments," where the "rush of juices could almost be heard below the hiss of fertilization"—the sensual dream, the lost Paradise. The starved uplands of Flintcomb-Ash, with their ironic mimicry of the organs of generation, "myriads of loose white flints in bulbous, cusped, and phallic shapes," and the dun consuming ruin of the swede field—the mockery of impotence, the exile. Finally, that immensely courageous use of setting, Stonehenge and the stone of sacrifice. Obvious as these symbolisms are, their deep stress is maintained by Hardy's naturalistic premise. The earth exists here as Final Cause, and its omnipresence affords constantly to Hardy the textures that excited his eye and care, but affords them wholly charged with dramatic, causational necessity; and the symbolic values of setting are constituted, in large part, by the responses required of the characters themselves in their relationship with the earth.

Generally, the narrative system of the book—that is, the system of episodes—is a series of accidents and coincidences (although it is important to note that the really great crises are psychologically motivated: Alec's seduction of Tess, Clare's rejection of her, and the murder). It is accident that Clare does not meet Tess at the May-walking, when she was "pure" and when he might have begun to court her; coincidence that the mail cart rams Tess's wagon and kills Prince; coincidence that Tess and Clare meet at Talbothays, *after* her "trouble" rather than before; accident that the letter slips under the rug; coincidence that Clare's parents are not at home when she comes to the vicarage; and so on. Superficially it would seem that this type of event, the accidental and coincidental, is the very least credible of fictional devices, particularly when there is an accumulation of them; and we have all read or heard criticism of Hardy for his excessive reliance upon coincidence in the management of his narratives; if his invention of probabilities and inevitabilities of action does not seem simply poverty-stricken, he appears to be too much the puppeteer working wires or strings to make events conform to his "pessimistic" and "fatalistic" ideas. It is not enough to say that there is a certain justification for his large use of the accidental in the fact that "life is like that"—chance, mishap, accident, events that affect our lives while they remain far beyond our control, are a very large part of experience; but art differs from life precisely by making order out of this disorder, by finding causation in it. In the accidentalism of Hardy's universe we can recognize the profound truth of the darkness in which life is cast, darkness both within the soul and without, only insofar as his accidentalism *is not itself accidental* nor yet an ideology-obsessed puppeteer's manipulation of character and event; which is to say, only insofar as the universe he creates has aesthetic integrity, the flesh and bones and organic development of a concrete world. This is not true always of even the best of Hardy's novels; but it is so generally true of the construction of *Tess*—a novel in which the accidental is perhaps more preponderant than in any other Hardy—that we do not care to finick about incidental lapses. The naturalistic premise of the book—the condition of earth in which life is placed—is the most obvious, fundamental, and inexorable of facts; but because it is the physically "given," into which and beyond which there can be no penetration, it exists as mystery; it is thus, even as the basis of all natural manifestation, itself of the quality of the supernatural. On the earth, so conceived, coincidence and accident constitute order, the prime terrestrial order, for they too are "the given," impenetrable by human *ratio,* accountable only as mystery. By constructing the *Tess*-universe on the solid ground (one might say even literally on the "ground") of the earth as Final Cause, mysterious cause of causes, Hardy does not allow us to forget that what is most concrete in experience is also what is most inscrutable, that an overturned clod in a field or the posture of herons standing in a water mead or the shadows of cows thrown against a wall by evening sunlight are as essentially fathomless as the procreative yearning, and this in turn as fathomless as the sheerest accident in event. The accidentalism and coincidentalism in the narrative pattern of the book stand, thus, in perfectly orderly correlation with the grounding mystery of the physically concrete and the natural.

But Hardy has, with very great cunning, reinforced the *necessity* of this particular kind of narrative pattern by giving to it the background of the folk instinctivism, folk fatalism, and folk magic. If the narrative is conducted largely by coincidence, the broad folk background rationalizes coincidence by constant recognition of the mysteriously "given" as what "was to be"—the folk's humble presumption of order in a rule of mishap. The folk are the earth's pseudopodia, another fauna; and because they are so deeply rooted in the elemental life of the earth—like a sensitive animal extension of the earth itself—they share the authority of the natural. (Whether Hardy's "folk," in all the attributes he gives them, ever existed historically or not is scarcely pertinent; they exist here.) Their philosophy and their skills in living, even their gestures of tragic violence, are instinctive adaptations to "the given"; and because they are indestructible, their attitudes toward events authoritatively urge a similar fatalism upon the reader, impelling him to an imaginative acceptance of the doom-wrought series of accidents in the foreground of the action.

We have said that the dilemma of Tess is the dilemma of moral consciousness in its intractable earthy mixture; schematically simplified, the signifying form of the *Tess*-universe is the tragic heroism and tragic ineffectuality of such consciousness in an antagonistic earth where events shape themselves by accident rather than by moral design; and the *mythological* dimension of this form lies precisely in the earth's antagonism—for what is persistently antagonistic appears to have its own intentions, in this case mysterious, supernatural, for it is only thus that earth can seem to have "intentions." The folk are the bridge between mere earth and moral individuality; of the earth as they are, separable conscious ego does not arise among them to weaken animal instinct and confuse response—it is the sports, the deracinated ones, like Tess and Clare and Alec, who are morally individualized and who are therefore able to suffer isolation, alienation, and abandonment, or to make others so suffer; the folk, while they remain folk, cannot be individually isolated, alienated, or lost, for they are amoral and their existence is colonial rather than personal. (There is no finer note of this matter—fine in factual and symbolic precision, and in its very inconspicuousness—than the paragraph describing the loaded wagons of the migrating families:

> The day being the sixth of April, the Durbeyfield wagon met many other wagons with families on the summit of the load, which was built on a well-nigh unvarying principle, as peculiar, probably, to the rural laborer as the hexagon to the bee. The groundwork of the arrangement was the position of

> the family dresser, which, with its shining handles, and finger marks, and domestic evidences thick upon it, stood importantly in front, over the tails of the shaft-horses, in its erect and natural position, like some Ark of the Covenant which must not be carried slightingly.

Even in the event of mass uprooting, the folk character that is preserved is that of the tenacious, the colonial, the instinctive, for which Hardy finds the simile of the hexagon of the bee, converting it then, with Miltonic boldness, to its humanly tribal significance with the simile of the Ark of the Covenant.) Their fatalism is communal and ritual, an instinctive adaptation as accommodating to bad as to good weather, to misfortune as to luck, to birth as to death, a subjective economy by which emotion is subdued to the falling out of event and the destructiveness of resistance is avoided. In their fatalism lies their survival wisdom, as against the death direction of all moral deliberation. There is this wisdom in the cheerful compassion of the fieldwomen for Tess in her time of trouble: the trouble "was to be." It is in Joan Durbeyfield's Elizabethan ditties of lullaby:

> I saw her lie do-own in yon-der green gro—ve;
> Come, love, and I'll tell you where.

—the kind of ditty by which women of the folk induce maturity in the child by lulling him to sleep with visions of seduction, adultery, and despair. It is in the folk code of secrecy—as in Dairyman Crick's story of the widow who married Jack Dollop, or in Joan's letter of advice to her daughter, summoning the witness of ladies the highest in the land who had had their "trouble" too but who had not told. Tess's tragedy turns on a secret revealed, that is, on the substitution in Tess of an individualizing morality for the folk instinct of concealment and anonymity.

While their fatalism is a passive adaptation to the earthy doom, the folk magic is an active luxury: the human being, having a mind, however incongruous with his animal condition, has to do something with it—and if the butter will not come and someone is in love in the house, the coexistence of the two facts offers a mental exercise in causation (though this is not really the "rights o't," about the butter, as Dairyman Crick himself observes; magical lore is not so dainty); yet the magic is no less a survival wisdom than the fatalism, inasmuch as it does offer mental exercise in causation, for man cannot live without a sense of cause. The magic is a knowledgeable mode of dealing with the unknowledgeable, and it is adaptive to the dooms of existence where moral reason is not adaptive, for moral reason seeks congruence between human intention and effect and is therefore always inapropos (in Hardy's universe, tragically inapropos), whereas magic seeks only likenesses, correspondences, analogies, and these are everywhere. Moral reason is in complete incommunication with the "given," for it cannot accept the "given" as such, cannot accept accident, cannot accept the obscure activities of instinct, cannot accept doom; but magic can not only accept but rationalize all these, for the correspondences that determine its strategies are themselves "given" —like is like, and that is the end of the matter. As the folk fatalism imbues the foreground accidents with the suggestion of necessity, the folk magic imbues them with the suggestion of the supernaturally motivated; and motivation of whatever kind makes an event seem "necessary," suitable, fitting. The intricate interknitting of all these motifs gives to Hardy's actually magical view of the universe and of human destiny a backing of concrete life, as his evocation of the earth as Cause gives to his vision the grounding of the naturalistic.

The folk magic is, after all, in its strategy of analogy, only a specialization and formalization of the novelist's use of the symbolism of natural detail, a symbolism of which we are constantly aware from beginning to end. Magical interpretation and prediction of events consist in seeing one event or thing as a "mimicry" of another—a present happening, for instance, as a mimicry of some future happening; that is, magic makes a system out of analogies, the correlative forms of things. Poets and novelists do likewise with their symbols. Burns's lines: "And my fause luver staw my rose, / But ah! he left the thorn wi' me," use this kind of mimicry, common to poetry and magic. When a thorn of Alec's roses pricks Tess's chin, the occurrence is read as an omen—and omens properly belong to the field of magic; but the difference between this symbol which is an omen, and the very similar symbol in Burns's lines, which acts only reminiscently, is a difference merely of timing—the one "mimics" a seduction which occurs later, the other "mimics" a seduction and its consequences which have already occurred. And there is very little difference, functionally, between Hardy's use of this popular symbol as an *omen* and his symbolic use of natural particulars—the chattering of the birds at dawn after the death of Prince and the iridescence of the coagulated blood, the swollen udders of the cows at Talbothays and the heavy fertilizing mists of the late summer mornings and evenings, the ravaged turnip field on Flintcomb-Ash and the visitation of the polar birds. All of these natural details are either predictive or interpretive or both, and prediction and interpretation of events through analogies are the profession of magic. When a piece of blood-stained butcher paper flies up in the road as Tess enters the gate of the vicarage at Emminster, the occurrence is natural while it is ominous; it is realistically observed, as part of the "given," while it inculcates the magical point of view. Novelistic symbolism *is* magical strategy. In *Tess,* which is through and through symbolic, magic is not only an adaptive specialization of the "folk," but it also determines the reader's response to the most naturalistic detail. Thus, though the story is grounded deeply in a naturalistic premise, Hardy's use of one of the commonest tools of novelists—symbolism—enforces a magical view of life.

Logically accommodated by this view of life is the presentation of supernatural characters. Alec D'Urberville does not appear in his full otherworldly character until late in the book, in the episode of the planting fires, where we see him with pitchfork among flames—and even then the local realism of the planting fires is such as almost to absorb the ghostliness of the apparition. The usual form of his appearance is as a stage villain, complete with curled mustache, checked suit, and cane; and actually it seems a bit easier for the reader to accept him as the Evil Spirit itself, even with a pitchfork, than in his secular accouterments of the villain of melodrama. But Hardy's logic faces its conclusions with superb boldness, as it does in giving Angel Clare his name and his harp and making him a minister's son; if Alec is the Evil One, there will be something queer about his ordinary tastes, and the queerness is shown in his stagy clothes (actually, this melodramatic stereotype is just as valid for a certain period of manners and dress as our own stereotype of the gunman leaning against a lamppost and striking a match against his thumbnail). Alec is the smart aleck of the Book of Job, the one who goes to and fro in the earth and walks up and down in it, the perfectly deracinated one, with his flash and new money and faked name and aggressive ego. If he becomes a religious convert even temporarily it is because he is not really so very much different from Angel (the smart aleck of the Book of Job was also an angel), for extreme implies extreme, and both Angel and Alec are foundered in egoism, the one in idealistc egoism, the other in sensual egoism, and Angel himself is diabolic enough in his prudery. When Alec plays his last frivolous trick on Tess, lying down on one of the slabs in the D'Urberville vaults and springing up at her like an animated corpse, his neuroticism finally wears, not the stagy traditional externals of the Evil Spirit, but the deeply convincing character of insanity—of that human evil which is identifiable with madness. Both Angel and Alec are metaphors of extremes of human behavior, when the human has been cut off from community and has been individualized by intellectual education or by material wealth and traditionless independence.

Between the stridencies of Angel's egoism and Alec's egoism is Tess—with her Sixth Standard training and some anachronistic D'Urberville current in her blood that makes for spiritual exacerbation just as it makes her cheeks paler, "the teeth more regular, the red lips thinner than is usual in a country-bred girl": incapacitated for life by her moral idealism.

capacious of life through her sensualism. When, after Alec's evilly absurd trick, she bends down to whisper at the opening of the vaults, "Why am I on the wrong side of this door?" her words construct all the hopelessness of her cultural impasse. But her stabbing of Alec is her heroic return through the "door" into the folk fold, the fold of nature and instinct, the anonymous community. If both Alec and Angel are spiritually impotent in their separate ways, Tess is finally creative by the only measure of creativeness that this particular novelistic universe holds, the measure of the instinctive and the natural. Her gesture is the traditional gesture of the revenge of instinct, by which she joins an innumerable company of folk heroines who stabbed and were hanged—the spectacular but still anonymous and common gesture of common circumstances and common responses, which we, as habitual readers of newspaper crime headlines, find, unthinkingly, so shocking to our delicate notions of what is "natural." That she goes, in her wandering at the end, to Stonehenge, is an inevitable symbolic going—as all going and doing are symbolic—for it is here that the earthiness of her state is best recognized, by the monoliths of Stonehenge, and that the human dignity of her last gesture has the most austere recognition, by the ritual sacrifices that have been made on these stones.

The Mayor of Casterbridge as Tragedy

by John Paterson

As a man of his time and place, Thomas Hardy was ill-equipped to meet the challenge of tragedy in its traditional form. Although the romantic and scientific humanisms to which his expatriation in London had exposed him did not exclude a tragic vision of human experience, they were incompetent, by their denial of moral and religious universals, to provide that framework of theme and form which could alone make peace with a tragic vision. Hence the maimed achievements of *The Return of the Native* and *Jude the Obscure.* In the absence of a justice, an ethical substance, which is beyond man's power to shape or control but to which, at the same time, he is necessarily responsible, the disasters in which these works culminate are deprived of a moral and hence fully tragic significance. Celebrating the human at the expense of the superhuman, they cannot justify the ways of God to man.

Hardy was not, however, exclusively or even primarily a man of his century. As the citizen of a provincial Dorset which had had no news of Swinburne and Darwin, he inherited a traditional moral wisdom not yet damaged by the romantic and scientific inspirations which were everywhere shaking the confidence of the modern imagination. In *Far from the Madding Crowd* and *The Woodlanders,* for example, he could magnify not the romantic agonies of those condemned, like the Eustacias and the Judes, to live in a world without justice or dignity but the modest pieties of the Oaks and the Winterbornes, their decent adoration of a Nature that was still a mystery and a miracle, still the earnest of a moral consciousness in the universe. Their diabolical antagonists, the Sergeant Troys and Dr. Fitzpiers, invite in fact not the fatuous indulgence of the romantic imagination but the horror and disgust of the medieval imagination in the presence of Dr. Faust. Even in *The Return of the Native,* the "tragic" apotheosis in death of the rebellious Eustacia Vye is criticized retroactively by the comic apotheosis in marriage of Diggory Venn and

"*The Mayor of Casterbridge* as Tragedy," by John Paterson. From *Victorian Studies* III (December 1959), pp. 151-172.

Thomasin Yeobright[1] who have, like the Oaks and the Winterbornes, come to terms with central headquarters. As the beneficiary of a prenineteenth century culture whose primitive decencies neither Swinburne nor Darwin had entirely confounded, Hardy's imagination could still be possessed, evidently, by what Keats has nostalgically called "our deep eternal theme," by "the fierce dispute, / Betwixt damnation and impassioned clay" that authorizes the form and substance of traditional tragedy.

Hence the lonely and peculiar significance in the literature of modern times of *The Mayor of Casterbridge*. Temporarily freed from the disabling humanistic biases of his age, exploiting a level of the mind to which his romantic sympathies and naturalistic assumptions could not penetrate, Hardy here assumes what the literature of tragedy after Shakespeare has not found it easy or possible to assume: the existence of a moral order, an ethical substance, a standard of justice and rectitude, in terms of which man's experience can be rendered as the drama of his salvation as well as the drama of his damnation. Reviving a body of beliefs about man and fate, nature and society, that were once the ordinary possession of the Western imagination, he exploits a wisdom that makes possible the achievement of tragedy in the heroical sense of a Sophocles or a Shakespeare.

I

The traditional basis of *The Mayor of Casterbridge* as tragedy emerges at once in the plainly fabulous or hyperbolical quality of its first episode. Discouraged by his failure to get on in the world and impatient of ordinary domestic restraints, Michael Henchard, the journeyman haytrusser, arrives at the fair at Weydon-Priors, steeps himself in the alcoholic brews of the furmity-woman, and in a drunken moment sells his wife to a sailor for five guineas. Clearly calculated to startle the imagination, to appeal to its sense for the grand and the heroic in human experience, Henchard's act of violence bears the same relation to the novel as the betrayal of Cordelia and the murder of Laius to *Lear* and *Oedipus*.[2]

[1] As Hardy was himself to confess in the celebrated footnote on p. 473 of the British Wessex edition (1912), he was forced, by editorial pressure and the necessities of serial publication, to provide for a happy ending. The allegedly extraneous sixth book of *The Return of the Native* is less inapposite, however, than Hardy and some of his critics would lead one to believe. His attitude to Eustacia's romantic revolts, to the extraordinary and the tragic in human experience, is not after all wholly uncritical. Hence the celebration of the ordinary and the comic in human experience which is the domesticating effect of the sixth book is not altogther foreign to the novel as originally conceived. The implications of his footnote notwithstanding, in other words, Hardy in effect converted editorial necessity into artistic virtue.

[2] D. A. Dike has explored some of the analogies between *The Mayor of Casterbridge* and *Oedipus Rex* in his "A Modern Oedipus: *The Mayor of Casterbridge*," *Essays in Criticism*, II (1952), 169-179.

Arousing such forces of retribution as will not be satisfied with less than the total humiliation of the offender and the ultimate restoration of the order offended, it will come to represent, like its counterpart in *Lear* and *Oedipus,* the violation of a moral scheme more than human in its implications.

That such is indeed its significance is underlined by its dramatic isolation in the structure of the novel, by the fact that twenty years intervene between the shocking event that commands the attention of the first two chapters and the events of the chapters that follow. For the primary effect of this structural peculiarity is to dramatize the causal relation between Henchard's crime and punishment. Recording the remorseless private and public deterioration of the protagonist, the novel enacts the indignation of the moral order whose serenity his act of impiety has violently affronted. Forsaken by Farfrae, blasted by the disclosure that Elizabeth-Jane is not his daughter, and deprived of the love and loyalty of Lucetta; humiliated by the revelations of the furmity-woman and ruined in a trade war with his Scottish antagonist; crushed by his public rebuke on the occasion of the Royal Visit, rejected by the "daughter" whose affection had consoled him in defeat, and reduced in the end to the starkest of deaths, Henchard will be forced, like Oedipus and Faust and Lear, to rediscover in suffering and sorrow the actuality of the moral power he had so recklessly flouted.

The actuality of this power is otherwise expressed in the inexorability with which the guilty past asserts, as in *Hamlet* and *Oedipus,* its claim to recognition and atonement. The series of fatal reappearances that challenges and undermines Henchard's illegitimate power—i.e., Lucetta's, the furmity-woman's, Newson's as well, of course, as Susan Henchard's ("Mrs. Henchard was so pale that the boys called her 'The Ghost'" [pp. 94-95])[3]—schematizes the determined revenge of a supernatural authority for which a wrong left uncorrected and unpunished is intolerable. This sinister theme is early adumbrated in the mayor's proud refusal to make restitution for the damaged wheat he has sold to the community. "But what are you going to do to repay us for the past?" an indignant townsman challenges him from the street. "If anybody will tell me how to turn grown wheat into wholesome wheat," the arrogant man replies with an irony of which he is, in the pride of his office, tragically unconscious, "I'll take it back with pleasure. But it can't be done" (p. 41). Henchard thus defines in allegorical terms the conditions of his crime and punishment, his answer pointing up not only the irrevocability of that other

[3] All page references will be to Harper's "Modern Classics" edition (1922) which is more easily accessible than the definitive Wessex edition. The discrepancies between the American and British editons are not such as to affect the position taken in this essay.

and profounder crime buried in his past but also the uncanny pertinacity with which it will return, as the agent of a wounded moral intelligence, to haunt and destroy his life.

The authenticity of a moral intelligence beyond man's power to control is verified in the heroic imagination of Henchard himself. For it is the measure of his grandeur, the measure of his dissociation from such mere victims of naturalistic or unconscious force as Tess and Jude and Eustacia, that he should acknowledge from the very beginning the extrahuman and specifically moral agency of the opposition that has set itself against him. On the morning after the sale of his wife, for example, he seeks as it were to propitiate the offended powers by presenting himself in the local church and swearing to give up drinking for twenty years. He will come to feel, as disaster overwhelms him, "that some power [is] working against him" (p. 219), that he has fully deserved the opposition of a "sinister intelligence bent on punishing him" (p. 144). His recognition of a justice beyond his power to control will be solemnized, finally, not only in the great words with which he leaves Casterbridge[4] but also in the heroic self-condemnation of his last will and testament (p. 384).

The universality of Henchard's experience is guaranteed by its re-enactment in the story of Lucetta Le Sueur. For one thing, she has sought, in the willful and impious fashion of the mayor himself, to dissociate herself from the past: "my ancestors in Jersey," she says defensively, "were as good as anybody in England. . . . I went back and lived there after my father's death. But I don't value such past matters . . ." (p. 173).[5] More to the point, however, in having lived in sin with Henchard in Jersey, she too has been guilty of a moral indiscretion in the past. Indeed, in rejecting her old lover and electing to marry Farfrae, she has refused, once again like her more heroic male counterpart, to recognize and make restitution for her crime. "I won't be a slave to the past—," she cries pathetically, when the demoniacal Henchard seeks forcibly to legalize their old association, "I'll love where I choose!" (p. 204). At the very moment, however, when her love-letters have been burned and she thinks herself free from the consequences of her delinquency, she hears the sounds of the skimmington ride which will publish her shame and even-

[4] "I — Cain — go alone as I deserve — an outcast and a vagabond. But my punishment is *not* greater than I can bear!" (p. 361).

[5] Her irreligious disrespect for the past is more indirectly suggested in her frivolous description of its trophies in the local museum: "there are crowds of interesting things," she tells Elizabeth without conviction, "skeletons, teeth, old pots and pans, ancient boots and shoes, bird's eggs — all charmingly instructive" (p. 178). Her careless impiety has in fact been underscored by the piety in death of her rival and foil, for Susan Henchard's dust has been said to mingle "with the dust of women who lay ornamented with glass hair-pins and amber necklaces, and men who held in their mouths coins of Hadrian, Posthumus, and the Constantines" (p. 153).

tually bring about her death. Her melodramatic and middle-class re-enactment of Henchard's authentic moral drama bears witness, like Gloucester's prose re-enactment of Lear's crime and punishment, to the reality of an order whose indignation, once provoked, can neither be appeased nor controlled.

Henchard's terrible retrogression obeys, certainly, a law so distinct and irrefutable in its logic as to suggest an origin more supernatural than natural. Reduced to the humble trade with which he began, discarding the shabby-general suit of cloth and the rusty silk hat which had been the emblems of his illegitmate power, taking again to the drink he had twenty years before repudiated, leaving Casterbridge exactly as he had entered it, revisiting Weydon-Priors, the scene of the original crime, and dying at last, broken in body and spirit, on the barren wastes of Egdon Heath, Henchard travels with every stage of his decline and fall the long road by which he had come, embraces with every step the past he had denied, and rediscovers, like Lear, in the conditions of his going out the conditions of his setting forth. Having, as Tess and Jude have not, exchanged his humanity for worldly power and prestige, he is systematically deprived of that for which he had exchanged his humanity. Guilty, in a sense that Tess and Jude are not, of pride offensive to the gods, his suffering and death acquire a value to which theirs canot quite lay claim. The fate that presides over Henchard's destruction as the witness of a moral intention in the universe is hardly interchangeable, indeed, with the vulgar and even brutish fate that presides, either as crass casualty or as unwitting opposition, over the destruction of the Tesses and the Judes and the Eustacias.[6]

[6] The critical consensus would have it that fate for Hardy was always synonymous either with a perverse and even willful Chance or with an exclusively social or natural Necessity. His weakness as a tragedian, Arthur Mizener believes, inheres in his naturalistic assumption "that there can be only one kind of reality . . ." ("*Jude the Obscure* as a Tragedy," *Southern Review*, VI [1940], 202). Presupposing that "the nature of inanimate things is unconscious and undesigning," Hardy sees events, writes Jacques Barzun, as "chance collidings of willfull and indifferent forces among themselves . . ." ("Truth and Poetry in Thomas Hardy," *Southern Review*, VI [1940], 184). Generalizations appropriate for *Tess* and *Jude*, however, meet in the case of *The Mayor of Casterbridge* with unexpectedly stiff resistance. Assuming as it does more than "one kind of reality," its events suggesting not so much "chance collidings of willful and indifferent forces" as a logic or pattern beyond man's power to control and even to understand, *The Mayor of Casterbridge* can fairly be called a *lusus naturae*. It may be objected that the novel is unique only insofar as the hero's character creates the events leading to his downfall. In the last analysis, however, these events follow a logic, a pattern, in which the hero as character may participate but for which he himself is not finally responsible. The logic or the pattern acquires a reality of its own independent of the hero's particular contribution. As in much Shakespearean tragedy, in other words, character itself becomes a part or instrument of that general fate which presides, on behalf of a supernature, over the course of human affairs.

In its mysterious remoteness and refinement, fate in *The Mayor of Casterbridge* has much in common with Hegel's sublime and indestructible "ethical substance." The conflict upon which the novel is founded does not suggest, after all, the grotesquely unequal contest between good and evil in which a malevolent "superhumanity" triumphs, as in *Tess* and *Jude* and to a certain extent in *The Return of the Native,* over an innocent and helpless humanity. It suggests, rather, the more equal, the more ambiguous, conflict that occurs when, to the discomfiture of a supernatural wisdom within whose bounds all merely natural oppositions are absorbed and reconciled, one great good is asserted at the expense of another. In this context, the conditions of Henchard's heroic grandeur—his pride, his passion, his ambition—are exactly the conditions of his downfall and destruction. They invite the correction of that absolute wisdom for which the more modest humanity of Elizabeth-Jane and Donald Farfrae is equally sympathetic.

Thus while Henchard stands for the grandeur of the human passions, for the heroism of spirit that prefers the dangerous satisfactions of the superhuman to the mild comforts of the merely human, Farfrae and Elizabeth stand for the claims of reason and thought, for the spirit of moderation that is prepared to come to terms with merely human possibilities. Elizabeth-Jane's Cordelia is said to feel "none of those ups and downs of spirit which beset so many people without cause; . . . never a gloom in [her] soul but she well knew how it came there . . ." (p. 100). Her would-be father, on the other hand, his morale destroyed by his crime, is victimized by mysterious and rebellious depressions which he can neither understand nor control. With her "field-mouse fear of the coulter of destiny," Elizabeth declines to adorn herself in the pomp and pride of fine clothing: "I won't be too gay on any account. It would be tempting Providence to hurl mother and me down . . ." (p. 101). With his leonine pride and contempt of Fortune, on the other hand, Henchard makes love to his own destruction, affecting in his first appearance as chief magistrate "an old-fashioned evening suit, an expanse of frilled shirt . . . ; jewelled studs, and a heavy gold chain" (p. 37).

Again, if Henchard suggests the passionate extremities of King Oedipus, Farfrae suggests the less spectacular appeal to reason and compromise for which Creon stands. "In my business, 'tis true that strength and bustle build up a firm," says the mayor, unconsciously allegorizing the terms of their opposition as well as the basis of his own failure: "But judgment and knowledge are what keep it established. Unluckily, I am bad at science, Farfrae; bad at figures—a rule o'thumb sort of man. You are just the reverse . . ." (p. 55).[7] The conflict between the passion of the one

[7] In his symbolic acknowledgment of his brotherhood with the Scotchman—"Your forehead, Farfrae, is something like my poor brother's—now dead and gone . . ."

and the reason of the other is thus dramatized as a conflict between the rugged individualist and the organization man, between primitive and modern ways of doing business. In his victory over Henchard's gallant but corrupt and self-defeating Mark Antony, Farfrae in fact recalls, as much in his narrowness as in his shrewdness, the not altogether attractive figure of Octavius Caesar. He brings to the firm an order and regularity of which the owner is rendered, by the very largeness of his nature, mentally incapable: "the old crude *viva voce* system of Henchard, in which everything depended upon his memory, and bargains were made by the tongue alone, was swept away. Letters and ledgers took the place of 'I'll do't,' and 'you shall hae't' . . ." (p. 103). Later, identifying himself with the new mechanization, Farfrae will be responsible for introducing a modern sowing machine while Henchard, identifying himself with custom and tradition, will remain true to "the venerable seed-lip [which] was still for sowing as in the days of the Heptarchy" (p. 191). Indeed, for all the irregularity of his behavior, the mayor is moved by profound emotions to which, in his rudimentary piety, he cannot or will not be unfaithful. As the Fortinbras, as the Octavius Caesar, of the drama, on the other hand, Farfrae is ready, not long after Lucetta's death, to dishonor the emotion to which he once had thrilled. "There are men," Hardy remarks, and he must have had Henchard in mind, "whose hearts insist upon a dogged fidelity to some image or cause . . . long after their judgment has pronounced it no rarity . . . and without them the band of the worthy is incomplete. But Farfrae was not of those. . . . He could not but perceive that by the death of Lucetta he had exchanged a looming misery for a simple sorrow" (p. 348).

The novel does not commemorate, then, as *Tess* and *Jude* commemorate, the total degradation of the good and the true. Henchard's defeat and Farfrae's accession to power simply reassert, however painfully, the necessary balance between two great values with equal claims to recognition and fulfillment: the grandeur that would transcend the limits of the human condition and the moderation that is satisfied to live within these limits. The fate that controls the world of *The Mayor of Casterbridge* resembles, to this extent, not the brutal and insentient force that presides over *Tess* and *Jude* but the ideal justice and wisdom that Hegel found presiding over the tragic drama of Sophocles and Shakespeare.

II

In the end, of course, Henchard carries within him, in the perverse instinct for betraying his own best interests, the seeds of his own down-

(p. 54)—Henchard appears to recognize, albeit momentarily, the interdependency between reason and passion which his behavior consistently and tragically refutes.

fall and disaster. *The Mayor of Casterbridge* is not, however, any more than *Lear* and *Oedipus,* a study in the impulse to self-destruction. Presupposing a concept of man as traditional as its concept of fate, the novel defines the disharmonies of Henchard's mind and imagination within an ethical and religious rather than a psychiatric or scientific frame of reference.

Founding itself upon an ancient psychology, *The Mayor of Casterbridge* celebrates, first of all, the subordination of the passions that link man with nature to the reason that unites him with God. It is Henchard's tragedy that, like Lear and Othello, he reverses and destroys this order. For when he sells his wife to a sailor for five guineas in violation of the profoundest moral tact, it is at a moment when, under the spell of the furmity-woman, he has allowed the passions to distort and deform the reason. Indeed, the surrender to passion responsible for the original crime will, in spite of his heroic resolution to give up drinking for twenty years, repeat itself in those sudden angers and indignations that alienate Farfrae, Elizabeth, and Lucetta, among others, and eventually deprive him of the ordinary consolations of love and friendship. The precarious balance between reason and passion will be re-established only at the very end when, thoroughly scourged and chastised, all passion spent, Henchard is displaced by the Farfraes and Elizabeths in whose persons the claims of reason are piously acknowledged.[8]

The novel rests, however, not only on the hierarchic psychology that enjoins the subordination of passion to reason but also on the hierarchic cosmology that enjoins the subordination of the human to the superhuman. Henchard's tragedy is that he has, in repudiating his solidarity with the human community, subverted the order that has placed man in the middleground between God and nature. Hence his explicit identification with Dr. Faustus, the archetypal representative of human rebellion: Henchard could be described, Hardy writes, "as Faust has been described —as a vehement gloomy being who had quitted the ways of vulgar men without light to guide him on a better way" (p. 131). Indeed, in selling his wife to a sailor who will later return to claim his due, in joining with Farfrae to make his damaged wheat whole again (that is, to manipulate and defraud nature,[9] in approaching the conjurer Fall for illegitimate insights into the future course of the weather, Henchard is discovered in

[8] Thus in the last pages of the novel, Elizabeth is celebrated in having, unlike Henchard, discovered the secret "of making limited opportunities endurable," in having cultivated "those minute forms of satisfaction that offer themselves to everybody not in positive pain" (p. 385).

[9] "To fetch it [the damaged wheat] back entirely is impossible," Farfrae tells him; "Nature won't stand so much as that, but here you go a great way towards it" (p. 53).

the attitude and situation made legendary in the story of the diabolical doctor.

Hence the traditional pattern of his decline and fall. In contriving to be more than human, Henchard inevitably becomes a great deal less than human. Arrogating powers and prerogatives that rightly belong to the gods, he forfeits, like Faust and Lear and Othello before him, his own humanity. This retrogression is first of all apparent in his brutal loneliness, in his increasing alienation from the human community. It is also apparent, however, though more indirectly, in the elemental or natural imagery with which he is persistently associated. Troubled by the presence of Elizabeth-Jane, he moves "like a great tree in a wind" (p. 141). After the cruel discovery that she is not after all his daughter, he greets her in a manner described as "dry and thunderous" (p. 192). His habit, after his estrangement from Farfrae, is to look "stormfully past him" (p. 132) and in their grim trial of strength in the loft, they rock and writhe "like trees in a gale" (p. 314).

At the very last, of course, the mayor is restored to the human community from which he has willfully separated himself. In marching Abel Whittle off to work without his breeches and exposing him to public humiliation, Henchard had committed once more, at the level of the comic and pathetic, the startling crime at Weydon-Priors. Once again he had dishonored, as Cain to the Abel of his servant and factotum, the sacred bond that unites man with even the lowliest of his kind. For when the antiheroic terms of Abel's creation are granted, his nature is ironically revealed as essentially continuous with the mayor's: he is, in all but the pomp and pride of office, Michael Henchard's own brother. "There is sommit wrong in my make, your worshipful!" the poor man confesses in terms that describe his master as well as himself; "especially in the inside . . ." (pp. 111-112). Indeed, Abel reacts to his public humiliation with a gloomy and morbid sensitivity that recalls Henchard himself in the days of his decline and fall: "Yes—I'll go to Blackmoor Vale half naked as I be, since he do command; but I shall kill myself afterwards; I can't outlive the disgrace; for the women-folk will be looking out of their winders at my mortification all the way along, and laughing me to scorn as a man 'ithout breeches! You know how I feel such things, Maister Farfrae, and how forlorn thoughts get hold upon me. Yes—I shall do myself harm—I feel it coming on!" (p. 113). Hence the significance of the novel's final episodes in which Henchard dies abandoned by all but his simple and stubbornly loyal workman. He has rediscovered in the figure of a hapless and dim-witted laborer, as Lear has rediscovered in a fool and a madman, that brotherhood with all men to which he had in the pride of his nature and his office been unfaithful. The novel invokes, in short, as *The Return of the Native* and *Jude the Obscure* with their humanistic orientation do not, the traditional notion that man has been confined not unjustly to a fixed place in the hierarchy of being and is inspired to go his willful way only at the risk of the direst penalties.

III

As the particular terms of Henchard's deterioration may already have suggested, the novel's concept of nature is in many respects as traditional as its concept of man and fate. Certainly, there is no equivalent in *The Mayor of Casterbridge* for the grotesque image of an Egdon Heath that dwarfs and ultimately overwhelms a helpless humankind. Where nature does enter the novel, it enters as a force obedient and instrumental to a moral order whose rights and claims take priority over man's. Like Oedipus in murdering his father and like Lear in denying his daughter, Henchard affronts, in casting off wife and child, a nature that antedates both Wordsworth and Darwin.

The barbarous violence of his deed and the Babylonian character of the fair that is appropriately its setting are opposed, for example, to a piety in nature that is a reflex of a piety in the universe:

> The difference between the peacefulness of inferior nature and the wilful hostilities of mankind was very apparent at this place. In contrast with the harshness of the act just ended within the tent was the sight of several horses crossing their necks and rubbing each other lovingly as they waited in patience to be harnessed for the homeward journey. Outside the fair, in the valleys and woods, all was quiet. The sun had recently set, and the west heaven was hung with rosy cloud . . . (p. 13).[10]

The specifically moral agency of this nature becomes most obvious, however, in the catastrophic weather that eventually insures the defeat and humiliation of the hero. For if the rains and tempests that control the world of *The Mayor of Casterbridge* do not perform in the violent and dramatic terms of the storm in *Lear,* they bear in the end the same significance. They reflect, as the symptom of a demoralization in nature, the demoralization of the order that Henchard's unnatural act has, much in the manner of Lear's, produced. Insofar, too, as they confound his designs at the same time that they cooperate with Farfrae's, they reveal the ex-

[10] The sense in which the hero's crime has violated, and separated him from, a profound morality in nature is elsewhere suggested by the floral imagery with which he is identified in the days of his prelapsarian innocence: "he looked a far different journeyman from the one he had been in his earlier days. Then he had worn clean, suitable clothes, light and cheerful in hue; leggings yellow as marigolds, corduroys immaculate as new flax, and a neckerchief like a flower-garden" (p. 264.).

tent to which he has lost the power to "sympathize" with, to intuit, its mysteries. Finally and more especially, they enforce, as the agents of the superhuman, the powerful claims which Henchard's guilty humanity has flouted and abrogated.

The presidency of a rational power in the universe is apparent not alone, however, in the anthropomorphism of the novel's rains and tempests.[11] It is also apparent in the power of the conjurer Fall to divine the mysteries of the weather. More than a mere concession to local color, more than a symptom of the amateur anthropologist's interest in the folklore of his native region, the weird prophet to whom Henchard comes for help has a function in the novel not unlike that of the oracle in *Oedipus.* The authenticity of his wisdom, the accuracy of his prognostications, argues, as the Delphic oracle argues, the existence of an order beyond man's power to alter or control. Hence it is one aspect of the general armistice towards which the novel moves that the hero is restored in the end to that rudimentary natural order whose decencies he had flouted and over whose mysteries he had sought to prevail. Returned to the primitive world of Abel Whittle where time is told by the sun (p. 383), he perishes in a mud hovel scarcely distinguishable in its dilapidation from the natural world surrounding it and in fact resembling Lear's humble refuge in the storm. The concept of nature upon which *The Mayor of Casterbridge* is founded antedates, then, the permissive nature invoked by nineteenth century transcendentalism and the mechanistic nature invented by nineteenth century science. It operates, like man and fate within a traditional moral frame of reference.

IV

The traditional basis of the novel is nowhere more distinct than in the anachronistic theory of society upon which it is predicated. Isolated and dissociated from a nineteenth century whose unity has been undermined by science, industry, and democracy, Casterbridge suggests, with its agrarian economy, with its merchant aristocracy and its rude population of mechanics, artisans, and laborers, a primitive hierarchic society. Thus Henchard resembles less the modern mayor than the tribal chieftain and is in fact displaced by Farfrae not in a democratic vote but, figuratively

[11] The irritability of an intelligent and moral power confronted by the mayor's continuing perversity—he has virtually driven Elizabeth from his house—is intimated in the ominously repeated "smacking of the rope against the flag-staff" (p. 165). Later, when the weather turns to accomplish his ruin, it performs as the agent of a virtually conscious design: "the sunlight would flap out like a quickly opened fan, throw the pattern of the window upon the floor of the room in a milky, colourless shine, and withdraw as suddenly as it had appeared" (p. 218).

if not literally, in a rude trial of strength. His status and stature as a tragic hero are not affected, certainly, by his membership, at the novel's most superficial level, in the antiheroic middle class. He is not after all the mayor of Dorchester, the provincial town whose reality is continuous with London and Liverpool and Manchester, but the mayor of Casterbridge, the provincial capital whose historical associations are more Roman and Hebraic than English.[12] Hence, although he is greater in will and energy than the Christopher Coneys and Solomon Longways, he is at the same time, in his taciturnity, in his fatalism, in his grotesque and often brutal humor, their true apotheosis, their "hero" in the epic sense. In his physical resemblance to the town of Casterbridge itself—they are both described in terms of squares and rectangles, for example—he becomes the very symbol of the place, his leadership acquiring to this extent a supernaturalistic rather than a merely naturalistic sanction.

Hence the virtually religious interdependence of the man and the city. Participating, like nature, in a universal moral organization, society is demoralized, as Henchard himself has been demoralized, by the outrage for which no atonement has been made. In receiving and rewarding a man whose ancient crime has gone unacknowledged and uncorrected, Hardy's city has invited, like the Thebes of Sophocles and the Denmark of Shakespeare, the disapprobation of the gods—a plague, a profound social and political disturbance—from which it will not be released until the guilty party has been publicly identified and punished.

The pollution of the provincial capital is first of all suggested in the imagery of damp and decay that conditions the atmosphere of the novel.[13] It is even more strongly suggested, however, by the frequent allusions to the corrupt and criminal past that evidently underlies—and the analogy

[12] The novel is literally saturated with allusions to Hebraic and, more notably, as the Latin root of "Casterbridge" would suggest, to Roman, life and literature. It is worth noting, in this connection, that the Saul-David legend was apparently employed by Hardy to frame, and give historical depth to, his "contemporary" narrative (See Julian Moynahan's demonstration in "*The Mayor of Casterbridge* and the Old Testament's First Book of Samuel: A Study of Some Literary Relationships," *PMLA*, LXXI [1956], 118-130). Henchard's analogy with Saul as well as with Oedipus supports the notion developed in the following pages that the archetype of the diseased monarch is fundamental to the hero's conception.

[13] In the early chapters, for example, the mayor has sold the bakers grown wheat, wheat damaged by damp, and debased the bread of an embittered population. Later, when the weather turns to defeat his speculations, the air itself feels "as if cress would grow in it without other nourishment" (p. 218). Imagined as the "mildewed leaf in the sturdy and flourishing Casterbridge plant" (p. 294), Mixen Lane, the haunt of criminals and the very sign and symptom of the town's moral dis-ease, is described in nearly symbolic terms as stretching out "like a spit into the moist and misty lowland" (p. 293). Shortly thereafter, the secret of Lucetta's past will spread through the town "like a miasmatic fog" (p. 308).

with Henchard's own case is unmistakable—the apparently innocent appearance of the city. "Casterbridge is a old hoary place o' wickedness . . . ," one of its gloomier citizens acknowledges. " 'Tis recorded in history that we rebelled against the King one or two hundred years ago, in the time of the Romans, and that lots of us was hanged on Gallows Hill, and quartered, and our different jints sent about the country like butcher's meat . . ." (p. 59). To bear out this depressed description, the violent history of the Roman amphitheater outside the town is developed in lugubrious detail:

> Apart from the sanguinary nature of the games originally played therein, such incidents attached to its past as these: that for scores of years the town-gallows had stood at one corner; that in 1705 a woman who had murdered her husband was half-strangled and then burnt there in the presence of ten thousand spectators. . . . In addition to these old tragedies, pugilistic encounters almost to the death had come off down to recent dates in that secluded arena. . . (p. 81)[14].

Later in the novel, depressed and embittered by the disclosure that he is not Elizabeth's father, Henchard encounters in a walk by the river a half-phantasmagorical scene emblematic not only of his own crime and guilt but also of the crime and guilt that attaches to Casterbridge itself:

> Here were the ruins of a Franciscan priory, and a mill attached to the same, the water of which roared down a back-hatch like the voice of desolation. Above the cliff, and behind the river, rose a pile of buildings, and in the front of the pile a square mass cut into the sky. It was like a pedestal lacking its statue. This missing feature . . . was, in truth, the corpse of a man; for the square mass formed the base of the gallows, the extensive buildings at the back being the county gaol. In the meadow where Henchard now walked the mob were wont to gather whenever an execution took place, and there to the tune of the roaring weir they stood and watched the spectacle (p. 145).

Later still, an allusion is made to a large square called Bull Stake, hidden, significantly, between the Market House and the Church and stained, like the amphitheater and the priory, by a history of brutality and suffering: "a stone post rose in the midst, to which the oxen had formerly been tied for baiting with dogs to make them tender before they were

[14] "Persons sitting with a book or dozing in the arena," the novel goes on to report, "had, on lifting their eyes, beheld the slopes lined with a gazing legion of Hadrian's soldiery as if watching the gladiatorial combat; and had heard the roar of their excited voices . . ." (p. 82).

killed in the adjoining shambles. In a corner stood the stocks" (pp. 219-220).

The demoralization of the present by the corruption of the past is perhaps most vividly allegorized in the description of Lucetta's Casterbridge house and, specifically, in the despcription of its structural peculiarity. The front it offered to the world was "Palladian," the novel records, "and like most architecture erected since the Gothic age was a compilation rather than a design. But its reasonablesness made it impressive" (p. 160). Like Henchard and Lucetta herself, however, the house has a guilty secret. Its reasonable exterior conceals ugly and grotesque passions, passions associated here with the Gothic. For one thing, the secret exit Elizabeth discovers in the rear, an ancient archway significantly described as "older even than the house itself," has for its keystone a sinister mask which evokes once again the theme of a hidden decay and disease: "Originally the mask had exhibited a comic leer . . . but generations of Casterbridge boys had thrown stones at the mask, aiming at its open mouth; and the blows thereon had chipped off the lips and jaws as if they had been eaten away by disease." More significantly, the door and the mask conjure up once again the imagery of the vile and violent crimes in the past: "The position of the queer old door and the odd presence of the leering mask suggested . . . intrigue. By the alley it had been possible to come unseen from all sorts of quarters in the town—the old play-house, the old bull-stake, the old cock-pit, the pool wherein nameless infants had been used to disappear" (p. 161).

Like its maimed and guilt-haunted ruler, then, Casterbridge is demoralized and disabled by a grisly past.[15] Infected, like Thebes and Denmark, by the strong stench of time and human evil, it suggests nothing so much, in fact, as a grim and unhallowed wasteland. For one thing, the local peasantry are plainly discovered in a harsher and more skeptical light than they were in *Under the Greenwood Tree, Far from the Madding Crowd,* and even *The Return of the Native.* This reinterpretation in part registers a developing realistic bias in Hardy already adumbrated in *The Trumpet-Major* and eventually dominant in *Tess* and *Jude.* More exactly, however, it cooperates with the larger purposes of *The Mayor of Casterbridge,* a brutalized populace bearing witness, like the pimps and

[15] This is not to suggest that as a "cause" of the city's demoralization, the criminality of its past history operates on the same level with the criminality of its chief magistrate. It enters the novel only at the level of reference and allusion and not at the level of the action and to this extent serves no more than a symbolic function. The city's gruesome history acts, in short, less as a direct cause of its discomposure than as an analogy with the history of Michael Henchard. Indeed, insofar as he is haunted by the same history of crime and passion as Casterbridge itself, the virtually religious basis of his rulership—the interdependence of the man and the city—is once again verified.

whores of *Measures for Measure* and the gravediggers of *Hamlet,* to the moral delinquency of a society that has winked at crime and, in a metaphorical sense at least, offended the gods.

The demoralization of the folk, their disillusioned and even cynical way of looking at things, is emphasized in being juxtaposed with the romantic idealism of Donald Farfrae, the Fortinbras-like visitor from the brisker and more bracing climate of the Scottish world to the north. Celebrating in a sentimental song the loveliness of his homeland, he evokes in Casterbridge's hollow men a response at once comic and disenchanted. "Danged," says one, "if our country down here is worth singing about like that! When you take away from among us the fools and the rogues, and the lammigers, and the wanton hussies, and the slatterns, and such like, there's cust few left to ornament a song with in Casterbridge, or the country round" (p. 59). "We be bruckle folk here," adds Christopher Coney, defining at once the sterility of the landscape and the brutalization of its inhabitants, "the best o' us hardly honest sometimes, what with hard winters, and so many mouths to fill, and God a'mighty sending his little taties so terrible small to fill 'em with. We don't think about flowers and fair faces, not we—except in the shape o' cauliflowers and pigs' chaps" (p. 60).[16]

The local demoralization is perhaps rendered most dramatically in the sinister community of Mixen Lane. Without precedent in the novels that antedate *The Mayor of Casterbridge,* these polluted precincts harbor a peasantry no longer redeemed, as even Christopher Coney and Solomon Longway are redeemed, by their whimsicality and humor: "Vice ran freely in and out certain of the doors of the neighbourhood; recklessness dwelt under the roof with the crooked chimney; shame in some bow-windows; theft (in times of privation) in the thatched and mud-walled houses by the sallows. Even slaughter had not been altogether unknown here. In a block of cottages up an alley there might have been erected an altar to disease in years gone by" (pp. 293-294). Far from celebrating its charm and picturesqueness, the novel contemplates the delinquent proletariat of Casterbridge with something resembling aristocratic irony and disdain. The inn called Peter's Finger is described as "the church of Mixen Lane" (p. 295). Satirically defined as "a virtuous woman who years ago had been unjustly sent to gaol as an accessory to something or other

[16] Indeed, for all his whimsy Christopher will later be guilty of a moral dereliction not significantly different from Henchard's. Acting from an ineluctable moral premise ("Why should death rob life o' fourpence?") and in violation of the profoundest moral tact ("And when you've used 'em, and my eyes don't open no more, bury the pennies, good souls, and dont ye go spending 'em . . ."), he will rifle the grave of Susan Henchard for the four ounce pennies that serve as weights for her eyes (p. 137).

after the fact," the landlady has "worn a martyr's countenance ever since, except at times of meeting the constable who apprehended her, when she winked her eye" (p. 296). Her customers are described, meanwhile, with a nearly bitter irony, as "ex-poachers and ex-gamekeepers whom squires had persecuted without a cause . . ." (p. 296). The monstrous rites of the skimmington ride will in fact expose on the level of action this deterioration of the folk. Having terrorized a helpless woman, they will slink "like the crew of Comus" back to the miasmal suburbs from which they have momentarily emerged; questioned by the constables, they will answer with a sinister and dishonorable evasiveness (p. 324).

In the end, of course, the denizens of Mixen Lane are no more condemned for their moral dereliction than are Shakespeare's pimps and gravediggers. They are less the causes of the moral and social disorder than its victims. They express the bitterness and despair of a society whose magistrates, in having offended against justice, have forfeited their clear moral authority to rule. For the demoralization of the city is apparent not alone in the brutalization of the lower orders. It is also apparent in the brutalization of those proud merchant princes who, in having welcomed and celebrated a man offensive to the gods, in having become infected by the mayor's pride and arrogance, have submitted their humanity to base and ugly distortions.[17]

It is therefore one aspect of the city's ordeal that its safety and stability are threatened throughout by serious internal conflicts. As in *Hamlet* and *Lear,* the disturbance of the moral order expresses itself in the disturbance of the social order. The discontinuity between the moral order that Henchard has insulted and the social order that has received and rewarded him is made evident almost at once. Twenty years after the original crime, Susan enters the provincial capital expecting with good reason to find the culprit occupying the stocks: she finds him instead presiding arrogantly over a civic banquet as the wealthiest and most powerful man

[17] At the banquet held in the mayor's honor, for example, they are described in terms that suggest a fallen, a bestialized, humanity: "the younger guests were talking and eating with animation; their elders were searching for tit-bits, and sniffing and grunting over their plates like sows nuzzling for acorns" (p. 38). Later unmanned, like Henchard himself twenty years earlier, by drink, they undergo Circean transformations: "square-built men showed a tendency to become hunchbacks; men with a dignified presence lost it in a curious obliquity of figure, in which their features grew disarranged and one-sided; whilst the heads of a few who had dined with extreme thoroughness were somehow sinking into their shoulders, the corners of their mouth and eyes being bent upwards by the subsidence" (p. 44). At the scene of the market, finally, these Bulges, Brownlets, Kitsons and Yoppers, whose gross and cacophonous names define the rudimentariness of their spiritual condition (p. 176), are described in terms of an elemental imagery that suggests, as in Henchard's case, a less than complete humanity: they are described as "men of extensive stomachs, sloping like mountain sides; men whose heads in walking swayed as the trees in November gales" (pp. 174-175).

in the community. Hence, while the mayor and the members of the local oligarchy hold court in the King's Arms for all the world like depraved Roman emperors, a surly populace, alienated by the corruption of its bread, gathers in the outer darkness of the street on the point of revolt. "As we plainer felows bain't invited," one citizen remarks in unconscious criticism of the insolence of high office, "they leave the winder-shutters open that we may get jist a sense o't out here" (p. 36). "They can blare their trumpets and thump their drums, and have their roaring dinners," a local Madame Lafarge has declared in terms that point up the Roman character of the revels, "but we must needs be put-to for want of a wholesome crust" (p. 33).

The corruption of those in power will eventually be exposed, of course, with the reappearance and trial of the furmity-woman, the agent of the mayor's original moral subversion. Charged with committing an outrage on the church wall, charged in effect with an irreligious act not different from that for which Henchard, her judge, has gone unpunished, she publicizes the crime he has concealed for twenty years and exposes therewith the discrepancy between the social order of which he is the head and the moral order to which he has done violence. She not only represents, then, the past's determined and inexorable reassertion of its rights and bears witness, in her own moral delinquency, to the brutalization of the lower classes already discoverable in Christopher Coney and the maimed citizens of Mixen Lane. She also expresses their revulsion against the social and political order whose mandate to rule and administer justice has, by the fact of its own moral disability, been rendered fraudulent. "It proves," says she, delivering the moral of the occasion, "that he's no better than I, and has no right to sit there in judgment upon me" (p. 232). The moral inadequacy of Henchard's society is in fact underlined by Hardy's farcical treatment of the whole episode. For if, in his tragic embarrassment, the mayor recalls the figure of Duke Angelo, the arresting constable Stubberd recalls, and indeed fulfills the same function as, Shakespeare's clownish constable Elbow. Regarding the furmity-woman "with a suppressed gaze of victorious rectitude" (pp. 230-231), Stubberd reflects, in his physical decrepitude, in his ignorance and absurd self-righteousness, the mortal impotence of the society whose law he has been hired to enforce.

The disharmony and confusion to which Henchard's original act of impiety has exposed the city becomes climacteric, finally, in the nearly savage violence of the skimmington ride. For the hidden imposthume that silently undermines the moral stability of the town has not, in spite of Henchard's public degradation, been fully removed. In refusing like the mayor to acknowledge the crime in her past, in marrying the man who has supplanted him as the town's chief merchant and magistrate,

Lucetta has in effect perpetuated the ancient wrong.[18] Furthermore, in publicly repudiating the sadly deteriorated Henchard on the occasion of the Royal Visit, Farfrae as well as Lucetta becomes guilty of the same pride, of the same offense against human solidarity, of which the fallen mayor himself had been found guilty.

In this light, the skimmington ride expresses the demoralization and confusion of a social order that has continued willfully to dissociate itself from the moral order. If, as Farfrae not altogether wrongly suspects, the organizers of the barbaric rite have been inspired by "the tempting prospect of putting to the blush people who stand at the head of affairs" (p. 346), it is because their claims to rulership have been fraudulent and dishonest. Indeed, the moral incompetence of the society over which Farfrae and Lucetta prevail is dramatized, as in the episode of the furmity-woman's trial, by the comedy of its cowardly constabulary. Described as shrivelled men—"yet more shrivelled than usual, having some not ungrounded fears that they might be roughly handled if seen" (p. 323)—Stubberd and his crew conceal in a water-pipe the staves that are the instruments of their office and take refuge up an alley until the skimmington ride is over.

At the very last, of course, the agonies of this divided and demoralized society are permitted to subside. With the total eclipse of Henchard and Lucetta and the marriage of Farfrae and Elizabeth-Jane, the social order is brought once again into harmony with the moral order. In marrying Lucetta with her pride and her guilt and her fine clothing, Farfrae had compromised his right to rule, had aroused, like Henchard in his day, the animosity of his citizen-subjects.[19] However, in uniting himself with Elizabeth-Jane who has declined, unlike Lucetta, to antagonize the superintending powers, Farfrae restores himself to the good graces of the folk and brings to an end the civil division that had registered the resentment of an affronted moral order.[20] Hence, in the novel's final passages, the restoration of the society whose authority Henchard and Lucetta

[18] The Royal Visit over which she and her husband preside suggests in fact the same barbaric pride and arrogance as the civic banquet over which the guilty Henchard had presided earlier in the novel: Lucetta is defined as Farfrae's Calphurnia (p. 307) and the official carriages are described as rattling "heavily as Pharaoh's chariots down Corn Street" (p. 308).

[19] "How folk do worship fine clothes!" one good citizen had bitterly remarked at the time of Farfrae's marriage to Lucetta. "I do like to see the trimming pulled off such Christmas candles," another had ominously declared. Indeed, their preference for Elizabeth was made explicit on this same occasion: "now there's a better-looking woman than she that nobody notices at all . . ." (p. 308).

[20] "As a neat patching up of things I see much good in it," says Christopher Coney, giving the assent of the folk to the new dispensation (p. 356).

had jeopardized, the reconciliation of the classes whose mutual hostility had threatened its total collapse, can be celebrated in the mild dominion of an Elizabeth-Jane who perceives "no great personal difference between being respected in the nether parts of Casterbridge and glorified at the uppermost end of the social world" (p. 385).

In the context of this novel, then, the social order acquires a virtually religious sanction of which it is almost wholly deprived in the naturalistic contexts of *Tess* and *Jude*. Michael Henchard is not, like the protagonists of the later novels, crucified by a brutal and depraved society. Disabled, on the contrary, by *his* crime and guilt, society emerges not as the victimizer but as the victim. Its corruption and demoralization register, as in *Oedipus* and *Hamlet,* the corruption and demoralization of its chief magistrate. They register the disapprobation of a universal order whose morality the defection of the hero has profoundly disturbed. Like fate and nature, society here operates within a traditional moral frame. The sociology of the novel is as archaic as its psychology and cosmology.

V

To argue that *The Mayor of Casterbridge* observes the traditional norms of tragedy is not of course to argue that it has no realistic basis whatsoever. It would hardly be a novel if it did not admit something of the life of its particular time and place. The presence of the conjurer Fall and the incident of the skimmington ride bear witness to the amateur anthropologist's authentic interest in the folkways of a dying culture. Indeed, Hardy was himself to acknowledge in his preface (p. v) that the story was specifically inspired by three events in the real history of the Dorchester locality: the sale of a wife, the uncertain harvests which preceded the repeal of the Corn Laws, and the visit of a member of the royal house. To describe the dominating motive of the novel as therefore realistic, however, would be not only to underestimate, but also to leave largely unexplained, the great vitality that it ultimately generates. It would be to ignore the fact that its realistic data are in the end assimilated and controlled by the tragic form, and that it is this form and not the content, not its fidelity to the data of social history, that finally accounts for its perennial power. Wife-sale may well have been a virtual commonplace in the rural England of the nineteenth century,[21] and such magicians as the conjurer Fall may still have frequented the countryside of Wessex. But their appearance in *The Mayor of Casterbridge* as the *matériel* of two of its most crucial episodes is adequately explained less

[21] Miss Ruth Firor has suggested so much (*Folkways in Thomas Hardy* [Philadelphia, 1931], p. 237) as indeed has Hardy himself at the beginning of ch. iv.

by their reference to aspects of contemporary reality than by their reference to the novel's artistic necessities, by their adaptation as stations in the tragic martyrdom of Michael Henchard. Again, Hardy may well have been concerned, as a social historian, with the new mechanization, with the decay of the primitive agriculture that had been practised since the days of the Heptarchy. Quite clearly, however, this conflict between the old method and the new is exploited not for the sake of history but for the sake of the novel: it defines and develops the tragic conflict between Henchard and Farfrae, between the old god and the new. The novel is not damaged as tragedy, in other words, as *Tess* and *Jude* were to be damaged, by a preoccupation with social history or social issues.[22] Cut off from contemporary experience as the later novels are not, *The Mayor of Casterbridge* repudiates prose fiction's characteristic willingness to admit, more undiscriminatingly than is possible for epic and tragedy, the unblessed life of time and history.[23] This is so much the case that, as has already been pointed out, the atmosphere of the novel is more Roman and Hebraic than English: it evokes not so much the world of London, Liverpool, and Manchester as the world of Thebes, Padan-Aram, and ancient Rome.

To argue, finally, that *The Mayor of Casterbridge* satisfies the traditional norms of tragedy is not to argue that the celebrant of nineteenth century romantic and scientific doctrines is altogether suppressed. If the novel assumes, in its concepts of man and fate, nature and society, a traditional frame of reference tolerant of tragedy, there are inevitably occasions when the Swinburnian and Darwinian Hardy reasserts himself with results that make for a reduction of the tragic temperature. After he has identified an order in nature as the delicate reflex of a moral order in the universe, he must pay his respects to the contemporary scientific doctrine that has taken nature out of its traditional frame: "in presence of this scene after the other, there was a natural instinct to abjure man as the blot on an otherwise kindly universe; till it was remembered that . . . mankind might some night be innocently sleeping when these quiet objects were raging aloud" (p. 13; see above, p. 161). And having

[22] Jacques Barzun has pointed out that "no reform of the divorce laws or the entrance requirements of Oxford would by itself alter the chances of Tess' and Jude's coming to happier ends" ("Truth and Poetry in Thomas Hardy," p. 188). This is another way of saying, however, that these issues have an interest in and for themselves that the conflict between the old and the new agriculture cannot claim. Certainly, these questions do dominate *Tess* and *Jude* as the agricultural question does not dominate *The Mayor of Casterbridge*.

[23] Which is to question Arthur Mizener's assertion that Hardy "never freed himself wholly from the naturalistic assumption that narrative must be significant historically rather than fabulously" ("*Jude the Obscure* as a Tragedy," p. 196).

decided that the ugly weathers of the novel expressed the reaction of a just and morally intelligent fate, he must temporarily reassert his humanistic allegiances and openly commiserate with a cruelly persecuted humanity: the impulse of the peasantry, he remarks, "was well-nigh to prostrate themselves in lamentation before untimely rains and tempests, which came as the Alastor of those households whose crime it was to be poor" (pp. 211-212).[24]

Not even the traditional symbolism of Mixen Lane as the cancer that undermines the sanity and health of the Casterbridgean city-state is proof against an author tempted momentarily to humanistic apologetics: "yet amid so much that was bad needy respectability also found a home. Under some of the roofs abode pure and virtuous souls whose presence there was due to the iron hand of necessity, and to that alone" (p. 295). Most glaringly of all, perhaps, the balance between the heroic passion of Henchard, on the one hand, and the modesty of Farfrae and Elizabeth, on the other, is at times upset by the author's insurgent romantic sympathies. Rebelling against the traditional frame he has himself set up, rebelling against the moral dispensation that Henchard himself has been great enough to accept as right and just, Hardy will bitterly revile the mediocrities who have supplanted his doomed and suffering protagonist. Elizabeth's "craving for correctness" he denounces as "almost vicious" (p. 248); Farfrae he mocks as celebrating the "dear native country that he loved so well as never to have revisited it" (p. 373).

The outrage and indignation of the nineteenth century humanist in the presence of a suffering mankind, common enough in *Tess* and *Jude* and indeed the primary condition of their creation, are not, however, the predominating motives of *The Mayor of Casterbridge*. These emotions may flare momentarily at the surface of the novel; but they do not penetrate to or issue from its vital center. They appear after all only at the superficial level of authorial commentary and are contradicted and ultimately overwhelmed by the novel's fundamental assumptions, by the traditional moral or religious values rendered at the crucial level of character and action, form and structure. Hence the novel's emergence as one of the truly remarkable anachronisms in the history of English literature. Rejecting the disabling doctrine of the nineteenth century and exploiting the enabling doctrine of a time still capable of vibrating

[24] Indeed, Henchard's heroic recognition of the moral authority of the power that has humbled his pride, a recognition irrefutably validated in the narrative structure of the novel, is at one point repudiated as bearing witness to his fetichism: "Henchard, like all his kind, was superstitious, and he could not help thinking that the concatenation of events this evening had produced was the scheme of some sinister intelligence bent on punishing him. Yet they had developed naturally" (p. 144).

to the vision of a just and ordered universe, *The Mayor of Casterbridge* approximates, as perhaps no novel before or since has approximated, the experience of tragedy in its olden, in its Sophoclean or Shakespearean, sense.

Jude the Obscure

by A. Alvarez

Jude the Obscure is Hardy's last and finest novel. Yet its publication in 1895 provoked an outcry as noisy as that which recently greeted *Lady Chatterley's Lover.* The press attacked in a pack, lady reviewers became hysterical, abusive letters poured in, and a bishop solemnly burnt the book. The fuss may seem to us, at this point in time, incredible and even faintly ridiculous, but its effect was serious enough: ". . . the experience," Hardy wrote later, "completely cur[ed] me of further interest in novel-writing." After *Jude* he devoted himself exclusively to his poetry, never returning to fiction.

What caused the uproar? It was not Hardy's fatalism; after *Tess* his public had learned to live with that and even love it. Nor was his attack on social and religious hypocrisy particularly virulent, though there was certainly a good deal of entrenched resentment of his criticism of those two almost equally venerable institutions: marriage and Oxford. Zola's name was invoked by one or two reviewers, but not seriously. The real blow to the eminently shockable Victorian public was the fact that Hardy treated the sexual undertheme of his book more or less frankly: less frankly, he complained, than he had wished, but more frankly than was normal or acceptable.

Despite the social criticism it involves, the tragedy of *Jude* is not one of missed chances but of missed fulfillment, of frustration. It is a kind of *Anna Karenina* from the male point of view, with the basic action turned upside down. Where Anna moves from Karenin to Vronsky, from dessica-tion to partial satisfaction, Jude, swinging from Arabella to Sue, does the opposite. For all his—and Hardy's—superficial disgust, Jude and Arabella are, physically, very much married: their night at Aldbrickham after years apart is made to seem the most natural thing in the world; Jude's subsequent shame is prompted less by the act itself than by his anger at miss-

"*Jude the Obscure,*" by A. Alvarez. (Originally entitled "*Jude the Obscure:* Afterword.") From *Jude the Obscure* by Thomas Hardy (New York: New American Library, 1961). Afterword copyright © 1961 by New American Library, Inc. Reprinted by permission of the author.

ing Sue and fear that she will somehow find out. On the other hand, his great love for Sue remains at its high pitch of romance and fatality largely because she never really satisfies him. Hardy himself was quite explicit about this in a letter he wrote after the novel was published:

> One point . . . I could not dwell upon: that, though she has children, her intimacies with Jude have never been more than occasional, even when they were living together (I mention that they occupy separate rooms, except towards the end, and one of her reasons for fearing the marriage ceremony is that she fears it would be breaking faith with Jude to withhold herself at pleasure, or altogether, after it; though while uncontracted she feels at liberty to yield herself as seldom as she chooses). This has tended to keep his passion as hot at the end as at the beginning, and helps to break his heart. He has never really possessed her as freely as he desired.[1]

So Jude's tragedy, like every true tragedy, comes from inner tensions which shape the action, not from any haphazard or indifferent force of circumstance. Jude is as frustrated by Sue, his ideal, intellectual woman, as he is by Oxford, his equally shining ideal of the intellectual life. Frustration is the permanent condition of his life.

I am not, of course, suggesting that the book has no theme beyond the sexual relations of Jude, Sue, Arabella, and Phillotson. That was D. H. Lawrence's interpretation in his wonderfully perceptive, startlingly uneven *Study of Thomas Hardy*. But then, Lawrence was writing not as a critic but as an imaginative artist who owed a great personal debt to Hardy. His critical method was simply to retell Hardy's plots as though he himself had written them, isolating only what interested him. The result was considerable insight and an equally considerable shift of emphasis away from the novel Hardy actually wrote.

Obviously, *Jude the Obscure* does have its declared social purpose: to criticize a system which could, for mainly snobbish reasons, keep out of the universities "one of the very men," as Sue says, "Christminster was intended for when the colleges were founded; a man with a passion for learning, but no money, or opportunities, or friends. . . . You were elbowed off the pavement by the millionaires' sons." A figure who for Thomas Gray, a Cambridge don elegizing in his country churchyard, was an object of mildly nostaligic curiosity, became in Hardy's work a living, tragic hero. And by this shift of focus Hardy helped make the issue itself live. In his postscript of 1912 he wrote "that some readers thought . . . that when Ruskin College[2] was subsequently founded it should have been

[1] *The Later Years of Thomas Hardy* by F. E. Hardy, 1930, p. 42.

[2] Ruskin, Oxford, was the first college designed to provide opportunities at the university for working-class men who, for one reason or another, had not had a chance to

called the college of Jude the Obscure." Hardy may not have had as direct an influence on social reforms as Dickens; but he helped.

Yet *Jude the Obscure* is clearly more than a criticism of the exclusiveness of the major English universities. Surprisingly early in the book Jude realizes that his Christminster ambitions are futile. After that, though the university remains an obsession with him, it plays very little part in the novel itself. Instead, it is a kind of subplot echoing the main theme in slightly different terms, just as Gloucester and his sons repeat on a smaller scale the tragedy of King Lear and his daughters. But with this difference: that Jude is the hero of both the main plot and the subplot. Christminster may drop out of the major action, but his continuing obsession with it repeats, in another tone of voice, his obsession with Sue. In the beginning, both Sue and the university seem objects of infinitely mysterious romance; both, in the end, land Jude in disillusion. Both seem to promise intellectual freedom and strength; both are shown to be at bottom utterly conventional. Both promise fulfillment; both frustrate him. All Jude's intellectual passion earns him nothing more than the title "Tutor of St. Slums," while all his patience and devotion to Sue loses him his job, his children, and finally even his title of husband.

Hardy himself knew perfectly well that the Christminster, social-purpose side of the novel was relatively exterior to its main theme. Years later, when there was talk of turning *Jude* into a play, he wrote: "Christminster is of course the tragic influence of Jude's drama in one sense, but innocently so, and merely as cross obstruction." [3] There is, however, nothing exterior in the part Sue plays in Jude's tragedy. At times, in fact, she seems less a person in her own right than a projection of one side of Jude's character. Even Phillotson remarks on this: "I have been struck," he said, "with . . . the extraordinary sympathy, or similarity, between the pair. He is her cousin, which perhaps accounts for some of it. They seem to be one person split in two!" And, in harmony with the principle by which all the major intuitions in the novel are given to the men, Jude himself perceives the same thing: when he lends Sue his clothes after she has escaped from the training college and arrived, soaking wet, at his lodgings, "He palpitated at the thought that she had fled to him in her trouble as he had fled to her in his. What counterparts they were! . . . Sitting in his only arm-chair he saw a slim and fragile being masquerading as himself on a Sunday, so pathetic in her defencelessness that his heart felt big with the sense of it." The situation, in which the hero dresses in his own clothes his wet, lost, desperate double, is exactly the

go to a university after leaving school; it has since been supplemented by a wide system of government and local grants.

[3] F. E. Hardy, *op. cit.*, p. 249.

same as that of the masterpiece of double identity, Conrad's *The Secret Sharer*.

Considering the ultimate differences between Sue and Jude, Hardy perhaps thought that their similarities merely emphasized the contrasts of which, he wrote, the book was full: "Sue and her heathen gods set against Jude's reading the Greek testament; Christminster academical, Christminster in the slums; Jude the saint, Jude the sinner; Sue the Pagan, Sue the saint; marriage, no marriage; &c., &c." [4] But the geometrical neatness of Hardy's plan does not make his psychological insight any less profound or compelling. All through the book Sue is Jude "masquerading as himself on a Sunday." As even her name implies (Sue, Hardy says himself, is a lily, and Bridehead sounds very like maidenhead), she is the untouched part of him, all intellect, nerves, and sensitivity, essentially bodiless. That is why her most dramatic and typical appearances have always something ghostly about them. When, for example, Jude suddenly and guiltily comes across her after his night with Arabella at Aldbrickham, "Sue stood like a vision before him—her look bodeful and anxious as in a dream." Or, when she unexpectedly returns to Phillotson in his illness, and does her odd, characteristic conjuring trick with the mirror: "She was in light spring clothing, and her advent seemed ghostly —like the flitting in of a moth." It is this combination of nonphysical purity with exaggeratedly sharp intellect and sensitivity which preserves her for Jude as an object of ideal yearning, hopeless and debilitating. It is a yearning for his own lost innocence, before his Christminster ambitions were diverted by Arabella. Even when he finally rounds on her, after all their years and tragedies together, he can still only call her "a sort of fey, or sprite—not a woman!" Despite everything he can do, she remains a bodiless idea, an idea of something in himself.

Sue and Arabella are, in fact, like the white and black horses, the noble and base instincts, which drew Plato's chariot of the soul. But because Hardy too had a passion for Sue's kind of frigid purity ("She is," he wrote, "a type of woman which has always had an attraction for me"), he exaggerated the case against Arabella almost to the point of parody. Lawrence wrote:

> He insists that she is a pig-killer's daughter; he insists that she drag Jude into pig-killing; he lays stress on her false tail of hair. That is not the point at all. This is only Hardy's bad art. He himself, as an artist, manages in the whole picture of Arabella almost to make insignificant in her these pig-sticking, false-hair crudities. But he must have his personal revenge on her for her coarseness, which offends him, because he is something of an Angel Clare.

[4] F. E. Hardy, *op. cit.*, p. 42.

Where Hardy thought Arabella "the villain of the piece," Lawrence tried to make her out the heroine. Both views are wrong—not because Sue is any more or less of the heroine than Arabella, but because *Jude the Obscure* is fundamentally a work without any heroines at all. It has only a hero. I will return to this. Lawrence was, however, right when he said that Arabella survives Hardy's deliberate coarsening of her. The artist does her justice against the grain of his tastes. So it is she, not Sue, who shows flashes of real intelligence:

> "I don't know what you mean," said Sue stiffy. "He is mine if you come to that!"
>
> "He wasn't yesterday."
>
> Sue coloured roseate, and said "How do you know?"
>
> "From your manner when you talked to me at the door. Well, my dear, you've been quick about it, and I expect my visit last night helped it on. . . ."

And it is also she, not Sue, who really wants Jude:

> In a few moments Arabella replied in a curiously low, hungry tone of latent sensuousness: "I've got him to care for me: yes! But I want him to more than care for me; I want him to have me—to marry me! I must have him. I can't do without him. He's the sort of man I long for. I shall go mad if I can't give myself to him altogether! I felt I should when I first saw him!"

With fewer exclamation marks and without the moralizing qualification "of latent sensuousness"—as though that were so reprehensible!—Arabella's words would sound more frank and serious than any protestation Sue manages in the whole book. Similarly, despite everything, it is Arabella whom Jude really wants physically. There is no doubt about this from the moment when, without a flicker of distaste, he picks up the pig's pizzle she has thrown at him:

> . . . somehow or other, the eyes of the brown girl rested in his own when he had said the words, and there was a momentary flash of intelligence, a dumb announcement of affinity *in posse,* between herself and him, which, so far as Jude Fawley was concerned, had no sort of premeditation in it. She saw that he had singled her out from the three, as a woman is singled out in such cases. . . . The unvoiced call of woman to man, which was uttered very distinctly by Arabella's personality, held Jude to the spot against his intention—almost against his will, and in a way new to his experience.

This may have in it none of the refinement of Jude's passion for Sue, but it is considerably more human and spontaneous. Jude, after all, fell in love with Sue's photograph before he fell in love with Sue herself; and the first time she saw him "she no more observed his presence than that of the dust-motes which his manipulations raised into the sunbeams." So they are never really married because the connection between them is of the sensibility, not of the senses. The only real moment of ecstasy Jude shares with Sue is bodiless, precipitated by the scent and brilliance of the roses at the agricultural show. "The real marriage of Jude and Sue was," as Lawrence said, "in the roses." So it is Arabella who gets the last word; however much Hardy may have disliked her in principle, artistically he acknowledged the sureness of her physical common sense, to the extent at least of allowing her to make the final, unqualified judgment of the tragedy:

> "She may swear that on her knees to the holy cross upon her necklace till she's hoarse, but it won't be true!" said Arabella. "She's never found peace since she left his arms, and never will again till she's as he is now!"

Yet although his final attitude to Sue may have been ambiguous, in creating her Hardy did something extraordinarily original: he created one of the few totally narcissistic women in literature; but he did so at the same time as he made her something rather wonderful. Her complexity lies in the way in which Hardy managed to present the full, bitter sterility of her narcissism and yet tried to exonerate her.

Bit by bit even Jude is made to build up the case against her: she is cold, "incapable of real love," "an epicure of the emotions," and a flirt; she wants to be loved more than she wants to love; she is vain, marrying Phillotson out of pique when she learns that Jude is married, and going to bed with Jude only when Arabella reappears on the scene; she is even cruel, in a refined way, her deliberate, "epicene" frigidity having killed one man before the novel even starts. Yet despite all this, Jude loves her. Part of his love, of course, is rooted in frustration: he wants her endlessly because he can never properly have her. And he loves her, too, because he loves himself; he has in himself a narcissism which responds to hers, a vanity of the intellectual life, of his ideals and ambitions, of the refinement of intellect and sensibility which he had first projected onto Christminster.

But the truth and power of the novel lie in the way in which Jude, in the end, is able to understand his love for Sue *without lessening it.* Until the closing scenes, he manages to make her conform to his ideal by a kind of emotional sleight of mind: he dismisses his glimpses of the unchanging conventionality below the bright surface of her nonconformity by invoking both his own worthlessness and that vague marriage-curse which has been the lot of his family. The turning point is the death of the children:

> One thing troubled him more than any other; that Sue and himself had mentally travelled in opposite directions since the tragedy: events which had enlarged his own views of life, laws, customs, and dogmas, had not operated in the same manner on Sue's. She was no longer the same as in the independent days, when her intellect played like lambent lightning over conventions and formalities which he at that time respected, though he did not now.

Where Jude matures as a man, reconciling himself to the endless tragedies and disappointments until he can accept them more or less without self-pity, Sue remains fixed in her narcissism. She does not change, she simply shapes her outer actions to the commonplaces which at heart had always ruled her. Convention—which she calls High Church Sacramentalism—is simply a way of preserving her vanity intact. To break her self-enclosed mould would mean laying herself open to the real tragedy of her relationship with Jude—of which she, not Fate, is the main instrument—and thus giving herself to him completely. Because she is unable to do this, she denies the true marriage between them and perverts it to fit a conventional idea of matrimony. Arabella may occasionally have turned whore for practical ends—that, presumably, is how she raised the money to make Jude drunk before remarrying him—but it is Sue whom he accuses, when she returns to Phillotson, of "a fanatic prostitution." What began as intellectual freedom ends as prostitution to an idea. So when Jude finally turns on her with the cry "Sue, Sue, you are not worth a man's love!" he is passing judgment not only on her but also, because he never once denies that he loves her, on something in himself. That cry and Arabella's closing words represent a standard of maturity which Jude only slowly and painfully attains.

There is something puzzling about *Jude the Obscure* as a work of art: in impact it is intensely moving; in much of its detail it is equally intensely false. The dialogue, for example, is, with very little exception, forced and awkward. Even granted the conventional formalities of the time, no character ever properly seems to connect with another in talk. Despite all the troubles they have seen together, Jude and Sue speak to each other as though they had just been introduced at a vicarage tea-party; as a result, their grand passion becomes, on their own lips, something generalized, like the weather or religion or politics. They are, in Sue's own words, "too sermony." Conversely, Arabella, apart from her few moments of truth and an occasional, ponderous slyness, is reduced to a kind of music-hall vulgarity of speech. Widow Edlin is archly folksy and Father Time is almost a caricature of Hardy at his most Hardyesque. The only people who seem able to talk more or less naturally to others are the solitaries, Phillotson and, in a slighter way, Vilbert.

It may be that Hardy had very little ear for dialogue; it is something he rarely does well. But his clumsiness in *Jude* is more than a fault, it is part of the nature of the work. For the essential subject of the novel is not Oxford, or marriage, or even frustration. It is loneliness. This is the one condition without which the book would show none of its power. When they are together the characters often seem amateurishly conceived, and sometimes downright false. But once they are left to themselves they begin to think, feel, act, and even talk with that strange poignancy which is uniquely Hardy's. The brief, almost cursory paragraph in which Jude tries to drown himself after the failure of his first marriage is a far more effective and affecting scene than, for example, the elaborately constructed pig-killing—and largely, I think, because nothing is said. None of the emotional impact is lost in heavy moralizing or awkwardness. When Jude is on his own, as he is for a great deal of the novel, walking from one village to the next, one Christminster college to another, then he emerges as a creation of real genius.

The novel's power, in fact, resides in that sustained, deep plangency of note which is the moving bass behind every major incident. This note is produced not by any single action but by a general sense of tragedy and sympathetic hopelessness which the figure of Jude provokes in Hardy. And the essence of this tragedy is Jude's loneliness. He is isolated from society because his ambitions, abilities, and sensibility separate him from his own class while winning him no place in any other. He is isolated in his marriage to Arabella because she has no idea of what he is about, and doesn't care. He is isolated in his marriage to Sue because she is frigid. Moreover, the sense of loneliness is intensified by the way in which both women are presented less as characters complete in themselves than as projections of Jude, sides of his character, existing only in relation to him. In the same way, the wonderfully sympathetic and moving treatment of Phillotson in the scenes at Shaston—his surprising delicacy and generosity and desolating loneliness—is essentially the same as the treatment of Jude. The two men, indeed, are extraordinarily alike: they are both in love with the same woman, both fail in much the same way at Christminster, both inhabit the same countryside and suffer the same loneliness. Their difference is in age and ability and passion. Phillotson, in short, is as much a projection of Jude as the two women. He is a kind of Jude Senior: older, milder, with less talent and urgency, and so without the potentiality for tragedy. In one sense, the entire novel is simply the image of Jude magnified and subtly lit from different angles until he and his shadows occupy the whole Wessex landscape. And Jude in turn is an embodiment of the loneliness, deprivation, and regret which are both the strength and constant theme of Hardy's best poetry. Hardy may have been perfectly justified in denying that the book was at all autobiographical, but it is a supremely vivid dramatization of the state of mind out of which Hardy's poetry emerged.

This is why Father Time fails as a symbol. He is introduced in one of the most beautiful passages of the novel:

> He was Age masquerading as Juvenility, and doing it so badly that his real self showed through crevices. A ground-swell from ancient years of night seemed now and then to lift the child in this his morning-life, when his face took a back view over some great Atlantic of Time, and appeared not to care about what it saw.

And he is finally left in a paragraph of equal force:

> The boy's face expressed the whole tale of their situation. On that little shape had converged all the inauspiciousness and shadow which had darkened the first union of Jude, and all the accidents, mistakes, fears, errors of the last. He was their nodal point, their focus, their expression in a single term. For the rashness of those parents he had groaned, for their ill assortment he had quaked, and for the misfortunes of these he had died.

But in between these two points, his ominous remarks, desolation, and self-consciously incurable melancholy are so overdone as to seem almost as though Hardy had decided to parody himself. Even the death of the children, and Father Time's appalling note—"*Done because we are too menny*"—is dangerously close to being laughable: a situation so extreme, insisted on so strongly, seems more appropriate to *grand guignol* than to tragedy. But Hardy, I think, was forced to overdraw Father Time because the child is redundant in the scheme of the novel. What he represents was already embodied in fully tragic form in the figure of Jude. There was no way of repeating it without melodrama.

The power of *Jude the Obscure* is, then, less fictional than poetic. It arises less from the action or the fidelity of the setting than from the wholeness of the author's feelings. It is a tragedy whose unity is not Aristotelian but emotional. And the feelings are those which were later given perfect form in Hardy's best poetry. The work is the finest of Hardy's novels because it is the one in which the complex of emotions is, despite Father Time, least weakened by melodrama, bad plotting, and that odd incidental amateurishness of detail by which, perhaps, Hardy, all through his novel-writing period, showed his dissatisfaction with the form. It is also the finest because it is the novel in which the true Hardy hero is most fully vindicated, and the apparently fascinating myth of immaculate frigidity is finally exploded. But I wonder if Hardy was not being slightly disingenuous when he claimed that the treatment of the book by the popular reviewers had turned him, for good, from the novel to poetry. After *Jude the Obscure* there was no other direction in which he could go.

Poetry and Belief in Thomas Hardy

by Delmore Schwartz

I

It is natural that beliefs should be involved in poetry in a variety of ways. Hardy is a rich example of this variety. For that reason, it would be well to distinguish some of the important ways in which belief inhabits poetry.

Some poetry is written in order to state beliefs. The purpose of the versification is to make the doctrine plain. Lucretius is the obvious and much-used example, and Dante is probably another, although there is some dramatic justification for most passages of philosophical statement and discussion in the *Paradiso*.

Some poetry employs beliefs merely as an aspect of the thoughts and emotions of the human characters with which it is concerned. Almost every dramatic poet will serve as an example of this tendency. Human beings are full of beliefs, a fact which even the naturalistic novelist cannot wholly forget; and since their beliefs are very important motives in their lives, no serious poet can forget about beliefs all of the time. One doubts that any serious poet would want to do so.

It is not difficult to distinguish the two poetic uses of belief from each other. The first kind is generally marked by the forms of direct statement, the second kind by a narrative or dramatic context. And when there is a shift in purpose, when the dramatic poet begins to use his characters merely as mouthpieces to state beliefs, the shift shows immediately in the surface of the poetry. The poet's use of his medium and his attitude toward his subject are always reflected strikingly in the looking glass of form.

Between these two extremes, there exist intermediate stages of which Hardy provides a number of examples. It is commonplace, in addition, that a poet may begin with the intention of stating a belief—or perhaps

"Poetry and Belief in Thomas Hardy," by Delmore Schwartz. From the Hardy Centennial number (VI, 1940) of *The Southern Review*.

merely some observation which interests him—and conclude by modifying belief and observation to suit the necessities of versification, the suggestion of a rhyme or the implication of a metaphor.

But there is a prior way in which beliefs enter into a poem. It is prior in that it is inevitable in the very act of writing poetry, while the previous two ways may conceivably be avoided. The poet's beliefs operate within his poem whether he knows it or not, and apart from any effort to use them. This fundamental operation of belief can be seen when we consider a Christian poet's observations of Nature, and then compare them to similar observations on the part of a Romantic poet, such as Wordsworth or Keats. The comparison can be made more extreme with ease, if we substitute a Russian or a Chinese poet, using descriptive passages. It should be evident that poets with different beliefs when confronted with what is nominally the same object do not make the same observations. The same shift because of belief occurs in the slightest detail of language; such common words as *pain, animal, night, rock, hope, death, the sky* must of necessity have different powers of association and implication for the Christian poet and one whose beliefs are different. It is a simple fact that our beliefs not only make us see certain things, but also prevent us from seeing other things; and in addition, or perhaps one should say at the same time, our understanding of the language we use is changed.

In Hardy's poetry, these three functions of belief all have an important part. Another and equally important factor is at work also. With the tone, the attitude implied by the tone, and often with the explicit statement of his poem, Hardy says with the greatest emphasis: "You see: this is what Life is." And more than that, he says very often: "You see: your old conception of what Life is has been shown to be wrong and foolish by this example."

One hesitates to make a simple synopsis of Hardy's beliefs. It is not that there is anything inherently obscure in them, but that they exist in his poetry so close to the attitudes, feelings, tones, and observations which make them different from their abstract formulation. For the purpose of lucidity, however, it is worthwhile saying that Hardy believed, in the most literal sense, that the fundamental factor in the nature of things was a "First or Fundamental Energy," as he calls It in the foreword to *The Dynasts.* This Energy operated without consciousness or order throughout the universe and produced the motions of the stars and the long development of the forms of life upon our own planet. Hardy did not hold this view simply, though on occasion he stated it thus. Stated thus, his writing would be an example of philosophical poetry. But this view is only one moment of his whole state of mind and does not by any means exist by itself. It is a view which Hardy affirms in active opposition, first of all, to the view that an intelligent and omnipotent Being ruled the universe; second of all, in active opposition to what he knew of the nature of human life as something lived by human beings who in their conscious striving blandly disregarded the fact that they were merely products of the First or Fundamental Energy. Thus Hardy's state of mind is one example of the conflict between the new scientific view of Life which the nineteenth century produced and the whole attitude toward Life which had been traditional to Western culture. Hardy is a partisan of the new view, but acutely conscious always of the old view. He holds the two in a dialectical tension. Indeed there are moments when it seems that Hardy is merely taking the Christian idea of God and the world, and placing a negative prefix to each of God's attributes. The genuine atheist, by contrast, is never so concerned with the view which he has rejected. Or if he is so concerned, he is, like Hardy, a being who is fundamentally religious and essentially possessed by a state of mind in which an old view of Life and a new one contest without conclusion.

There are certain poems in which this conflict is stated explicitly. In the lyric called "A Plaint to Man," the false God of Christianity is personified and given a voice, and with that voice he addresses mankind, resuming the doctrine of evolution:

> When you slowly emerged from the den of Time,
> And gained percipience as you grew,
> And fleshed you fair out of shapeless slime,
>
> Wherefore, O Man, did there come to you
> The unhappy need of creating me—
> A form like your own—for praying to?

This false God, being told that mankind had need of some agency of hope and mercy, tells mankind that he, God, dwindles day by day "beneath the deicide eyes of seers," "and tomorrow the whole of me disappears," so that "the truth should be told, and the fact be faced"—the fact that if mankind is to have mercy, justice, and love, the human heart itself would have to provide it.

In another poem, "God's Funeral," the ambiguity of Hardy's attitude becomes increasingly evident. The God of Christianity is being escorted to his grave by a long train of mourners who are described in Dantesque lines and who have thoughts which are overheard by the protagonist of the poem and which rehearse the history of monotheism from the standpoint of a higher criticism of the Bible. Among the funeral throng, however, the protagonist sees many who refuse to believe that God has died:

> Some in the background then I saw
> Sweet women, youths, men, all incredulous,
> Who chimed: "This is a counterfeit of straw,
> This requiem mockery! Still he lives to us!"
>
> I could not buoy their faith: and yet
> Many I had known: with all I sympathized;
> And though struck speechless, I did not forget
> That what was mourned for, I, too, long had prized.

This confession that Hardy, too, had prized what he was so concerned to deny must be remembered for the light it gives us upon Hardy's poetry as a whole. In other poems, the wish to believe in the dying God is frankly declared. "The Oxen," a poem which will require detailed attention, tells of an old Christmas story that the oxen kneel at the hour of Christ's nativity, and the poet declares in the most moving terms that if he should be asked at Christmas to come to the pen at midnight to see the oxen kneel, he would go "in the gloom, Hoping it might be so!" In *The Dynasts,* this desire is given the most peculiar and pathetic form of all. The hope is stated at the very end that the Fundamental Energy which rules the nature of things will continue to evolve until It takes upon Itself the attribute of consciousness—"Consciousness the Will informing till It fashions all things fair!"—and thus, or such is the implication, becomes like the God of Christianity, a God of love, mercy, and justice.

At the same time, there is a decisive moment of Hardy's state of mind which is directly opposed to this one. Hardy works without end to manipulate the events in the lives of his characters so that it will be plain that human life is at the mercy of chance and the most arbitrary circumstances. Hardy not only makes his Immanent Will of the universe an active power of evil, but he engages his characters in the most incredible conjunctions of unfortunate accidents. There is such an intensity of interest in seeing chance thwart and annihilate human life that the tendency of mind seems pathological until one remembers that chance and coincidence have become for Hardy one of the primary motions of the universe. It is Providence, which is functioning in reverse; the poet has attempted to state a definite view of life in the very working out of his plot.

And at the same time also, the older and stronger view of Life inhabited the poet's mind at a level on which it was not opposed. Hardy inherited a substratum of sensibility of a definite character and formed by definite beliefs which denied the scientific view his intellect accepted. He inherited this sensibility from his fathers, just as he inherited the lineaments of his face, and he could as soon have changed one as the other. Hardy was convinced that the new scientific view was the correct one; he was convinced intellectually, that is to say, that Darwin, Huxley, Schopenhauer, Hartmann, and Nietzsche had attained to the truth about Life. But at the same time, he could not help seeing Nature and human life in the light which was as habitual as walking on one's feet and not on one's hands. He could not work as a poet without his profound sense of history and sense of the past, his feeling for the many generations who had lived and died in his countryside before him; and his mind, like theirs, naturally and inevitably recognized human choice, responsibility, and freedom, the irreparable character of human acts and the undeniable necessity of seeing life from the inside of the human psyche rather than from the astronomical-biological perspective of nineteenth century science. But more than that, he could not work as a poet without such entities as "spectres, mysterious voices, intuitions, omens and haunted places," the operations of the supernatural in which he could not believe.

II

The cosmology of nineteenth century science which affected Hardy so much has had a long and interesting history in the culture of the last forty years. Its effects are to be seen in the novels of Theodore Dreiser, in the plays of Bernard Shaw, the early philosophical writing of Bertrand Russell, the early poetry of Archibald MacLeish, and the poetry of Robinson Jeffers. A prime American example is Joseph Wood Krutch's *The Modern Temper,* where it is explicitly announced that such things as love and tragedy and all other specifically human values are not possible to modern man. The example of Bertrand Russell suggests that of I. A. Richards, whose sincerity ritual to test the genuineness of a poem works at least in part by envisaging the "meaninglessness" of the universe which follows or seemed to follow from the scientific view; and the example of Krutch suggests some of the best poems of Mark Van Doren, where the emptiness of the sky, the departure of the old picture of the world, is the literal theme. This array of examples, and the many others which might be added, should not only suggest how modern a poet Hardy is; they should also suggest how variously the scientific view may enter into the poet's whole being, what different attitudes it may engender, and how differently the poet's sensibility may attempt to handle it.

It is nothing if not fitting that I. A. Richards should look to Hardy for his perfect example in *Science and Poetry,* the book he has devoted to precisely this question, the effect of the scientific view upon the modern poet. Mr. Richards is at once very illuminating, I think, and very wrong in what he says of Hardy. It would not be possible for anyone to improve upon the appreciation of Hardy's virtues implicit in the three pages Mr. Richards devotes to him; but it would be equally difficult to invert the truth about Hardy as completely as Mr. Richards does in the interests of his general thesis. He quotes a remark about Hardy made by J. Middleton Murry: "His reaction to an episode has behind it and within it a reaction to the universe." And then his comment is: "This is not as I should put it were I making a statement; but read as a pseudo-statement, emotively, it is excellent; it makes us remember how we felt. Actually it describes just what Hardy, at his best, does not do. He makes no reaction to the universe, recognizing it as something to which no reaction is more relevant than another."

On the contrary, Hardy is almost always bringing his reaction to the universe into his poems. It is true that he sees the universe as something to which no reaction is more relevant than another; but it is just that view of the neutral universe which prepossesses Hardy almost always and gives much of the power to the most minute details of his poems. Perhaps one ought not to say Hardy's beliefs, but Hardy's disbeliefs; whichever term is exact, the fact is that his beliefs or disbeliefs make possible the great strength of his verse. We can see that this is so if we examine some of the poems in which Hardy's beliefs play a direct part.

THE OXEN

Christmas Eve, and twelve of the clock.
  "Now they are all on their knees,"
An elder said as we sat in a flock
  By the embers in hearthside ease.

We pictured the meek mild creatures where
  They dwelt in their strawy pen,
Nor did it occur to one of us there
  To doubt they were kneeling then.

So fair a fancy few would weave
  In these years! Yet, I feel,
If someone said on Christmas Eve,
  "Come; see the oxen kneel,

"In the lonely barton by yonder coomb
  Our childhood used to know,"
I should go with him in the gloom,
  Hoping it might be so.

The belief in this poem is of course a disbelief in the truth of Christianity. The emotion is the wish that it were true. But it must be emphasized that this emotion, which obviously motivates the whole poem, depends upon a very full sense of what the belief in Christianity amounted to; and this sense also functions to provide the poet with the details of the Christmas story which serves as the example of Christianity. It is Hardy's sensibility as the son of his fathers which makes possible his realization of the specific scene and story; this sensibility itself was the product of definite beliefs, to refer back to the point made at the beginning that we see what we do see because of our beliefs. But for the whole poem to be written, it was necessary that what Hardy's sensibility made him conscious of should be held against the scientific view which his intellect accepted. Both must enter into the poem. This is the sense in which a reaction to the universe, if one must use Mr. Murry's terms, is involved in Hardy's reaction to the Christmas story. Hardy, remembering the Christmas Story of childhood, cannot help keeping in mind the immense universe of nineteenth century science, which not only makes such a story seem untrue, but increases one's reasons for wishing that it were true. His sensibility's grasp of the meaning of Christmas and Christianity makes such a choice of detail as calling the oxen "meek mild creatures" likely, perfectly exact, and implicit with the Christian quality of humility. His intellectual awareness of the new world-picture engenders the fullness of meaning involved in the phrase, which is deliberately emphasized by the overflow, "In these years!" A reaction to the universe is involved in this phrase and in addition a reaction to a definite period in Western culture.

If we take a negative example, one in which Hardy's beliefs have operated to produce a poor poem, this function of belief will be seen with further definition. The following poem is as typical of Hardy's failures as "The Oxen" is of the elements which produced his successes:

THE MASKED FACE

I found me in a great surging space,
At either end a door,
And I said: "What is this giddying place,
With no firm-fixéd floor,
That I knew not of before?"
"It is Life," said a mask-clad face.

I asked: "But how do I come here,
Who never wished to come;
Can the light and air be made more clear,
The floor more quietsome,
And the door set wide? They numb
Fast-locked, and fill with fear."

The mask put on a bleak smile then,
And said, "O vassal-wight,
There once complained a goosequill pen
To the scribe of the Infinite
Of the words it had to write
Because they were past its ken."

Here too Hardy's picture of the universe is at work and Hardy is intent upon declaring his belief that Life is beyond human understanding. But there is a plain incongruity between the vaguely cosmological scene which is declared to be Life in the first stanza and the stenographic metaphor for human life in the last stanza, which, apart from this relationship, is grotesque enough in itself. There is no adequate reason in the poem why a giddying place with no firm-fixéd floor should be beyond understanding, and it is not made so by being entitled: Life. It reminds one rather of the barrel-rolls at amusement parks and by no means of the revolutions of day and night which Hardy presumably had in mind. The masked face is probably intended to designate the Immanent Will; but here again, there is a gulf between what Hardy meant by that Will and any speaking face, and the gulf cannot be annulled merely by the device of personification. Moreover, it is difficult enough to see the human being as a goose-quill pen; when the pen complains, the poem collapses because too great a weight of meaning has been put upon a figure which was inadequate at the start.

In poems such as these, and they are not few, Hardy has been merely attempting to versify his beliefs about the universe, and neither his mastery of language nor his skill at versification can provide him with all that he needs. He needs his sensibility; but his sensibility works only when the objects proper to it are in view. When it is required to function on a cosmological scene, it can only produce weak and incommensurate figures. It is possible for a poet to make poetry by the direct statement of his beliefs, but it is not possible for such a poet as Hardy. The true philosophical poet is characterized by an understanding of ideas and an interest in them which absorbs his whole being. Hardy was interested in ideas, too; but predominantly in their bearing upon human life. No better characterization could be formulated than the one Hardy wrote for his novel, *Two on a Tower:* "This slightly-built romance was the outcome of a wish to set the emotional history of two infinitesimal lives against the stupendous background of the stellar universe, and to impart to readers the sentiment that of these contrasting magnitudes the smaller might be the greater to them as men."

III

Hardy failed when he tried to make a direct statement of his beliefs; he succeeded when he used his beliefs to make significant the observations which concerned him. This contrast should suggest that something essential to the nature of poetry may very well be in question. It is a long time since the statement was first made that poetry is more philosophical than history; the example of Hardy provides another instance of how useful and how illuminating the doctrine is. The minute particulars of Hardy's experience might have made a diary, history, or biography; what made them poetry was the functioning of Hardy's beliefs. The function of belief was to generalize his experience into something neither merely particular, which is the historian's concern; nor merely general, which is the philosopher's; but into symbols which possess the qualitative richness, as Mr. Ransom might say, of any particular thing and yet have that generality which makes them significant beyond their moment of existence, or the passing context in which they are located. And here again an examination of a particular poem will make the discussion specific:

A DRIZZLING EASTER MORNING

And he is risen? Well, be it so. . . .
And still the pensive lands complain,
And dead men wait as long ago,
As if, much doubting, they would know
What they are ransomed from, before
They pass again their sheltering door.

I stand amid them in the rain,
While blusters vex the yew and vane;
And on the road the weary wain
Plods forward, laden heavily;
And toilers with their aches are fain
For endless rest—though risen is he.

It is the belief and disbelief in Christ's resurrection which not only make this poem possible, but make its details so moving. They are not only moving; the weary wain which plods forward heavily and the dead men in the graveyard are envisaged fully as particular things and yet become significant of the whole experience of suffering and evil just because the belief exists for Hardy and provides a light which makes these particular things symbols. *Without the belief, it is only another rainy morning in March or April.* In passing, it should be noted that both belief and disbelief are necessary; the belief is necessary to the disbelief. And both are responsible here as elsewhere for that quality of language which is Hardy's greatest strength. The mere use of such words as *men, doubting, door, rain,* has a richness of implication, a sense of generations of human experience behind it; this richness is created immediately by the modifying words in the context, *pensive, weary, plod, vex, heavily,* and other workings of the words upon each other; but fundamentally by Hardy's ability to see particulars as significant of Life in general. He would not have had that ability without his beliefs and disbeliefs, though it is true that other poets get that ability by other means and other beliefs.

IV

Once we remember that good poems have been produced by the use of different and contradictory beliefs, we are confronted by the problem of belief in the modern sense.

There are good reasons for supposing that this is not, in itself, a poetic problem. But at any rate, it is true enough that many readers are profoundly disturbed by poems which contain beliefs which they do not accept or beliefs which are in direct contradiction to their own. Hardy's beliefs, as presented explicitly in his poems, offended and still offend his readers in this way.

In turn, the poet is wounded to hear that his poems are not enjoyed because his beliefs are untrue. Throughout his long career, both as poet and as novelist, Hardy was intensely disturbed by criticism on such a basis.

In the "Apology" to *Late Lyrics and Earlier,* Hardy spoke out with the tiredness and anger of an author who has suffered from reviewers for fifty years. His answer is curious and defective, however. He points out that the case against him is "neatly summarized in a stern pronouncement . . . 'This view of life is not mine.' " But instead of defending himself by pointing to all the great poetry which would be elminated if it were judged merely on the basis of its agreement with the reader's beliefs, Hardy concedes the basic issue to his critics by claiming that his beliefs are better than they have been painted. He defends himself by saying that he is not a pessimist, but "an evolutionary meliorist." No one but another evolutionary meliorist could be persuaded by this kind of argument.

On another occasion, in the introduction to *The Dynasts,* Hardy attempts to solve the problem by requiring Coleridge's temporary "suspension of disbelief which constitutes poetic faith." But this formula would seem to provide for no more than the convention of theatrical or fictive illusion. When the curtain rises, we must suspend disbelief as to whether we see before us Elsinore, a platform before the castle. If we do not, then there can be no play. The case seems more difficult, at least on the surface, when we are asked to accept alien beliefs.

Now there are two ways in which we tend to handle alien beliefs. One of them is to reject those poems which contain beliefs we regard as false. This is an example of judging poetry in terms of its subject, considered in abstraction, and the difficulties are obviously numerous. For one thing, as has been said, we would have to reject most great poetry. Certainly we would have to do without Homer, and without Dante or Shakespeare.

The other alternative, which is in any case preferable to the first, is to judge poetry wholly in terms of its formal character. But this is an act of unjustifiable abstraction also. For it is evident that we enjoy more in a poem, or at least the poem presents more to us, than a refined use of language.

What we need, and what we actually have, I think, is a criterion for the beliefs in a poem which is genuinely a poetic criterion. In reading Hardy when he is successful, in "A Drizzling Easter Morning," we find that the belief and disbelief operate upon the particular *datum* of the poem to give it a metaphorical significance it would not otherwise have. To repeat, without both belief and disbelief it is only another rainy morning in the spring. Conversely, in "The Masked Face," the asserted belief, instead of generalizing the particulars of the poem, merely interferes with them and fails to give them the significance they are intended to have.

In both instances, we are faced with a relationship between the belief in the poem and its other particulars. This is a relationship *internal* to the poem, so to speak. It is not a question of the relationship of the poet's beliefs to the reader's. In "The Masked Face," for example, the inadequacy proceeds from the relationship between the belief that Life is beyond human understanding, and the goose-quill pen which is required to represent the human mind.

It might be objected that this internal relationship between the belief and the rest of the poem is in turn good, or not good, in terms of what the given reader himself believes. Thus it might seem that for a reader who shares Hardy's beliefs, the goose-quill pen was an adequate figure for the human mind. Actually this cannot be so, unless the reader is not interested in poetry but merely in hearing his beliefs stated. If the reader is interested in poetry, the poem itself cannot give him the poetic experience of Life as beyond human understanding, which is its intention. The details of the poem, as presented in the context which the belief and the versification provide, do not do the work in the reader's mind which is done by such an element in "A Drizzling Easter Morning," as the weary wain, which plods forward, laden heavily. And one reason why they lack that energy is their relationship, within the poem, to the belief the poem asserts. Whether or not the reader shares Hardy's beliefs, even if he shares them completely, the goose-quill pen is an inadequate figure for what it is intended to signify in the context. The belief in the poem fails to make it adequate, and this is a poetic failure, just as, in "The Oxen," the kneeling animals are a poetic success because of the disbelief, whether the reader himself disbelieves in Christianity or not.

And again, it might be objected that only valid beliefs, in the end, can operate successfully upon the other elements of any poem. Once more we must refer back first to the fact that poets have written good poetry based upon opposed beliefs, and then to the point made at the start, that there is a basic way in which beliefs have much to do with the whole character of a poet's sensibility, with what he sees and does not see. The subject of poetry is experience, not truth, even when the poet is writing about ideas. When the poet can get the whole experience of his sensibility into his poem, then there will be an adequate relationship between the details of his poem and the beliefs he asserts, whether they are true or not. For then he is getting the actuality of his experience into his poem, and it does not matter whether that actuality is illusory or not; just as the earth may be seen as flat. The functioning of his sensibility guarantees his asserted beliefs; it guarantees them as aspects of experience, though not as statements of truth. The philosophical poet, as well as any other kind, must meet this test. The details of his poem are neither dramatic, nor lyrical, but there is the same question of the relationship between his asserted ideas and the language, tone, attitude, and figures which constitute the rest of the poem.

At any rate, by adopting this point of view, we avoid the two extremes, the two kinds of abstraction, which violate the poem as a concrete whole. And it is especially necessary to do this in Hardy's case, for it is unlikely that many readers will hold Hardy's beliefs as he held them. In the future we are likely to believe less or more; but we will not be in the same kind of intellectual situation as Hardy was.

The important thing is to keep Hardy's poetry, to keep as much of it as we can, and to enjoy it for what it is in its utmost concreteness. And if this is to be accomplished, it is necessary that we keep Hardy's beliefs *in* his poetry, and our own beliefs outside.

A Literary Transference

by W. H. Auden

I cannot write objectively about Thomas Hardy because I was once in love with him.

Until my sixteenth year I read no poetry. Brought up in a family which was more scientific than literary, I had been the sole autocratic inhabitant of a dream country of lead mines, narrow-gauge tramways, and overshot waterwheels. But in March, 1922, I decided to become a poet and for the next twelve months browsed about in the school library, taking up some poet for a few weeks, then dropping him for another, De la Mare, W. H. Davies, and even A. E., without finding what I really wanted.

I have yet to meet a poetry-lover under thirty who was not an introvert, or an introvert who was not unhappy in adolescence. At school, particularly, maybe, if, as in my own case, it is a boarding school, he sees the extrovert successful, happy, and good and himself unpopular or neglected; and what is hardest to bear is not unpopularity, but the consciousness that it is deserved, that he is grubby and inferior and frightened and dull. Knowing no other kind of society than the contingent, he imagines that this arrangement is part of the eternal scheme of things, that he is doomed to a life of failure and envy. It is not till he grows up, till years later he runs across the heroes of his school days and finds them grown commonplace and sterile, that he realizes that the introvert is the lucky one, the best adapted to an industrial civilization, the collective values of which are so infantile that he alone can grow, who has educated his phantasies and learned how to draw upon the resources of his inner life. At the time however his adolescence is unpleasant enough. Unable to imagine a society in which he would feel at home, and warned by some mysterious instinct from running back for consolation to the gracious or terrifying figures of childhood, he turns away from the human to the nonhuman: homesick he will seek, not his mother, but mountains or autumn woods, friendless he will mutely observe the least shy of the wild animals, and the growing life within him will express itself in a devotion to music and thoughts upon mutability and death. Art for him will be something infinitely precious, pessimistic, and hostile to life. If it speaks of love, it must be love frustrated, for all success seems to him noisy and vulgar; if it moralizes, it must counsel a stoic resignation, for the world he knows is well content with itself and will not change.

Deep as first love and wild with all regret,
O death in life, the days that are no more.

* * *

Now more than ever seems it sweet to die
To cease upon the midnight with no pain.

* * *

That dead men rise up never
That even the weariest river
   Winds somewhere safe to sea.

* * *

Lovers lying two and two
Ask not whom they sleep beside
And the bridegroom all night through
Never turns him to the bride.

That to the adolescent is the authentic poetic note and whoever is the first in his life to strike it, whether Tennyson, Keats, Swinburne, Housman or another, awakens a passion of imitation, and an affectation which no subsequent refinement or sophistication of his taste can ever entirely destroy. In my own case it was Hardy in the summer of 1923; for more than a year I read no one else, and I do not think that I was ever without one volume or another of the beautifully produced Wessex edition in my hands: I smuggled them into class, carried them about on Sunday walks, and took them up to the dormitory to read in the early morning, though they were far too unwieldy to be read in bed with comfort. In the autumn of 1924 there was a palace revolution after which he had to share his kingdom with Edward Thomas, until finally they were both defeated by Eliot at the battle of Oxford in 1926.

Besides serving as the archetype of the Poetic, Hardy was also an expression of the Contemporary Scene. He was both my Keats and my Carl Sandburg.

To begin with, he looked like my father: that broad unpampered moustache, bald forehead, and deeply lined sympathetic face belonged to the other world of feeling and sensation (for I, like my mother, was a thinking-intuitive). Here was a writer whose emotions, if sometimes monotonous and sentimental in expression, would be deeper and more faithful than my own, and whose attachment to the earth would be more secure and observant.

> A ghost-girl-rider. And though, toil-tried,
> He withers daily,
> Time touches her not,
> But she still rides gaily
> In his rapt thought
> On that shagged and shaly
> Atlantic spot,
> And as when first eyed
> Draws rein and sings to the swing of the tide.
>
> * * *
>
> No shade of pinnacle or tree or tower,
> While earth endures,
> Will fall on my mound and within the hour
> Steal on to yours;
> One robin never haunt our two green covertures.

The many poems on The Place Revisited and Time Regained seemed to me profoundly moving not only because I could apply them to my own situation—I was unhappily in love—but also because I half suspected that my own nature was both colder and more mercurial, and I envied those who found it easy to feel deeply.

Further, the properties of Hardy's world were the properties of my own childhood: it was unsophisticated and provincial, and it was the England of the professional classes, clergymen, doctors, lawyers, and architects. A world still largely Victorian, in which one went to church twice on Sundays and had daily family prayers before breakfast, did not know divorced persons or artists, rode in pony traps or on bicycles to rub brasses or collect fossils, and relied for amusement on family resources, reading aloud, gardening, walks, piano duets, and dumb crambo; above all a world which had nothing to do with London, the stage, or French literature.

There were several Londoners at school, alarming elegant creatures—one even who was said to read Racine for pleasure. Looking back, I realize how lucky it was that I felt too gauche and frightened to get to know and imitate them, for their favorite authors could only have encouraged me into pretending a life which had no contact with my own experience: the dangers of too early a sophistication and contact with "modern" writers are so great and I have seen sterility result too often not to be skeptical about the value of any academic courses in the contemporary arts. I was fortunate indeed in finding the only poet who wrote of my world. I might so easily have become attached, for example, to one or other of the Georgians and learned little, for they were Londoners observing it from the outside.

> There's a ghost at Yell'ham Bottom chiding loud
> at the fall of the night,
> There's a ghost in Froom-side Vale, thin lipped and
> vague, in a shroud of white,
> There is one in the railway train whenever I do not
> want it near,
> I see its profile against the pane, saying what I
> would not hear.

* * *

> Thus I, faltering forward
> Leaves around me falling,
> Wind oozing thin through the thorn from norward,
> And the woman calling.

* * *

> Icicles tag the church-aisle leads,
> The flag-rope gibbers hoarse,
> The home-bound foot-folk wrap their snow-flaked heads,
> Yet I still stalk the course—
> One of us . . . Dark and fair He, dark and fair She, gone·
> The rest—anon.

* * *

> Yet God knows, if aught He knows ever, I loved the
> Old Hundredth, Saint Stephen's,
> Mount Zion, New Sabbath, Miles-Lane, Holy Rest, and
> Arabia, and Eaton.

* * *

> I reach the marble-streeted town,
> Whose "Sound" outbreathes its air
> Of sharp sea-salts;
> I see the movement up and down
> As when she was there.

Ships of all countries come and go,
The bandsmen boom in the sun
A throbbing waltz;
The schoolgirls laugh along the Hoe
As when she was one.

All these things were part of my life and so I could follow Hardy's reflections about them, which were old-fashioned enough to come within my comprehension, and modern enough to educate.

Hardy had been born in an agricultural community virtually untouched by industrialism and urban values, and when he died its disintegration was almost completed. The conflict between science and Faith which worried Tennyson, worried him but he had to live longer and so to go beyond Tennyson's compromise. The pessimism of Schopenhauer, the determinism of Spinoza were not of course final solutions, but they were a necessary and progressive step in development for certain people placed in a certain situation.

It is not a question of historical date only. Baudelaire and Rimbaud faced conditions in Paris which provincial England did not have to face until after the Great War. That is why they now seem so modern. But no society or individual can skip a stage in their development, though they may shorten it. Whatever its character, the provincial England of 1907, when I was born, was Tennysonian in outlook; whatever its outlook the England of 1925 when I went up to Oxford was The Waste Land in character. I cannot imagine that any other single writer could have carried me through from the one to the other.

But Hardy was a creative artist and, therefore, much more than a nursemaid whom one could outgrow. The most importunate problem of our age is the problem of individuation. The antagonists who compete for our loyalty and faith and whom the Victorians knew as Dogma and Science are now called The Individual and the Collective, the Conscious Ego and the Unconscious Id, the Willed and the Determined, and it is in respect to this that Hardy's poetry is of most distinctive and permanent value. The Victorians were confident individualists, just because the collective ties of earth and tradition were still strong. Our own generation was born too late to experience either tradition or the passion for individual emancipation; and we are only too apt in consequence to abandon ourselves to a morbid worship of the Collective.

What I valued most in Hardy, then, as I still do, was his hawk's vision, his way of looking at life from a very great height, as in the stage directions of *The Dynasts,* or the opening chapter of *The Return of the Native.* To see the individual life related not only to the local social life of its time, but to the whole of human history, life on the earth, the stars, gives one both humility and self-confidence. For from such a perspective the difference between the individual and society is so slight, since both are so insignificant, that the latter ceases to appear as a formidable god with absolute rights, but rather as an equal, subject to the same laws of growth and decay, and therefore one with whom reconciliation is possible.

No one who has learned to do this can ever accept either an egocentric, overrational Humanism which fondly imagines that it is willing its own life, nor a pseudo-Marxism which rejects individual free-will but claims instead that a human society can be autonomous.

It was Hardy who first taught me something of the relations of Eros and Logos.

> —"Ah! knowest thou not her secret yet, her vainly
> veiled deficience,
> Whence it comes that all unwittingly she wounds the
> lives she loves?
> That sightless are those orbs of hers?—which bar to
> her omniscience
> Brings those fearful unfulfilments, that red ravage
> through her zones
> Whereat all creation groans. . . .
>
> . . . "Deal, then, her groping skill no scorn, no note of
> malediction;
> Not long on thee will press the hand that hurts the
> lives it loves;
> And while she plods dead-reckoning on, in darkness of
> affliction,
> Assist her where thy creaturely dependence can or
> may,
> For thou art of her clay.

To the questions, "Where does the Logos—*the consciousness the will informing till it fashion all things fair*—come from? Is it an external gift of grace or is it itself created by Eros?" Hardy gives no answer. In theory perhaps he thought like the Greeks, that consciousness was enough to convert the will. Today it seems doubtful if gnosis by itself is enough and probable that, since the machine has freed Eros from the ancient external disciplines, only an ascesis planned perhaps publicly but practiced individually can save us from the sufferings of anarchy or dictatorship. Be that as it may, we can only put such a question to ourselves because Hardy and others have made us see that it exists.

Hardy comforted me as an adolescent, and educated my vision as a human being, but I owe him another and, for me personally, an even more important debt, of technical instruction. Again I think that I was extremely fortunate in my choice. In the first place Hardy's faults as a craftsman, his rhythmical clumsiness, his outlandish vocabulary were obvious even to a schoolboy, and the young can learn best from those of whom, because they can criticize them, they are not afraid. Shakespeare or Pope would have dazzled and therefore disheartened. And in the second place no English poet, not even Donne or Browning, employed so many and so complicated stanza forms. Anyone who imitates his style will learn at least one thing, how to make words fit into a complicated structure and also, if he is sensitive to such things, much about the influence of form upon content.[1]

> The thick lids of Night closed upon me
> Alone at the Bill
> Of the Isle by the Race—
> Many-caverned, bald, wrinkled of face—
> And with darkness and silence the spirit was on me
> To brood and be still.

Such unusual verse forms help the imitator to find out what he has to say: conventional forms like the sonnet are so associated with a particular tradition of thoughts and attitudes that the immature writer can do little with them. On the other hand free verse which may appeal to him as looking easier, is in reality so difficult that it can only be used by those in whom intention and power of expression are one. Those who confine themselves to free verse because they imagine that strict forms must of necessity lead to dishonesty, do not understand the nature of art, how little the conscious artist can do and what large and mysterious beauties are the gift of language, tradition, and pure accident.

Hardy saved me from this and in addition taught me much about direct colloquial diction, all the more because his directness was in phrasing and syntax, not in imagery.

> I see what you are doing: you are leading me on. . . .
> Upon that shore we are clean forgot,
> Gentlemen.

* * *

He was a man who used to notice such things.

[1] Hardy's fondness for complicated verse structure is perhaps not unconnected with his training as an architect.

Here was a "modern" rhetoric which was more fertile and adaptable to different themes than any of Eliot's gas-works and rats' feet which one could steal but never make one's own.

Hardy was my poetical father and if I seldom read him now, it is, perhaps, because our relationship is so assured as no longer to need being made conscious. He is dead, the world he knew has died too, and we have other roads to build, but his humility before nature, his sympathy for the suffering and the blind, and his sense of proportion are as necessary now as they ever were.

THE SUNDIAL ON A WET DAY

I drip, drip here
In Atlantic rain,
Falling like handfuls
Of winnowed grain,
Which, tear-like, down
My gnomon drain,
And dim my numerals
With their stain,—
Till I feel useless,
And wrought in vain!

And then I think
In my despair
That, though unseen,
He is still up there,
And may gaze out
Anywhen, anywhere;
Not to help clockmen
Quiz and compare,
But in kindness to let me
My trade declare.

Hardy and the Poetry of Isolation

by David Perkins

I

The sense of personal isolation is one of the most obvious impressions conveyed by the literature of the nineteenth and twentieth centuries. That this should be so implies the convergence of widespread influences; but an artist has only himself to give to his work, and any voice he may lend to a general dilemma will be as he himself feels it rather than as a delegate from some historical era. One need not demonstrate Hardy's urgent preoccupation in his poetry with the hurt of aloneness. Its importance is marked not only by open statement in his poems, but also by the fact that the protagonist almost always appears as a solitary, an outsider, or an individual alienated from the life of his fellows. The intention here is rather to discuss what is individual in Hardy's own response. In Hardy's poetry the feeling of isolation does not primarily stem from the typical Victorian complaint that the forms of society themselves keep people apart. Nor does it arise, as in much of the poetry earlier in the century, from the experience of an inner light, of possessing sources of inspiration and insight unavailable to the generality of mankind. To feel that you have secret springs of insight entails some alienation; but as with Blake or Wordsworth, it also makes that insight more a cause of joy than of uneasiness. In Hardy, however, the ever-present sense of difference seems to have resulted only in unmingled discomfort. It is something from which the poet would wish to escape. Hence one may describe many of Hardy's poems as a fingering of the theme of isolation and an exploring of roads out of the dilemma—roads which are inevitably obstructed by a nagging honesty to his own experience. It is precisely in his sensitivity to the frustration and tragedy of human life that Hardy feels himself cut off from other men. Much that is usually termed his "pessimism" is a way of looking at things which he felt to be unshared and which prevented him from entering whole-heartedly into the state of mind of his fellows. An extreme example would be the poem "Mad Judy." "When

"Hardy and the Poetry of Isolation," by David Perkins, From *ELH*, XXVI (1959), pp. 253-270.

the hamlet hailed a birth," Judy was in the habit of crying, and conversely when a child died Judy would feast and sing. Naturally in the village Judy was thought to be mad. It is not simply that Hardy saw himself as a skeleton at a feast, although his poetry sometimes verges on such a self-description.[1] He was, indeed, unkindly reviewed as an unwelcome skeleton, but Hardy's lines "O, doth a bird deprived of wings / Go earth-bound wilfully" are a sufficient answer. The problem is more complex. Quite apart from the very painfulness of his point of view, the sense of difference itself created anxieties and self-doubt, and lent an increased urgency to a desire to find some antidote for tragic sensitivity.

There was, of course, the simple lack of reflection which Hardy's poetry dramatizes in unsophisticated, usually rustic persons. This would not be a possible resolution in any personal way; but Hardy seems at times to have known nostalgic attractions toward it, and to have felt imprisoned and excluded by his own sensitivity. Indeed, with a state of mind such as Hardy's, the shuffling unawareness which permits most people to ease through life without being perturbed by the general view of human suffering becomes a cause of bafflement. In a writer such as Swift, it may also release a powerful indignation; but Hardy seems to have been too gentle and too humble to assert himself in that way. In fact, the reservations implicit in humility gave Hardy's attitude much of its complexity. Perhaps Hardy's most successful exploration of the common mental attitude which permits men to slough their questionings occurs in "The Man He Killed." Here the extreme surface simplicity, the short, almost jingling meters, the colloquial idiom, the total absence of stock poetic associations, the unwillingness to employ the glitter of poetic phrase, bespeak a rigid artistic discipline and integrity in which all has been subordinated to an interplay of character and incident. The situation, of course, is simply that in battle two soldiers, "ranged as infantry, / And staring face to face," have fired on each other, and the survivor narrates that event. The poem turns on the character of the speaker revealed in his reactions to what has taken place. The speaker begins by stating that he had no personal quarrel with the man he killed. This naturally raises the question of why he killed him, and, pondering the question, the speaker can only say that it was "Because he was my foe." But he seems unsure and unsatisfied, and hence reiterates the explanation: "my foe of course he was; / That's clear enough." We are introduced, then, to a rather simple type of person, incapable of thinking past stock and ready-

[1] See, for example, "He Revisits his First School":

> to show in the afternoon sun,
> With an aspect of hollow-eyed care,
> When none wished to see me come there,
> Was a garish thing, better undone.

made answers ("he was my foe"), well-meaning and troubled by having killed a man toward whom he felt no rancor. At once the speaker goes on to recognize that the man was not his "foe" at all, but simply a man who happened, like himself, to have drifted into the army:

> He thought he'd 'list, perhaps,
> Off-hand like—just as I—
> Was out of work—had sold his traps—
> No other reason why.

At this point, the speaker having identified himself with the man he killed, convention would seem to suggest a revulsion from the killing, and a direct attack on war and the meaningless slaughter it involves. But this would take the poem outside the limited feeling and moral awareness of the speaker. Instead the speaker merely concludes:

> Yes; quaint and curious war is!
> You shoot a fellow down
> You'd treat if met where any bar is,
> Or help to half-a-crown.

The summing up leading to the conclusion that war is "quaint and curious" suggests that the speaker has resolved his problem and will be no more troubled by it. But in the reader the aroused sense of wrong is in no way satisfied by the words "quaint and curious." Instead, by the drastic understatement of the last stanza, Hardy forces the reader to face up to the situation more or less on his own, and exacts that "full look at the worst" which is a necessary prelude to any possible "Better." Hence it is by the limitations of the speaker that the poem makes its point. But the limitations of the speaker give an additional edge of irony to the poem. For the irony is not simply that two men who have no quarrel should fire on each other, being trapped in the blind moilings of the "Immanent Will." There is the further irony that a decent man, such as the speaker, should not be more disturbed, should be able to appease his discomfort with the words "quaint and curious."

Although the outlook of people such as the speaker in "The Man He Killed" is rooted in a limited awareness, it figures in Hardy's poetry as a ground of happiness. From this point of view, sensitivity or awareness may itself be felt as a burden or blight. Indeed, in Hardy this mode of feeling underlies a frequent metaphysical conceit by which "the birth of consciousness" on the earth is explained as a mutation, not expected or allowed for in the pattern of the cosmos, and the accidental cause of pain. It is not too much to say that when Hardy openly confronts this theme, and tries to storm it by the main gate, his poetry itself undergoes a kind of mutation, and at once reflects the division in Hardy's nature which Mr. Ransom has stressed—the philosopher feeling obligated to "expose nature" while "from the poet it usually got faithful perception and love." Paradoxically, it is these openly cosmological poems that have tended to be anthologized and more commonly known. Yet in them, as R. P. Blackmur says, Hardy, like Swift, becomes one of the great examples "of a sensibility violated by ideas." In these extreme instances, where he summons Nature directly to the bar of judgment, it is almost as though Hardy were trying to turn the tables on Wordsworth, whom he so closely parallels in other ways—in brooding sensitivity, in sympathy with the homely and concrete, in open recognition of the isolation of man from the larger course of things and in the yearning to overcome it. Wordsworth had voiced one of the great hopes of the nineteenth century when he attempted to find, in direct union with external nature and the Being that animates it, an escape from the human sense of alienation. Here Hardy's feelings naturally rebelled. But at his best he was simply content not to follow Wordsworth, and, except for relatively trivial personifications, to let nature serve only as a background in harmony or contrast with human suffering. Three-quarters of a century of novel writing intervening between Wordsworth and Hardy—not to mention Hardy's own experience in writing novels—made it far more difficult to bring in Nature successfully as a dramatic protagonist with a definite will and character: human problems inevitably edge themselves more to the forefront, and in a dramatic or novelistic way. Least of all could Nature be a friendly protagonist—a "nurse" or "foster-mother," as it was at times for Wordsworth. The more successful poems naturally accept this situation, and are successful partly because they do so. Hence Hardy's innocence and freshness—however dark the horizon around his scenes—the almost mute "humility before nature," of which Auden speaks: things are taken as they come, with a sympathy and tenderness further deepened by the implied questioning.

There is a violation, therefore, of both Hardy's own sensibility and his technical approach when nature abruptly emerges from the background as an abstraction, and speaks through a megaphone. With God so artificially introduced, Hardy maintained a controversy which had a *succès de scandale,* though it was seldom a ground of poetic success. Deserting drama for controversy, he tended to ventriloquize his perplexity. The question presented itself to Hardy's mind with utter simplicity—a simplicity he delighted to exhibit by attributing his views to children and peasants, or else to bullfinches, sheep, lonely trees, and other subhuman species. In the face of human suffering, God must be conceived either as malicious to cause, or powerless to prevent, or indifferent, or unaware.

Since Hardy was seldom willing to conceive Divinity as deliberately malicious, the fact of pain necessarily posited some alienation of human life from God. This, of course, appears in "God-Forgotten," which achieved notoriety by its bitter statement of the dilemma. "God-Forgotten," however, does not explore the reasons in the nature of God that may account for man's isolation. Various lyrics suggest a number of possibilities, all having in common the explanation that God is "unconscious." As in *The Dynasts* God usually figures as a blind working "by rote," "Sense-sealed" and "logicless." Mind or awareness is a uniquely human possession. But this aware consciousness, which characterizes neither nature nor God, is what feels the pain inherent in "change and chancefulness" and protests against it. The protest rises from a moral sense which is itself local to man. Hence it cannot be appeased by an appeal beyond human circumstances. Both the capacity to suffer and the protest against it show man's alienation from the way of things; the fact of consciousness itself is the ground of human isolation in the cosmos. We are treading familiar ground in speaking of lyrics like "God-Forgotten" and "New Year's Eve." It is perhaps enough to point out that so compulsive a desire to bring Nature forward and indict her for not being a "homely nurse" may suggest how far along the path Hardy temperamentally must have accompanied Wordsworth. Indeed we may see here a partial explanation of the bitterness, almost as from a betrayal, which underlies some of these lyrics. But Hardy's strong need to sympathize and the circumstances that drew it out are more important than the metaphysical program which lures him into direct controversy. Most of his poems, as he said more than once, were conceived as "dramatic monologues by different characters."

Persons frequently used as protagonists in Hardy's lyrics are lovers or old men obsessed with memories. In his presentation of love situations Hardy characteristically fastened not on the fact of union, but instead on whatever in the experience even of lovers discloses the hopeless loneliness of the human mind. A catalogue by dramatic scheme of Hardy's love lyrics would reveal not only the invariable nineteenth century stock of lovers estranged or lovers kept apart by social convention and class difference. It would also show a large number of poems in which the lovers live together in a semblance of union till one or the other is suddenly forced to recognize that he has been actually ignorant of the heart of his partner. The most obvious examples occur in tragedies of "crossed-fidelities," to adopt R. P. Blackmur's phrase, in which one of a married couple is discovered to have been secretly pining for an absent or defunct lover. But the theme also appears in an aspect which is a commonplace of present-day literature. One has only to think of Proust's large statement of the impossibility of knowing, possessing, and uniting with the person loved—an impossibility arising from the fact that each individual, like certain insects which live under water in their own bubble of air, creates and inhabits his own universe. In Hardy, whose attitudes were formed in an earlier era, this point of view is somewhat unexpected, and never comes to a full clarity of statement. But it can be felt as an undercurrent in a poem such as "The Sigh." Here the woman "sighed" the first time her lover kissed her, and the sigh seemed to imply "Some sad thought she was concealing." "Nothing seemed to hold" the lovers "sundered," so the speaker inevitably "wondered / Why she sighed." But though afterwards he "knew her throughly," he never learned the reason. Hence he continued even at the end of his life to half regret that she had sighed. The poem, as often in Hardy, is simply the recording of an incident with no effort to abstract from it an explanation of the feelings presented. But the regret must grow from the thought that at the time of their first kiss they actually had been slightly "sundered," that the speaker did not know her "throughly." Moreover, Hardy seems sometimes to have suspected that the mind itself bestows the charm or beauty it seems to find in the desired object. In "At Waking" the speaker suddenly sees his love beside him in "bare / Hard lines":

> Yea, in a moment,
> An insight that would not die
> Killed her old endowment
> Of charm that had capped all nigh.

Before this "vision appalling" her charm "vanished . . . like the gilt of a cloud." Both the former beauty and the "bare / Hard lines" are an "endowment" from the speaker. But if to love depends on a way of seeing, one cannot come together with what one loves because it has no objective existence.

It is mainly in the obsessive attention to the process of memory that Hardy dramatizes the subjective isolation of the individual. For the content of memory is felt to be inevitably personal. It is a rummage-room of past incidents and feelings which have no value or meaning except to the individual, and of which no one else has any knowledge. Moreover, the protagonist of Hardy's lyrics dwells largely in his memories. He lives surrounded by scenes and objects which recall some past event, and the past, continually dominating his attention, achieves a vividness greater than the present. He is one

> to whom these things,
> That nobody else's mind calls back,

Have a savour that scenes in being lack,
And a presence more than the actual brings.
["Places"]

In fact memory has an obsessive grip so powerful that it invades the present, leading to uncertainty and confusion, and making the speaker incapable of response to the immediate moment. In "The Old Neighbour and the New" the speaker tells of a visit to the "new rector" of the church:

But in the arm-chair I see
My old friend, for long years installed here,
Who palely nods to me.

As he listens to the conversation of the "new man," he is aware of "The olden face gazing upon" him, and can reply to the new rector's remarks only with a "vague smile."

And on leaving I scarcely remember
Which neighbour to-day I have seen,
The one carried out in September,
Or him who but entered yestreen.

In fact ghosts, which exist for Hardy largely as a personification of the process of memory, constantly intrude on his protagonist. In looking at "Old Furniture" he sees the "hands of the generations":

Hands behind hands, growing paler and paler,
As in a mirror a candle-flame
Shows images of itself, each frailer
As it recedes.

It often seems that the only possibility of meaningful social intercourse is with the dead. This appears in "Paying Calls" where the metaphor of social visiting creates a rather neat irony. The speaker casually states that he "Strayed here a mile and there a mile / And called upon some friends." He called on some he "had not see / For years past" and on "others who had been / The oldest friends of all." Though it was "mid-summer / When they had used to roam" he "found them all at home." The movement of the poem has been so slyly relaxed that it is only now that the reader begins to realize the situation:

I spoke to one and other of them
By mound and stone and tree
Of things we had done ere days were dim
But they spoke not to me.

Thus the haunting grip of past experience takes the speaker out of the present into a personal world of memory, but there is no consolation in that personal world. The dead do not speak to the protagonist of Hardy's poetry, or if they do it is usually to show his alienation from the past which the ghosts represent. In "Night in the Old Home," the speaker, alone by his fireside and obsessed with sad visions, receives a visit from his "perished" ancestors. The ghosts gather and sit quitely, regarding the speaker with a "strange upbraiding smile." The speaker seems to infer the reason of this "upbraiding"; for he describes himself rather apologetically as a "thinker of crooked thoughts upon Life in the sere," and asks the ghosts whether they "uphold" him. The ghosts, however, do not in the least "uphold" him. Instead, they seem to answer "O let be the wherefore! We fevered our years not thus: / Take of life what it grants" and so "watch Time away beamingly." The ghosts, being his ancestors, are those of the dead with which the protagonist might be expected to have the closest rapport. But instead the "upbraiding" ghosts contrast the contented unawareness they displayed in their lives with the "crooked thoughts" of the speaker, and there is even the suggestion that the speaker may be wrong in his obsessions. Hardy, however, had too much integrity, was too loyal to his own experience, to idealize unthinking acceptance as a mute wisdom, and as a whole the poem does not allow the speaker to seem wrong. Instead there is no reconciliation of the contrasted attitudes, and we are left with the speaker's sense of exclusion.

II

If the ease based on unthinking must be rejected, the feeling of isolation stemming from a tragic view still remains, and with it the uneasiness which a sense of being different provokes. And Hardy frequently allows the possibility that instead of seeing more than his fellows, the gloomy protagonist of his poetry may see less. He may be in some way deprived, crippled, and incapable of access to realms of truth which would bring joy if known. In "The Year's Awakening" a symbolism of the reasons is used, as in Shelley's "Ode to the West Wind," to suggest a hope for the future. In two stanzas, the speaker addresses respectively a "vespering bird" and a "crocus root," both of which are stirred by the approach of spring. But there is nothing in the atmosphere to suggest a "turn in temperature," since "weeks of cloud / Have wrapt the sky in a clammy shroud" of "weather life can scarce endure." Hence the focus of the poem is on the question four times addressed to the crocus and the bird: "How do you know" that spring is coming? In itself, this might suggest very little, but by reflection from other poems of Hardy it implies a knowledge which the speaker cannot attain, and which, if he could attain it, would be an honest source of joy. Of course, there is no suggestion in this poem, which is a rather trivial performance, of the source of this knowledge. But for Hardy, as for almost all the major English poets since Wordsworth, the origin of such knowledge would be in what we may call the visionary imagination—the imagination as it is felt sometimes to be intuiting beyond surface appearance the one reality at the core of things, and sometimes as presenting to the heart a symbol or vision which winds into this reality. In either case, only the visionary imagination can seize that knowledge which sustains the human spirit, and the psychological problem is always whether the intuitions of the imagination can be trusted. In the early years of the nineteenth century, poets seemed better able to sustain confidence, and in Blake, and sometimes in Wordsworth and Shelley, there are poems of sheer affirmation, emphasizing, as a corollary, the joyful transformation of human life when the heart securely possesses this imaginative insight. However, through the nineteenth century, there was a more or less general waning of confidence. Numerous poems, notably by Keats, dramatize the uncertainty, and the ecstasy of the early years ends in a state of mind where there is no faith at all. But the attractions of faith are still felt, and poems are written showing a stoic rejection of imaginative vision. This is perhaps the case in Arnold, where the vision is not of a transcendental reality, but of a past golden age created in poetic nostalgia and imagined without belief. Like every major poet of the century, Hardy felt the dilemma, though naturally he responded in a way modified by his own experience and needs. At times, he seems to have felt that there might be subjective sources of true insight and knowledge. But, in such cases, he had also to recognize that such sources were not available to him. It is this complex of attitudes which underlies one of his most successful poems, "The Darkling Thrush."

In the world of poetry, which is, of course, active in the mind of each individual reader, poems do not exist in disconnection, but, like all other experience, are constantly jostled and modified by references which they themselves magnetize. A poet will often count on this incipient association in building his poem. Of this "The Darkling Thrush" is a striking instance, and there are even verbal echoes suggesting that the "Ode to a Nightingale," in particular, may have been stirring in Hardy's consciousness (the "*Darkling* Thrush" recalling "*Darkling* I listen"; "*spectre*-gray" echoing "youth grows . . . *spectre*-thin"; "*full-hearted* evensong" paralleling "*full-throated* ease"; the thrush choosing to "*fling his soul*" with "so little cause for . . . such *ecstatic sound*," while the nightingale in Keats's ode is "*pouring forth thy soul* abroad / In such an *ecstasy*"). But far more important resemblances stem from the dramatic situation in "The Darkling Thrush." For the poem follows a number of lyrics in the nineteenth century which are constructed upon the speaker's emotions in suddenly hearing the song of a bird. In Shelley ("To a Skylark") and Keats ("Ode to a Nightingale"), the bird becomes a symbol of the visionary imagination, or of the soul in secure possession of vision and so lifted into ecstasy, and the speaker then aspires to an identification with the bird. The hope of such identification provides the drive or impetus of both poems, and, at least in Keats, the identification seems for a moment to take place. Average human experience ungraced by vision appears in both poems as a contrast to the symbolic connotations of the bird, and hence as the state of mind from which the speaker hopes to escape. In Hardy's poem, the bird has a similar—and I think more complicated—symbolic reference, but with the implication that there is no hope of closing the gap between speaker and bird. Through the course of the poem, the speaker remains mired in a state of mind which the "joy illimited" of the thrush is powerless to modify. In other words, instead of building on a hope and aspiration to share the joy of the thrush, the poem builds upon a hopeless contrast—a contrast all the more poignant from Hardy's characteristic manner of handling his symbol. For the thrush as a symbol is much more accessible (and potentially more encouraging) than Keats's nightingale or Shelley's skylark. It is itself growing old; it is as chained to the world of time and process as we. Hence identification with it is more possible. Having attributed so much to the nightingale, and associated it with the perfect and eternal, Keats, one feels, had little choice except to let it fly away; the nightingale is finally too remote from mortal life to share it ("no hungry generations tread thee down"). The only alternative would have been to surrender the dramatic situation entirely and to turn, as Shelley does with the skylark, to a hymn of praise and impassioned expression of desire to be like the bird. Hardy's greater realism keeps the symbol convincing and therefore open. For if the aging thrush can sing while subject as much to the burden of life as anything else—and while lacking, in this wintry landscape, all the Eden-like props with which the romantics surround their bird-symbols—the implication is that mortal joy, though rare, is certainly being attained. Hence the speaker hardly feels able to challenge the rightness of the bird's joy, but in humility and wistful nostalgia states his inability to share it; and the poem presents not a speaker who asserts a mournful pessimism as a necessary reflection from the facts of life, but rather one who feels himself to be incapable of seeing whole, being in some way stunted and incomplete.

The poem opens by depicting the speaker in a casual attitude—"I leant upon a coppice gate"—which seems to imply little expectation of any unusual occurrence. As is often the case in Wordsworth, the speaker's state of mind is presented indirectly through what he notices in the natural world and the way in which he chooses to describe it:

> I leant upon a coppice gate
> When Frost was spectre-gray,
> And Winter's dregs made desolate
> The weakening eye of day.
> The tangled bine-stems scored the sky
> Like strings of broken lyres,
> And all mankind that haunted nigh
> Had sought their household fires.

It is an extreme picture of cold desolation and disintegration. "Winter's dregs" is probably too abstract to be felt as a metaphor, but the word "dregs" contibutes to a sense of things petering out, as the "weakening eye of day" does even more powerfully. The comparison of "tangled bine-stems" to "strings of broken lyres" is both an exact visual observation and a vague extension of the death images suggested in the words "spectre" and "haunted." The root metaphor of "spectre," "dregs," and "broken lyres" seems to be of the aftermath of life and activity, or of a kind of inanimate life continuing after death, and the verb "scored," which was probably intended only to bear the meaning "traced lines upon," suggests, in conjunction with the "eye of day" figure, something especially unpleasant and almost malicious. The next four lines make the death metaphor explicit:

> The land's sharp features seemed to be
> The Century's corpse outleant,
> His crypt the cloudy canopy,
> The wind his death-lament.

The metaphor functions successfully as a comparison of the land to a corpse stretched out, and the "sharp features" of the land are aptly used to imply those of a corpse. But within the frame of the metaphor, to identify the corpse as that of the "Century" seems rather arbitrary and intrusive. However, the poem was dated "December 1900," and the ostensible, as opposed to the primary, theme of the poem may be the implication of some "Hope" for the century to come. But most obviously the poem presents the speaker looking on images of desolation and death, and oppressed by them:

> And every spirit upon earth
> Seemed fervourless as I.

But suddenly the speaker hears the "voice" of a thrush "among / The bleak twigs overhead." The thrush has itself every apparent reason to be dispirited since it is

> An aged thrush, frail, gaunt, and small,
> In blast-beruffled plume;

but it has chosen instead to "fling" its "soul / Upon the growing gloom" in a "full-hearted evensong / Of joy illimited." At this point in a different poem, a poem perhaps by an earlier poet, the speaker might have found himself cheered by the song of the thrush. But here the speaker remains "fervourless," unable to share the "joy" of the thrush, obstinately remarking in "terrestrial things" little "cause for carolings." Forced to recognize a contrast between himself and the thrush, he tries wistfully to account for it:

> So little cause for carolings
> Of such ecstatic sound
> Was written on terrestrial things
> Afar or nigh around,
> That I could think there trembled through
> His happy good-night air
> Some blessed Hope, whereof he knew
> And I was unaware.

The inability to share the kind of imaginative experience which constitutes a "blessed Hope" arises from a stubborn attention on the part of the speaker to his own perception, and a refusal to disown it. But some latitude is still allowed to a contrasting point of view, and this involves the speaker in a partial renunciation of the claims of his own experience. In this respect, the poem is rather unusual for Hardy. He is more likely to present the visionary experience without faith. As a first and tentative instance of this habit of mind we may take "The Impercipient." Perhaps because the poem is centrally Hardy's defense against attacks prompted by his somber expression and outlook, and because it gives a religious reference to the consolation of which he is deprived, the reservations are presented very indirectly. The poem is subtitled "At a Cathedral Service," and at once states the theme of alienation:

That with this bright believing band
  I have no claim to be,
That faiths by which my comrades stand
  Seem fantasies to me,
And mirage-mists their Shining Land,
  Is a strange destiny.

In its religious context, the sense of isolation appears as a want of belief, but the poem at once generalizes away from a specific reference to Christian faith. The dilemma is rather that the speaker is "always . . . blind / To sights" his "brethren see," and "cannot find" the "joys they've found." That this should be so is a "mystery," but it is one that consigns the speaker "To infelicity." The poem carries these implications into a metaphor:

I am like a gazer who should mark
  An inland company
Standing upfingered, with, "Hark! Hark!
  The glorious distant sea!"
And feel, "Alas, 'tis but yon dark
  And wind-swept pine to me!"

This stanza contains an example of the habit of mind which seems to have been Hardy's malady, and which he felt cut him off from other men. For the company have some impression, presumably through hearing, of a "distant sea"; but the speaker both hears and sees a "wind-swept pine" which, he feels, accounts for the impression animating the "company." In other words, by what seems to be a fuller awareness, based on both hearing and seeing, the speaker has in his own mind disintegrated the illusion which brings joy. Hence there is a suggestion of irony in the use of the word "shortcomings" in the next stanza:

Yet I would bear my shortcomings
  With meet tranquility,
But for the charge that blessed things
  I'd liefer not have be.
O, doth a bird deprived of wings
  Go earth-bound wilfully!

Throughout the poem, and especially in the image of a "bird deprived of wings," there is nostalgia for the beliefs and impressions which give joy to other people, a wanting to share them, and a feeling that he cannot. And the pathos is not weakened by the suggestion that the speaker's vision may be the truer—the nostalgia and the isolation are still present.

In Wordsworth, Shelley, and Blake, a primary symbol of the soul in possession of vision is, of course, the child. Because his focus is very different, Hardy seldom employs the symbol. But when he does, its use may be described as an act of piety to Wordsworth, whose influence spreads everywhere in his poetry. The poem "In a Waiting-Room" begins with a singularly grim description of a railway station. Pictures on the wall are "fly-blown" and "tarnished." A "Testament" open to the "Gospel of Saint John" has been scribbled over with calculations of profit and loss. Even the weather has a "mean hue," the morning being "sick as the day of doom." The adult persons in the waiting room seem "haggard" and "Subdued to stone." But some children enter "Like the eastern flame / Of some high altar" and are delighted with the pictures:

> Here are the lovely ships that we,
> Mother, are by and by going to see!
> When we get there it's 'most sure to be fine,
> And the band will play, and the sun will shine.

The poem then narrates that it continued to rain, and "we waited and still no train came in," but "the words of the child in the squalid room / Had spread a glory through the gloom." The comparison of children to an "eastern flame," a comparison bizarrely off-key with the rest of the poem, shows in its very straining the will to see the child as a Wordsworthian symbol. But the sudden "glory" to which the poem testifies is not communicated to the reader, and for the very good reason that it was not felt by the poet. For the harshness of the scene is what grips and oppresses the imagination, and the child's comments are insufficient to dispel this weight. Hence instead of an imaginative glimpse past surface appearances, the child's reaction is felt to be more that "wonder" which Johnson described as the "effect of novelty acting on ignorance." An even more striking failure occurs in "Midnight on the Great Western." Here the speaker sees a boy sitting in a train, and again a grim milieu is suggested in images of the "oily flame" and "sad beams" of the lamp. The boy, who has a "third-class seat," seems "listless" and "incurious . . . on all at stake." This attitude provokes the question:

> Knows your soul a sphere, O journeying boy,
>   Our rude realms far above,
> Whence with spacious vision you mark and mete

This region of sin that you find you in,
But are not of?

The question is prompted by the boy's seeming disconnection from his surroundings, and, doubtless, even more by a recollection of Wordsworth. But the previous stanzas have been a most unpromising prelude to a Wordsworthian question, and unlike Wordsworth, the speaker's speculation is merely a guess, with nothing in the presentation of the "listless" boy to justify its accuracy. Every reader has probably been "listless" and "incurious" in a "third-class seat," which may be itself sufficient to account for listlessness. Perhaps nothing better indicates Hardy's diminished faith than his few pathetic attempts to dress the child as an affirmative symbol of the visionary imagination.

In both poems just cited, the physical setting is noted with a realistic fidelity proceeding almost in contradiction to the over-all needs of the poem. This obsessive attention to the whole context of experience is very characteristic of Hardy. One has only to think of *The Dynasts,* which shows at least an intention to net every fish in the sea. Any narrowness which a reader may justly sense in Hardy is a narrowness of elucidation. Perhaps one might say that any experience may be given a "pessimistic" interpretation, but that "pessimism" does not itself limit the range of experience included. Now this wide spread of awareness very largely shapes the speaker's attitude in those poems which deal with the uncertainties of visionary insight. For it is precisely his honesty to a whole context which strips and disintegrates the momentary assertions of the imagination, converting what seemed to be a vision into an illusion. We have seen one instance of this in "The Impercipient." Perhaps the most successful symbol of the dilemma as Hardy felt it occurs in the poem, "In a Whispering Gallery." Here, as is not uncommon in Hardy's lyrics, the conception is more striking than the poem that resulted from it, but at least the intention is clear. In a whispering gallery the speaker hears a "whisper . . . Close, but invisible" which seems to be that of a "Spirit." It "brings" a "kindling vision," and "for a moment" the speaker is able to "rejoice, / And believe in transcendent things." To this point the poem seems to be taking a direction familiar in the work of Wordsworth or Blake, to be bent, that is, toward an annunciation of "transcendent things." But the poem at once proceeds to note the milieu within which the "whisper" is heard. The speaker is in a "gaunt gray gallery" on a "drab-aired afternoon." The weather is hazy, so that it is impossible to see across the gallery. Hence the speaker cannot know whether the "whisper" comes from some person on the other side of the gallery, or whether the "voice so near / Be a soul's voice floating here." Of course, that the question should be asked reveals that the trust in imagination is very insecure. Moreover, the title of the poem, the fact that the "spell" is only "for a moment," and that the original impression is of a "whisper," suggests that the "voice" belongs to "fleshed humanity," and that the "kindling vision" was based on illusion.

In general, then, Hardy recognizes two possible grounds of reconciliation. One is a resigned unawareness. Steeped in the common ways of daily incident, eyes lowered to what is immediately before one as a task or amusement, one need not notice the pain of life. The other road is more difficult to describe. In a sense it is a way of feeling of which Wordsworth and Blake are perhaps the main poetic voices in the century preceding Hardy. It is an escape from the obsession with sorrow through the visionary imagination leading one to a knowledge of "transcendent things," and making life a blessing by the knowledge of a truth beyond surface appearances. Both of these roads are blocked for Hardy by his helpless honesty to his own experience, which he can neither elude nor transform in accordance with what he might desire. The road of unawareness is more obviously rejected, though not without a nostalgia mingled with indignation for those who accept it. The road of vision is viewed with more complexity. First of all there is a general distrust of the visionary imagination itself. For within such experiences, whether recorded from the outside as by an onlooker, or as, for the moment, he himself seems to share them, there is a disintegrating honesty that reduces what seems to be vision to illusion. Hence there is a peculiar dilemma in which "Solace" can come only in "cleaving to the Dream" or vision. If by some "Blind" but "determined deftness" of "Fancy" one could escape the "power" of "heedfulness," it might be possible to "charm Life's lourings fair":

> If I have seen one thing
> It is the passing preciousness of dreams;
> That aspects are within us; and who seems
> Most kingly is the King.

But the consolation of "dreams" runs counter to our experience:

> For what do we know best?
> That a fresh love-leaf crumpled soon will dry,
> And that men moment after moment die,
> Of all scope dispossest.

And one cannot elude this knowledge. Faith in the dream drew the "dream-follower" to confusion and disaster. He attempted to impose the dream on reality, and in the confrontation he found "but a thing of flesh and bone / Speeding on to its cleft in the clay." The dream expired, and the dreamer "whitely hastened away."[2] But moving within the distrust of imagination, there is also the questioning, tentative openness of Hardy —a humility which could not finally measure life only against his own more programmatic ideas, and an honesty which, while it scrutinized the claims of imagination, could also turn upon itself. If at times he denied the validity of what the romantics called the visionary imagination, at other times he simply doubted his own capacity for it, feeling himself to be somehow incomplete. When this enters into his poetry, it creates a new dimension, as well as a certain pathos. It is indeed his humility and self-doubt that save Hardy, if he needs to be saved. Through them he achieves a more genuine and complex commitment of himself than the metaphysical lyrics or even the too-frequent ironic unmaskings of "change and chancefulness" release. For his sympathies did not fit him to be a prosecutor.

[2] "On a Fine Morning"; "A Young Man's Exhortation"; "The Dream-Follower."

The Dynasts as an Example

by Samuel Hynes

Sooner or later the artist involved with questions of meaning and belief (and this probably means every major artist) must feel the need to impose upon his ideas the complex organization which a long work requires. At the same time the conditions of belief in our time raise special problems for the artist with such intentions; he can neither assume a core of beliefs common to himself and his audience nor adopt the long forms which artists have traditionally used for such statements. Consequently, the long works which modern writers have produced have tended to be private, difficult, and eccentric—*Ulysses, The Cantos, The Waste Land,* and "The Comedian as the Letter C" have these qualities in common, if they have nothing else. None is epic in a traditional sense, though all have epic elements; none has a traditional hero; none depends on or asserts traditional values. They are epics for an age in which epic action is impossible.

The Dynasts is Hardy's venture into this realm of the modern epic. But for our purposes it is something more than that; it is Hardy's great effort to put his philosophical and poetic principles into practice on the largest possible scale. That tremendous scale makes *The Dynasts* useful as a test both of his principles and of the judgements we have thus far made of them.

Hardy must have sensed early in his career that lyric and anecdotal poetry could not give full and satisfactory expression to his thought—that he required a massive structure to support a modern epic. For over twenty years he pondered the shape that it should take, and made tentative, speculative entries in his notebooks. It appeared at last as *The Dynasts,* his most ambitious philosophical statement, in his most original form—the "epic-drama."

"*The Dynasts* as an Example." From *The Pattern of Hardy's Poetry* (Chapel Hill: University of North Carolina Press, 1956) by Samuel Hynes.

Some version of epic was, as Hardy saw from the first, the only possible vehicle for the philosophical statement that he intended. Traditionally, the epic has served didactic, philosophical, or religious purposes, embodying in a mythical history the values of the culture which produced it. In the epic hero it offers an image of the human potentialities implicit in those values. And it freely employs supernatural actors to dramatize the relation of man (in the person of the epic hero) to the controlling forces of the universe. It offers a canvas vast enough for a comprehensive statement within a single form, and it is unhampered by the restrictions of realism or probability.

In all these characteristics, the epic suited Hardy's aims, as the forms he had previously tried did not. The "philosophical" lyrics, as we have seen, could rarely support the weight of didacticism imposed upon them—the human figures, even those in the dramatic ballads, are too pallid to have much symbolic force, and the supernatural actors, when they appear, are generally felt to be extraneous. Even the great novels show in their defects the restrictions of a limited range, and of the demand for probability and realism implicit in the form as Hardy used it (most adverse criticisms of the novels are in these terms).

From the first, Hardy thought of his long poem as epic in scope, though not in form. The first entry in the notebooks relative to *The Dynasts,* dated May, 1875, reads: "Mem: A Ballad of the Hundred Days. Then another of Moscow. Others of earlier campaigns—forming altogether an Iliad of Europe from 1789 to 1815" (*Early Life,* p. 140). Six years later he entered this note: "A Homeric Ballad, in which Napoleon is a sort of Achilles, to be written" (*Early Life,* p. 191). The idea of the ballad-form did not survive—Hardy required, as he came to realize, "a larger canvas"—but the concept of an "Iliad of Europe" with Napoleon as the epic hero did.

The choice of subject matter was, given Hardy's habits of mind, almost inevitable. Hardy explains in the Preface to *The Dynasts* that

> The choice of such a subject was mainly due to three accidents of locality. It chanced that the writer was familiar with a part of England that lay within hail of the watering-place in which King George the Third had his favourite summer residence during the war with the first Napoleon, and where he was visited by ministers and others who bore the weight of English affairs on their more or less competent shoulders at that stressful time. Secondly, this district, being also near the coast which had echoed with rumours of invasion in their intensest form while the descent threatened, was formerly animated by memories and traditions of the desperate military preparations for that contingency. Thirdly, the same countryside happened to include the village which was the birthplace of Nelson's flag-captain at Trafalgar (p. vii).

It is true that, without these local materials, Hardy's epic would have been different in many particulars; but it would still, I think, have been an Iliad of Europe, and Napoleon would still have played his role as "a sort of Achilles." The notebook entries regarding *The Dynasts* range over some thirty years, but they make no mention of Dorset or of Captain Hardy; they deal primarily with two concerns: the form which the history of Napoleon and the Hundred Days should take, and the philosophical content which that history could be made to bear. It is oversimplifying to explain the attraction which Napoleon and the French Revolution had for Hardy as merely the result of "accidents of locality"; clearly the character and the events seemed to him to have a meaning which was relevant to his philosophic intentions.

Napoleon must have seemed to Hardy, and no doubt most modern readers would agree, the last figure in Western European history to whom epic stature could be ascribed. This point is important if we recall Hardy's view of the evolution of the "modern" personality (as set out in the first chapter of *The Return of the Native,* in the character of "Father Time" in *Jude,* and in various poems). If one accepts this notion of the *difference* of modern man, then one must find a modern hero, a modern epic story—classical themes will not do, because they represent man at a different stage of his evolution, less burdened by his own consciousness. (It is perhaps significant that Hardy rarely went outside his own century for material, and never successfully in a major work; *The Famous Tragedy of the Queen of Cornwall* is his most complete failure, partly because its traditional theme was not adaptable to Hardy's "modern" intentions.)

Furthermore, Hardy's Napoleon is, like other Hardy heroes, a man against the world—lonely and isolated even at the moment of his greatness. Hardy does not sentimentalize this isolation—Napoleon is not Childe Harold—but he does emphasize it, as he emphasized the isolation of Michael Henchard and Clym Yeobright and Jude Fawley. Man's alienation from men is an important aspect of Hardy's view of existence; it appears in the most characteristic situation of the lyric poems—the speaker alone, apart, out of place, "born out of due time"—as well as in the novels. Napoleon provided a dramatic example of the theme, a man lonely among multitudes.

Finally, Napoleon appears of all men the most self-determined, the absolute master of his fate, and this gives weight to the irony of a poem which was conceived in terms of "A spectral force seen acting in a man (e.g., Napoleon) and he acting under it—a pathetic sight—this compulsion" (*Later Years,* p. 227). An epic hero symbolizes the human condition as determined by the epic values. Napoleon stood, in Hardy's mind, as a dramatic symbol of man as Hardy saw him—struggling alone toward his own conception of his destiny—but helpless to alter his predetermined end. As darkness blots out Napoleon and the human scene for the last time in *The Dynasts,* the Spirit of the Years points the moral:

> Worthless these kneadings of thy narrow thought,
> Napoleon; gone thy opportunity!
> Such men as thou, who wade across the world
> To make an epoch, bless, confuse, appal,
> Are in the elemental ages' chart
> Like meanest insects on obscurest leaves
> But incidents and grooves of Earth's unfolding;
> Or as the brazen rod that stirs the fire
> Because it must.
>
> (*Dynasts,* III, VII, 9)

In Napoleon the paradox of human power and human helplessness, of will and necessity, emerges as a vast, cosmic irony.

Hardy's notes on *The Dynasts* follow, as I have said, two lines: the question of form and the question of philosophical content. Although Hardy saw the poem from the first as epic in scope, he apparently never thought of employing the traditional epic form; the forms he considered were those most natural to his talent and to his vision—the ballad and the drama. At first he seemed uncertain as to which was preferable; in 1889 he recorded his decision:

> For carrying out that idea of Napoleon, the Empress, Pitt, Fox, etc., I feel continually that I require a larger canvas. . . . A spectral tone must be adopted. . . . Royal ghosts. . . . Title "A Drama of Kings" (*Early Life,* p. 290).

From this date on the form was determined; in 1891 he changed the title to "A Drama of the Times of the first Napoleon," and he later refers to the work as "the Napoleon drama"—there is no further reference to ballads. The term *epic* is curiously absent from the notes, and indeed Hardy did not come to call *The Dynasts* an "epic-drama" until after it had been published.

On the question of philosophic content, however, Hardy's mind was clear from the beginning. The first notebook entry on the subject, dated 1881, outlines the philosophic scheme in substantially the form which it was to take twenty years later:

> Mode for a historical Drama. Action mostly automatic; reflex movement, etc. Not the result of what is called *motive,* though always ostensibly so, even to

the actors' own consciousness. Apply an enlargement of these theories to, say, "The Hundred Days"! (*Early Life*, p. 191).

The method by which this scheme could be made dramatic, however, was slower in evolving, and must have constituted the major problem of structure. Hardy began with a conviction that existing systems of belief were exhausted—not only as beliefs, but as materials for poetry:

> The old theologies [he wrote in an undated note] may or may not have worked for good in their time. But they will not bear stretching further in epic or dramatic art. The Greeks used up theirs: the Jews used up theirs: the Christians have used up theirs. So that one must make an independent plunge, embodying the real, if only temporary, thought of the age (*Later Years*, p. 104).

Circumstances seemed to him to force upon him an act of creation not required of earlier epic poets—he had first to create his own theology.

His "independent plunge" was not, however, as sudden as the remark above suggests. Hardy was personifying the forces which controlled his private world as early as 1866, when he wrote in "Hap":

> Crass Casualty obstructs the sun and rain,
> And dicing Time for gladness casts a moan.
> These purblind Doomsters had as readily strown
> Blisses about my pilgrimage as pain.
> (*Collected Poems*, p. 7)

Casualty and Time remain essentially the "Doomsters" of all his work, both poems and novels, though their names change, until they emerge in *The Dynasts* as The Immanent Will and The Spirit of the Years. In between, the motive force is called a Vast Imbecility, an Automaton, The President of the Immortals, and of course God (a term which is, for Hardy, a private personification of the mindless, indifferent force which propels the universe). Time is intermediately the Spinner of Years and the Time-Wraiths. A third term, Nature or "The Mother," is also present from the beginning; she seems to represent a pre-conscious evolutionary system, the physical world as it would work if man had not developed beyond expectations. Like the other spirits in Hardy's Olympus, she is powerless to change the way things are; in *The Dynasts* the Shade of the Earth calls her

> Dame Nature—that lay-shape
> They use to hang phenomena upon—

> Whose deftest mothering in fairest spheres
> Is girt about by terms inexorable!
>
> (I, I, 6)

But these private personifications did not provide in themselves a system expansive enough to perform the functions of the supernatural element in an epic. Hardy had still to create the vast metaphorical structure in which he embodied their separate meanings. By 1886 he had solved his problem; in that year he entered in his notebook the two ideas which form the framework of *The Dynasts* and give symbolic form to the philosophical content:

> The human race to be shown as one great network of tissue which quivers in every part when one point is shaken, like a spider's web if touched. Abstract realisms to be in the form of Spirits, Spectral figures, etc.
>
> The Realities to be the true realities of life, hitherto called abstractions. The old material realities to be placed behind the former, as shadowy accessories (*Early Life,* p. 232).

The idea of intervolved humanity, and the idea that reality is an attribute of the Spirit-world, defined the structure of the epic; Hardy had only to turn the scheme into a poem.

The organizing principle of this vast scheme remains essentially that of the lyrics—an antinomial juxtaposition of the apparent (human individuality and free will) and "the true realities of life." As in many of the lyrics, the spirit world has more reality, more specificity, than the human one. The major spirits—the Spirit of the Years, the Spirit of the Pities, the Spirits Ironic and Sinister—maintain their individuality throughout the piece, while men are submerged into the vast, blurring symbols of brain and nerves, which are intended to exhibit "as one organism the anatomy of life and movement in all humanity and vitalized matter" (*Dynasts,* I, Fore Scene).

The use of a single symbol for all of mankind, and Hardy's constant insistence on the mechanistic nature of human actions, gives to the human actors an almost allegorical quality, as though each individual man were merely another manifestation of the abstraction, Humanity. Hardy supports this view of his human figures with his suggestion, in the Preface, that they assume

> a monotonic delivery of speeches, with dreamy conventional gestures, something in the manner traditionally maintained by the old Christmas mummers, the curiously hypnotizing impressiveness of whose automatic style—that

of persons who spoke by no will of their own—may be remembered by all who ever experienced it (p. xi).

The most realistic human characters are generally anonymous—the men in the streets, the deserters, the harlots, the camp-followers—characters who are simply called "A Spectator" or "Third Woman." Such characters often have highly individualized scenes, but because they are anonymous, and because their responses to events, though vigorous, are uncomprehending and ineffectual, they do not sustain their individuality, but flow together into one stream of the "brain-like network of currents and ejections" which is the controlling Immanent Will. The Dynasts are less individualized, perhaps because they are seen in more public, less personal, circumstances; one general speaks and acts much like another, and the Parliamentary debates might well be the speeches of one rather dull M.P.

The spirit-personalities, on the other hand, are developed in some detail, particularly the three—the Spirit of the Years, the Spirit of the Pities, and the Spirit Ironic—who compose the principal antinomial pattern of the Overworld. The Spirit of the Years is, as he says, "unpassioned"; he is the eldest spirit, and age has brought resignation and acceptance of the immutable. The Spirit of the Pities is the youngest spirit, "a mere juvenile," says the Spirit Ironic, "who only came into being in what the earthlings call their Tertiary Age." His speeches are consistently compassionate of human suffering, and he emotionally resists the cold wisdom of the Years. The Spirit Ironic, like the Spirit of the Pities, speaks with a human voice, that is he expresses a human, emotional response to the inexorable Will; but because he is older, his response is ironic, not pitying. These three voices are always easily distinguishable from each other, and the attitudes which they express are clear and consistent.

By thus humanizing his abstractions and abstracting his humans, Hardy gives unity to an otherwise hopelessly diverse chronicle. And, more important to the philosophic aim, he forces upon the reader the central ironic point. The Spirits, he says, are "the true realities of life"; it is the ironic relation of their comments to the action, rather than the action itself, which dominates the poem and points the meaning. They thus provided Hardy with an opportunity which the lyrics, by their very nature, denied him—an opportunity to express his complex emotional response to the destinies of men in terms adequate to its complexity.

The two worlds of *The Dynasts,* and the interrelations with each and between the two, provide antinomial possibilities beyond any previous form that Hardy had tried. The principal opposition is drawn between earth and the Overworld, or more precisely between the degree of awareness possible to each. Humankind are, as the Spirits never tire of observing, automations, and as such are incapable of seeing the reality in which they are entrapped. It is only the Spirits who can recognize

> the intolerable antilogy
> Of making figments feel,
> (I, IV, 6)

which is Hardy's basic perception of the human condition.

On earth and in the Overworld, further complicating contrasts exist. Since men are blind to their mechanistic state, earthly antinomies take the form of dramatic ironies: a French streetwalker chants "*Jubilate* like the rest," ignorant of France's defeat at Trafalgar; King George blandly denies Pitt's need of aid and hastens his death; generals see victory in defeat and defeat in victory. Usually Hardy, who was not one to let an irony go unnoticed, underscores these points by inserting commentaries by the Spirit Ironic, the Spirit Sinister, or the Spirit of Rumour.

In the Overworld there are also oppositions. Different spirit-groups express different, often contradictory, attitudes toward the human events below them—pity or ironic amusement or sinister delight or the philosophic resignation of the convinced determinist. The Spirits never alter their views and are never reconciled to each other; they cannot be, since, as the Spirit of the Years teaches his fellow spirits,

> We are in Its hand . . . Here, as elsewhere,
> We do but as we may; no further dare.
> (I, II, 2)

In short, on earth and in the Overworld alike, the organizing principle is that eternal, irreconcilable conflict which was for Hardy the first (and only) principle of existence—the disparity between the way things ought to be (and often for men *seem* to be) and the way things are.

To say that the Spirits can see the way things are is not to say that they are real, even symbolically—Hardy is not asserting that such supernatural consciousnesses exist. The Spirits rather represent the ways in which man, if he were completely conscious of his place in the universe, might respond. Hardy was rigorously faithful to his monistic vision. In the Preface to *The Dynasts,* he writes: "The wide prevalence of the Monistic theory of the Universe forbade, in this twentieth century, the importation of Divine personages from any antique Mythology as ready-made sources or channels of Causation, even in verse," and he urges the reader to take the Spirits "for what they may be worth as contrivances of the fancy merely" (p. viii). The Spirits express the way things are, as ignorant man cannot, but they do not exist as forces—the universe of *The Dynasts,* like the universe of the shorter poems, is a monistic one, in which the only operative force is a nonteleological energy called The Immanent Will. The world is still, as Hardy says in the Preface, "unintelligible."

The central opposition set up in *The Dynasts* between the earth and the Overworld in terms of the awareness possible to each corresponds roughly to the dark and light worlds of the lyrics, and is supported, as in the lyrics, by diction and imagery. *The Dynasts* is Hardy's major *tour de force* in diction, as it is in other qualities. The metaphor on which he built his epic drama provided him with two groups of speaking voices which correspond to the two kinds of language which he set up in his diagram of diction: the Spirits of the Overworld employ poetic diction, while humanity speaks the language of common speech. This division, which is maintained meticulously through the drama's 19 acts and 130 scenes, gives verbal consistency and unity to each world; it also establishes diction as a symbolic extension of the philosophical distinction between the two worlds. The Spirits speak a rich private language which is as different as possible from common speech, which is not even quite English. The "Persons" in the drama, on the other hand, speak two varieties of common speech: one for the "Dynasts," the other for the people.

The dynasts speak in flat, formalized standard English, the result in part of Hardy's scrupulous fidelity to his sources—Hansard for the Parliament scenes, and a mass of histories, biographies, and memoirs for the rest. He wrote in his Preface to *The Dynasts* that ". . . whenever any evidence of the words really spoken or written by the characters in their various situations was attainable, as close a paraphrase has been aimed at as was compatible with the form chosen" (p. viii). The notes scattered through the text show that, even in translating from the French, Hardy strove above all for a close paraphrase. The common people speak, as one might expect, a more colloquial English which is, in the Wessex scences, enriched with dialectal and archaic forms. It remains plain, however, and free of Hardy's personal eccentricities of diction—it is closer to the style of the novels than to that of the poems.

Any scene from the Overworld set against any one from the world of men will show how distinct, how diametrically opposed the two styles of diction are. The Fore Scene of Part First is typical of the Overworld style. It is highly stylized, complex in syntax, polysyllabic and abstract in vocabulary, full of coinages; it bears the mark of Hardy's personality and thought in every line. It is packed with the language of mechanistic action (*rapt aesthetic rote, automatic, unweeting, pulsion of the Byss, clock-like laws, engines*) and of biology (*animalcula, fibrils, veins, tissues, nerves, pulses, lobule*); the latter introduces the biological image of men and things as a single organism exhibiting "the anatomy of life and movement in all humanity and vitalized matter" which recurs throughout the drama —an image of life as simply another kind of machine. In the Spirit scenes Hardy also used personal coinages and rare and obsolete words more freely than in even the most idiosyncratic poems—*pulsion, Byss, warefulness, closelier, reflexed, wareness* occur in the Fore Scene.

Any of the earth scenes will do for a comparison. The prose scenes of Wessex life show Hardy's command of local dialect, and sometimes also his talent for folk humor, though the humor is often more literary than local, more Shakespeare's Warwickshire than Hardy's, or George the Third's, Dorset. The Shakespearian influence is more apparent in the blank verse of the dynastic scenes, which is rarely very effective poetry, and is at its worst either turgid and pompous or simply lamely pedestrian. This exchange from the fourth act of Part First is typical, though far from the worst:

KING

And now he has left Boulogne with all his host?
Was it his object to invade at all,
Or was his vast assemblage there a blind?

PITT

Undoubtedly he meant invasion, sir,
Had fortune favoured. He may try it yet.
And, as I said, could we but close with Fox. . . .

(I, IV, 1)

The diction of these scenes is standard, undistinguished, and undistinguishable—all human characters speak in pretty much the same formal style. The device of setting this style in contrast to its opposite—the flat, unvarying speech of the blind leaders of humanity against the rich and various language of the omniscient Overworld—supports the antinomial, ironic view of events which is at the heart of *The Dynasts.*

The imagery of *The Dynasts* works in much the same systematic way to strengthen the central opposition between what men see, and what they would see if they were truly conscious. Men speak without metaphor, because their vision is a vision of things-as-things, and not as relationships. Metaphor is a mode of knowing, and since man cannot know, he can speak only in flat, discursive, unmetaphorical language. Knowledge belongs to the Overworld, to ideal consciousness, and so does metaphor and imagery. In *The Dynasts* Men describe; Spirits relate.

The scenes involving men are consequently rapid, strenuously active, and often highly dramatic, but they are poetically flat; in these qualities they demonstrate Hardy's view of man's fate—to be active, but ignorant. The speeches of men are expository and factual—they provide detail, but not meaning; frequently Hardy dispenses with human speech altogether, showing men's actions in dumb show, which becomes a kind of metaphor in itself of the limits of man's awareness.

The speeches of the Overworld figures, on the other hand, are rich in imagery, and this richness is primarily a function of the principal advantage which the Spirits have over mankind—a long-range perspective. The Spirits can see as whole the movements which men see as separate—armies clashing, navies maneuvering, populations fleeing. This panoramic view is in turn a symbol of their philosophical perspective, which is the main point. This is made clear in the stage directions which set up the cosmic structure of the poem in the Fore Scene: from the Overworld,

> Europe is disclosed as a prone and emaciated figure, the Alps shaping like a backbone, and the branching mountain-chains like ribs, the peninsular plateau of Spain forming a head,

and men and things can be seen

> with a seeming transparency . . . exhibiting as one organism the anatomy of life and movement in all humanity and vitalized matter. . . .

What the Spirits see here is the Immanent Will, that encompassing energy which determines all actions of "men and things." These two images—the emaciated figure of Europe and the anatomy of life—are the key images of *The Dynasts*; the subsequent action is simply a vast explication of the meanings implicit in them. Perspective is what men do not and cannot have, and so the lofty vision of the Overworld provides both an expansive perspective of vast "epic" actions, and an ironically contracting philosophical perspective of what those actions mean.

The conflicts in the Overworld, I have said, are unresolved. They are unresolved because individually the Spirits express conflicting aspects of Hardy's own attitudes toward experience—the endless, wrangling debate they carry on mirrors the state of Hardy's mind throughout his life. By separating his conflicting views Hardy was able to make his philosophical difficulties dramatic, and to avoid the confusion and inconsistency which mar philosophical lyrics like "The Sleep-Worker." But the difficulties remain, and compose the philosophical structure of the poem.

The most basic and recurrent conflict in the Overworld is that set up so clearly in "The Convergence of the Twain," between "human" aspirations and emotions on the one hand, and the blind mechanism of the Immanent Will on the other. The Immanent Will is not present in the action; or, to be more precise, it *is* the action, as we see it in the following stage direction:

> The scene assumes the preternatural transparency before mentioned, and there is again beheld as it were the interior of a brain which seems to manifest the volitions of a Universal Will, of whose tissues the personages of the action form portion (I, I, 6).

The spokesman for this "Universal Will" is the Spirit of the Years, an unemotional voice of the wisdom of experience, who laments nothing, hopes for nothing, and makes no teleological concessions. He argues throughout the poem the "Inadvertent Mind," and his last judgment of the drama of Napoleon is as relentlessly mechanistic as his first utterance:

> Thus doth the Great Foresightless mechanize
> In blank entrancement now as evermore
> Its ceaseless artistries in Circumstance . . . .
> (III, After Scene)

He speaks for the rationalistic side of Hardy's mind, the side which could not be content with anything less than a full look at the worst.

At the other pole of the antinomy stand the Spirit of the Pities and its Chorus, expressing Hardy's compassion and deep humanity. The group approximates, Hardy says in his Preface,

> "the Universal Sympathy of human nature—the spectator idealized" of the Greek Chorus; it is impressionable and inconsistent in its views, which sway hither and thither as wrought on by events (p. ix).

Pity is a rather inadequate term to describe this universal sympathy; Charity (in Saint Paul's sense) might be better, or simply Love.

The relation of the Pities to the Years is roughly that of an advocate before a justice (in which case the Immanent Will is the Law). Thus at Austerlitz the Pities plead their case:

> O Great Necessitator, heed us now!
> If it indeed must be
> That this day Austria smoke with slaughtery,
> Quicken the issue as Thou knowest how;
> And dull to suffering those whom it befalls
> To quit their lodgment in a flesh that galls!

and the Years replies:

> Again ye deprecate the World-Soul's way
> That I so long have told? Then note anew
> (Since ye forget) the ordered potencies,
> Nerves, sinews, trajects, eddies, ducts of It
> The Eternal Urger, pressing change on change,
> (I, VI, 3)

and we see once more the vision of mankind as the entangled network of a great, twitching brain. The plea has been thrown out of court.

The relation of Pities and Years is generally one of appeal and denial, or of question and answer (many of their exchanges are in the form of a catechism), and this is an appropriate relationship for the thesis and antithesis in an antinomial pattern. There is, however, one other important voice—that of the Spirit Ironic. In the Austerlitz scene, it is the Semichorus of Ironic Spirits who explicate to the Pities the vision of the great brain:

> O Innocents, can ye forget
> That things to be were shaped and set
> Ere mortals and this planet met?

They go on to summarize Hardy's view of evolution, describing how, in the past, they

> Beheld the rarest wrecked amain,
> Whole nigh-perfected species slain
> By those that scarce could boast a brain;
>
> Saw ravage, growth, diminish, add,
> Here peoples sane, there peoples mad,
> In choiceless throws of good and bad;
>
> Heard laughters at the ruthless dooms
> Which tortured to the eternal glooms
> Quick, quivering hearts in hecatombs.
> (I, VI, 3)

This sounds at first like more of the bleak mechanism of the Spirit of the Years; but in fact it is very different in tone. The Ironic Spirits accept the wisdom of the Years, but their response to it is as emotional as is that of the Pities; the account may be evolutionary, but the language is scarcely scientific or objective ("ravaged," "mad," "tortured," "quivering hearts"). For Hardy irony and pity, like tragedy and comedy, are simply alternate ways of responding to circumstance; and in fact the Pities do describe human life as tragedy, while the Ironic Spirits see it as comedy. Both of these responses are abundantly present in the lyric poems as well as in *The Dynasts,* and it would scarcely be an exaggeration to say that they were the only responses to experience available to Hardy. Those poems of which we are fondest are probably poems of the Pities, but there are plenty of Ironic poems as well: the "Satires of Circumstance," for example, are in this tone, and the Ancient Briton in "The Moth-Signal" is a grinning Ironic Spirit. The streak of cruelty which runs through the poems, in which Hardy seems almost to rejoice in the inevitable defeat of human fortunes, takes systematic form in *The Dynasts* as the Spirit Ironic. It is the other side of Pity, the reaction to suffering of a man who feels it too much.

It is the Pities who have the last speech:

> But—a stirring thrills the air
> Like to sounds of joyance there
> That the rages
> Of the ages
> Shall be cancelled, and deliverance offered from the darts that were,
> Consciousness the Will informing, till It fashion all things fair!
> (III, After Scene)

This final burst of "evolutionary meliorism" has seemed to some cirtics a contradiction of Hardy's pessimism, and a flaw in the poem as a whole, which should not be taken seriously. Nevertheless, there the speech is, and in a position which prevents our ignoring it; we *must* take it seriously if we take any of the poem seriously.

It is true that the final speech cannot be reconciled with a philosophy of unmitigated pessimism; but to see Hardy' thought as simply that is to miss completely the significance of his antinomial patterns, and to read into his thought a finality and a consistency which are not there. The Pities, as I have said, represent a deep compassion which is an essential part of Hardy's attitude toward existence, though it cannot easily be reconciled with the absolute determinism which the concept of the Immanent Will implies. But the point of *The Dynasts,* and of Hardy's philosophical verse in general, is not that the determinism of the Immanent Will is true and the human sympathy of the Pities sentimental and false. The Pities express, as Hardy says, the "Universal Sympathy of human nature"; while man endures, their attitude will be a valid one. The dialectic of *The Dynasts* is between these two attitudes; neither is urged as the whole truth, for though determinism may have all the evidence on its side, hope and compassion are inherent in human nature, and cannot be denied. Hardy's reason told him that man's fate was determined; yet he could urge man to face

> The fact of life with dependence placed
> On the human heart's resource alone,
> In brotherhood bonded close and graced
>
> With loving-kindness fully blown,
> And visioned help unsought, unknown.
> (*Collected Poems,* p. 306)

"Loving-kindness" is not from the vocabulary of determinism, but it is a common term in Hardy's poetry, and one must take it into account in considering the philosophical meaning of the poems, particularly of *The Dynasts.*

The Dynasts poses a philosophical problem—how can determinism and man's consciousness of injustice be reconciled?—but it offers no solution; the Pities have the final speech, but the speech is not a resolution. "Yes," Hardy wrote to his friend Clodd, "I left off on a note of hope. It was just as well that the Pities should have the last word, since, like *Paradise Lost, The Dynasts* proves nothing" (*Later Years,* p. 276).

Hardy is not quite right. Philosophically, *The Dynasts* does not prove anything: it is not in the nature of poetry to provide such proof. But technically, *The Dynasts* proves a good deal about Hardy as a poet. It proves, first of all, that Hardy could make his antinomial vision do the structural work of more involved and more consistent beliefs, in holding a complex poetic form together, but that he could not make a philosophy out of it; the ideas function in *The Dynasts* not as a system, but as the elements in that cosmic irony which was as close as he ever got to an answer. It proves, further, that his idiosyncratic patterns of diction and imagery could be made to function on a large scale, and with some delicacy of discrimination—that he could make odd words and odd perspectives seem necessary.

The Dynasts is not essentially different, either in thought or in style, from characteristic early lyrics—once again, development is not a valid consideration here. Rather it is a vast testing ground on which Hardy could discover the range and the limits of that thought and that style, and the right relationship between them. But, more than that, *The Dynasts* is a modern epic that works. It belongs among the great eccentric works of our time, and its greatness justifies its eccentricity.

Chronology of Important Dates

1840, June 2	Born at Upper Bockhampton, near Dorchester (Casterbridge).
1856-1861	Apprenticed to John Hicks, Dorchester architect.
1862-1867	Ecclesiastical architect's assistant, London.
1867-1868	Writes *The Poor Man and The Lady* (lost first novel).
1871	*Desperate Remedies,* first published novel.
1872	Marries Emma Lavinia Gifford. *Under the Greenwood Tree.*
1873	*A Pair of Blue Eyes.*
1874	*Far from the Madding Crowd.*
1876	*The Hand of Ethelberta.*
1878	*The Return of the Native.* Moves to London.
1880	*The Trumpet-Major.*
1881	*A Laodicean.*
1882	*Two on a Tower.*
1885	Settles at Max Gate, near Dorchester.
1886	*The Mayor of Casterbridge.*
1887	*The Woodlanders.*
1888	*Wessex Tales* (stories).
1891	*Tess of the D'Urbervilles. A Group of Noble Dames* (stories).
1894	*Life's Little Ironies* (stories).
1895	*Jude the Obscure.*
1897	*The Well-Beloved* (largely written before Jude).
1898	*Wessex Poems.*
1901	*Poems of the Past and the Present.*
1904, 1906, 1908	*The Dynasts* (Parts I, II, III).
1909	*Time's Laughingstocks* (poems).
1910	Awarded the Order of Merit.
1912	The first Mrs. Hardy dies.
1913	*A Changed Man* (stories first published 1881-1900).

1914	Marries Florence Emily Dugdale. *Satires of Circumstance* (poems).
1916	*Selected Poems.*
1917	*Moments of Vision* (poems).
1922	*Late Lyrics and Earlier.*
1923	*The Famous Tragedy of the Queen of Cornwall* (play).
1925	*Human Shows* (poems).
1928, January 11	Dies at Max Gate.
1928	*Winter Words* (poems published posthumously).

Notes on the Editor and Authors

ALBERT J. GUERARD, editor of this volume, was formerly Professor of English at Harvard, and is now a professor at Stanford. He has written critical books on Robert Bridges, André Gide, Joseph Conrad, and Thomas Hardy. He has also published six novels, including *The Hunted, Night Journey, The Bystander* and, most recently, *The Exiles.*

A[LFRED] ALVAREZ is a young English poet and critic, and the author of *Stewards of Excellence.*

W[YSTAN] H[UGH] AUDEN, the distinguished poet and essayist, has published many volumes, including *The Shield of Achilles* (1956) and *Times Three* (1960).

DONALD DAVIDSON, Professor of English at Vanderbilt, has published two volumes of essays and three volumes of poetry.

JOHN HOLLOWAY was Byron Professor of English of the University of Athens, and has been a University Lecturer at Cambridge since 1954 and a fellow of Queens' College since 1955. He is the author of *The Victorian Sage* (1953) and *The Charted Mirror* (1960).

SAMUEL HYNES, author of *The Pattern of Hardy's Poetry,* is a member of the English department at Swarthmore.

D[AVID] H[ERBERT] LAWRENCE (1885-1930), the famous novelist, poet, and essayist, felt himself indebted to Hardy.

JOHN PATERSON, Associate Professor of English at the University of California, is the author of *The Making of The Return of the Native,* a critical and textual study.

DAVID PERKINS, Associate Professor of English at Harvard, is the author of *The Quest for Permanence,* a study of Wordsworth, Shelley, and Keats. He has also published poetry.

DELMORE SCHWARTZ has distinguished himself in poetry, short story writing, and criticism. He won the Bollingen Prize for poetry in 1959.

DOROTHY VAN GHENT, author of *The English Novel: Form and Function,* teaches English at City College in New York.

MORTON DAUWEN ZABEL, author of *Craft and Character in Modern Fiction,* is a specialist on Conrad but has written on many other modern novelists. He is Professor of English at the University of Chicago.

Selected Bibliography

The authoritative text of Hardy's work is the Wessex Edition (24 vols.; London: Macmillan & Co., Ltd., 1912-1931); it embodies Hardy's final revisions. All the novels are included in the 1912 volumes. The American editions published by Harper & Brothers in 1915 ("Autograph Edition") and in 1920 ("Anniversary Edition") are essentially the same as the Wessex Edition. The *Collected Poems* (1919) did not become complete until the edition of 1930. The authoritative bibliography, and one that throws much light on composition and revision, Richard L. Purdy's *Thomas Hardy: A Bibliographical Study* (Oxford, 1954).

LIFE

The best introduction remains Florence Emily Hardy's *The Early Life of Thomas Hardy* (London, 1928) and *The Laters Years of Thomas Hardy* (London, 1930). These have been reissued in a single volume as *The Life of Thomas Hardy* (New York, London, 1962). It is probable that this biography was planned in detail and very largely written by Hardy himself. See Purdy, pp. 265-267, 273. Evelyn Hardy, *Thomas Hardy: A Critical Biography* (London, 1954) is a readable shorter work.

SELECTED STUDIES

The best single volume is the Thomas Hardy Centennial Issue of *The Southern Review,* Volume VI (Summer 1940). In addition to the essays reprinted here (by W. H. Auden, Donald Davidson, Delmore Schwartz, Morton Dauwen Zabel) there are others, nearly all of interest, by Howard Baker, Jacques Barzun, R. P. Blackmur, Bonamy Dobrée, F. R. Leavis, Arthur Mizener, Herbert J. Muller, Katherine Anne Porter, John Crowe Ransom, and Allen Tate.

Abercrombie, Lascelles, *Thomas Hardy: A Critical Study* (New York, 1912). A sensitive early analysis and summary of Hardy's attitude and art.

Brown, Douglas, *Thomas Hardy* (London, 1954). A brief and unassuming critique.

Firor, Ruth, *Folkways in Thomas Hardy* (Philadelphia, 1931). Available in paperback: New York: A. S. Barnes & Co., Inc., Perpetua Books.

Guerard, Albert J., *Thomas Hardy: The Novels and Stories* (Cambridge, Mass., 1949).

Hynes, Samuel L., *The Pattern of Hardy's Poetry* (Chapel Hill, 1961).

McDowall, Arthur, *Thomas Hardy: A Critical Study* (London, 1931).

Rutland, William, *Thomas Hardy: A Study of his Writings and their Background* (Oxford, 1938). A serious study of intellectual background.

Webster, Harvey C., *On a Darkling Plain* (Chicago, 1947). A good analysis of Hardy's thought and attitudes.